English Grammar for Writing

MARK HONEGGER

University of Louisiana, Lafayette

Houghton Mifflin Company

Boston   New York

Publisher: Patricia A. Coryell
Executive Editor: Suzanne Phelps Weir
Development Manager: Sarah Helyar Smith
Assistant Editor: Anne Leung
Senior Project Editor: Margaret Park Bridges
Senior Marketing Manager: Cindy Graff Cohen
Marketing Associate: Wendy Thayer

Cover and chapter opener image: "India Improv" by Ann Schroeder

Credits appear on page 283, which is an extension of the copyright page

Printed in the U.S.A.

Library of Congress Control Number: 2003109860

ISBN: 0-618-25189-8

23456789-QF-09 08 07 06 05

Contents

4   Phrases: The Art of Chunking   50

5   More on Phrases   63

6   Grammatical Roles: Distinguishing Identical Elements   78

7 Adverbials and Other Elements in the Clause   96

8 Passive? Tense? What's on That Verb?   108

9 Putting Words Together: Coordination, Subordination, and Parallelism   133

12 Word Choices 208

13 The Written Standard and the Oral Varieties of English 223

Appendix—The Grammatical Analysis of Literature 237

Selected Answers to Exercises 253

Glossary 277

Index 285

Preface

Who takes undergraduate grammar courses? The students in these classes can be quite diverse: English majors, education majors, communications majors, aspiring writers and editors, and students who simply hope to improve their college essays or their business reports. What all of these students have in common is a connection to writing and editing.

English Grammar for Writing is written for a person with little or no prior background in grammar. This assumption is based on my own experience teaching grammar at a variety of institutions, where I have found that most students did not know the basics of English well enough to analyze and discuss syntactic structure consistently and with confidence. Ironically, sometimes my honors students knew the least because they had followed academic tracks in school where they got to do "more interesting things" than study grammar. Hence, this book starts with the basics and attempts to explain each aspect of grammar along the way.

The coverage of grammar here is selective. *English Grammar for Writing* does not try to teach everything about the structure of English; rather, it focuses on those aspects of grammar that apply to punctuation and to matters of writing style such as passives and parallelism. It also includes a chapter on intonation and information structure, material that is not included in most grammar textbooks. This information can give students insights into the types of writing problems that can be hard to diagnose. Knowledge of grammar will equip students to precisely assess writing errors and to resolve fuzzy writing problems.

Many instructors have found success teaching grammar in the context of writing. This text reinforces the link between grammar and writing by showing how our understanding of structure enhances our understanding of writing. Teaching grammar in the context of writing works especially well for students who already have a relatively firm grasp of grammar; with a minimum of grammatical explanation, these students can find all kinds of interesting elements of their language.

For students who have only a tenuous grasp of grammar or who are not confident in their knowledge of grammar, however, it is not sufficient to teach grammar in a writing class. Language in real-world writing is too complex, too messy, to leave such students to their own devices in developing a sound understanding of the overall system of English. My experience is that all students can learn grammar if they are first introduced to simple, clear examples of the categories and terms that characterize English. And while there will always be exceptions to the rules and generalizations they are taught—language is, after all, one of the most complicated systems they will ever learn—the rules will be useful enough to provide a framework for understanding language coherently and systematically. Once this framework is in place, students can then apply their grammatical knowledge to real-world writing, whether they are working to improve the effectiveness of their assigned essays, analyzing poetry and prose for a literature class, or writing an office memo.

The Organization of the Book

English Grammar for Writing is a how-to book rather than a compendium. Each chapter builds on the previous ones, so students can understand how the whole system works together. The book begins by comparing writing with speech (Chapter 1), then moves to word classes (Chapters 2–3), followed by phrases and clauses or grammatical roles (Chapters 4–7). Tense and passives are introduced together (Chapter 8) because students often mistake one for the other. These topics are followed by subordination and coordination and modifiers (Chapters 9–10). The strong grammar foundation provided by the preceding chapters supports Chapter 11, which explains the importance of word order and word choice in writing to compensate for intonation in speech. The book concludes with the lexicon and varieties of English (Chapters 12–13) to round off students' overall appreciation of writing and of English. An appendix on using grammar in literature analysis enables instructors to incorporate this application into their grammar classes. The exercises throughout the book range from easy to difficult, and they encourage students to develop a robust knowledge of grammar by requiring different kinds of tasks: recognition, correction, composition, and even deliberate error production, the latter because some errors are hard to detect, so students need to learn about the problem in more than one way. Numerous sentence diagrams lay out grammar principles in an easy-to-read format.

Supplements for Student and Instructor

A website for students (<http://college.hmco.com/english>) provides additional exercises designed for the book, a step-by-step analysis of those sentences, and access to hundreds of other grammar exercises.

An Instructor's Resource Manual supplies complete answers for all exercises that are not open-ended and suggests discussion points that can be tied in with specific exercises. The corresponding instructors' website (<http://college.hmco.com/english>) provides a password-accessible version of the manual.

Acknowledgments

Many individuals have contributed to the writing of this book. I would especially like to thank my developmental editor, Mark Gallaher, for his many valuable suggestions. The following reviewers gave me the benefit of looking at the manuscript from many different perspectives, for which I am deeply grateful: Laura Bates, Indiana State University; Robert T. Brunner, Northern Virginia Community College; Avon Crismore, Indiana University–Purdue University, Fort Wayne; Douglas Downs, University of Utah; Morgan Gresham, Clemson University; Laura R. Micciche, East Carolina University; Sally L. Joyce, Keene State College; Rod Kessler, Salem State College; Barbara Kroll, California State University, Northridge; Claiborne Rice, University of Louisiana at Lafayette; Ravi Sheorey, Oklahoma State University; Beth Lee Simon, Indiana University–Purdue University, Fort Wayne; Donna Strickland, Southern Illinois University, Carbondale; John W. Taylor, South Dakota State University; Sarah Tsiang, Eastern Kentucky University

I have also benefited from the support of staff members at Houghton Mifflin, including Executive Editor Suzanne Phelps Weir, Development Manager Sarah Helyar Smith, Assistant Editor Anne Leung, and Senior Project Editor Margaret Park Bridges. My colleague, Dr. Mary Warner at Western Carolina University, has been a model of unswerving devotion to educating students. Finally, my wife, Rose, and my three daughters have also patiently borne the burden of birthing this book.

Mark Honegger
University of Louisiana, Lafayette

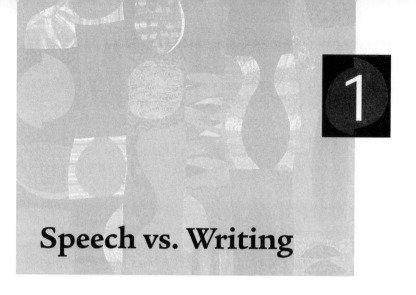

Speech vs. Writing

PREVIEW *This chapter provides a comparison between speech and writing, with a focus on the following issue: both modes of language have different resources for conveying what a sender wishes to communicate. Writing has fewer resources than speech, which puts it at a disadvantage. Learning to exploit those resources accurately and fully is the very purpose of this book, because the resources writing makes available are based on the structural properties, or grammar, of the English language.*

The Most Important Technology

We live in a technological world with all its marvels and complexities, and sometimes the technology overawes us. Efficiency, convenience, comfort, entertainment—all of these are at our fingertips. It is hard to imagine even going back to a world before technology, so much has it become integrated into the fabric of our lives. As you look around you at this splendid technological world, what would you say is its most important technology?

The first thing that comes to my mind is computers. Computers have influenced every facet of life, from video games to surgical procedures. Computer chips show up in a range of appliances that now can be called "smart." The widespread affordability of computers has given rise to that communications wonder called the Internet. Now the whole world is a mouse click away. What changes society will go through in the next few years because of computers and the Internet, no one can truly tell.

You might have thought of other influential technologies, too—for example, telecommunications has given us cell phones. Now you can go almost anywhere in the world and make or receive a phone call. Years ago, you could leave the office and truly be free of work, but today, your boss can track you down via pager or cell phone. Other wonders like bioengineering and genetic programming are radicalizing medicine and agriculture. Maybe in this new millennium every disease will be curable via gene resequencing.

However, none of these wonders is the most important technology today. There exists a technology that is even more indispensable to the human race than computers or the Internet or telecommunications, and it has already turned the world upside down for over four millennia. What is it?

This amazing technology is writing. Many readers may be surprised to think of writing as a technology because it does not appear to resemble the marvels mentioned above. Usually when we use the word *technology*, we think of applying science to some kind of industry or commerce. The word *technology* is also used to refer to the knowledge, methods, and materials needed to operate an industry or a commercial enterprise. Thus, using a line and a hook to catch fish is technology, albeit a simple one.

Writing consists of knowledge, methods, and materials. First, a large body of knowledge is required to write anything other people want to read. Then there are methods writers must master and engineered materials they must manipulate in order to produce a written message. However, writing is also an example of applying science to communication, because the written form of most languages is based on an analysis of a specific sound system and a specific system of meaning. It must be determined which sounds are important for conveying meaning and where words begin and end. For example, many Americans pronounce the *t* in *letter* as if it were a muddy *d*. However, we don't represent the actual pronunciation in the spelling of the word, because it turns out that it is not important for conveying meaning. Most of us don't even realize what actual consonant we articulate in the middle of *letter*. Likewise, in speech, words come to us in a more or less continual flow of sound, yet we must divide this flow of sound into distinct units if we are to represent language in writing.

Writers must also grapple with how to convey meaning. What words and punctuation marks should be used? What order should the words be put in? There are consequences to the choices writers make that are informed by the nature of language and the ways in which readers process language.

Writing has always been humanity's most important technology, and it continues to be so today. Consider the fact that it would be impossible to have discovered the other wonders of the modern world if we had not had centuries of writing, giving us the ability to store large amounts of knowledge and study and analyze it. Not only has writing given us today's technological wonders, but we all recognize that it is the foundation for their continuation. If Martians came tonight and zapped our brains so that the whole world lost its ability to write and read and couldn't regain it, we know that other sophisticated technologies could not continue. The information needed to manufacture and operate them is so complex and so copious that it could not be stored and used through purely oral means. Writing ensures that these technologies will continue; therefore, it controls the destiny of our world.

Remembering that writing is a technology can give us insight into the nature of writing. First, writing is something that needs to be learned. It is not a natural ability that springs into existence on its own. This is not true of our ability to speak. Speech (or sign language) develops naturally in us as infants. We are not taught our first language — instead, we are exposed to it. Writing, however, needs to be taught. In fact, writing has enough challenges to warrant that school systems in the United States devote twelve whole years to its development. One reason you go to school for this long is so that you can master both writing and reading with all their intricacies.

Second, because writing is a technology, there are technological aspects to master. For example, a lot of what a person learns when she learns about computers are conventions — the ways an entire industry has agreed to standardize how things are done so that people who don't know each other can work together. You can observe this use of convention when you look at a standard computer keyboard, where the letter keys are laid out in the following fashion:

q w e r t y u i o p

a s d f g h j k l

z x c v b n m

The keys don't have to be laid out in this sequence, and nothing prohibits computer manufacturers from choosing another sequence. In fact, some people find the order random and unhelpful, but because typewriters use this order and so many people have become used to the sequence, computers are usually sold with a QWERTY keyboard.

Writing works much the same way. A lot of what goes into writing is convention — socially agreed-upon rules that allow people who don't know each other to understand each other's writing. Convention is not the same as logical necessity. We could do things differently. However, it is useful that we all do things the same way so that all can participate in this community of writing.

Because writing is a technology, this book has a very specific focus with regard to teaching grammar. Its focus is on the teaching of grammar with an eye toward its application to writing and reading. It will not present grammar for grammar's sake, though that is sufficient reason for learning about grammar — being an educated person should include being knowledgeable about one's language. However, if you are reading this book, then my assumption is that you need to be able to write clearly and you need to consciously understand what is going on in writing, either because you will need to write in your career or because you will someday be teaching writing.

Though writing is a wondrous achievement, it is sadly underappreciated and ill understood. Part of my goal is to awaken in you an appreciation of written language in all of its brilliance. Some people are put off when asked to view writing as a technology, feeling that it dehumanizes writing. However, technology can actually help us to realize our humanity. An example of a humanizing technology is found in music. Much of the great and enduring music in the world, not to mention the popular music of today, depends on musical instruments that are manufactured through human technology. Human beings would not have been able to express their creativity and artistic sensibility through magnificent works such as Beethoven's *Fifth Symphony* without the violins and oboes and bassoons and other instruments that give sound to the notes on the page. Musical technology has served to make us more human, not less human.

In the same way, writing is a humanizing technology, something that allows us to express our humanity. Nevertheless, before we get into the nitty-gritty of this humanizing technology, we need to lay a foundation that establishes how writing works, and that is what we will do in this chapter. Let me then encourage you now to put on your best skeptic's hat and ask, "Okay, just what's so great about writing?"

Writing vs. Pictures

Writing is one of humanity's greatest tools, one that opens up a world of possibilities. Writing can do this because

1. *It is limited in its means.* English, for example, has 26 letters that come in two forms, uppercase and lowercase. It also has 12 major marks of punctuation. This means it is a small system language. In another, the writer might need to memorize thousands of symbols.

2. *It is unlimited in its output.* From this finite system, a writer can construct unlimited texts, unlimited in terms of size and unlimited with regard to the content that can be expressed.

This compactness of writing can be appreciated by comparing it to another human ability, that of making pictures. Numerous cultures that did not have a form of writing as we know it relied on pictographic communication. Consider, for example, the pictographic message below, sent by a Native American chief to the president of the United States as a message of friendship:

(From Henry R. Schoolcraft, *Historical and Statistical Information Respecting the Indian Tribes of America,* I. 418.)

Before you read further, try to figure out what the picture means.

How close did you come to the following explanation? The person in the house is the president. The two lines rising from the head of the first eagle identify it as the chief. He and the four warriors behind him are members of the eagle totem. The last warrior is a member of the catfish totem. The person in the lower left corner is also probably a chief. The lines connecting their eyes signify the idea of harmony, and the three houses at the bottom show that the Indians will adopt the customs of the whites.

Now, the picture is an ingenious method of communicating, and one can imagine the advantages of using pictures to communicate. They are aesthetically pleasing to look at. They have a kind of universality because they are not tied to specific languages. None of the objects in the picture represents any particular word either in the Native American language of the artist or in English. Rather they represent ideas or concepts, and insofar as these ideas and concepts are universal, these pictures could be recognized by viewers from many different languages and cultures. There is also more likely to be a resemblance between a picture and what it represents than between a word and what it represents. For example, people from diverse cultures and languages would probably understand that a picture of a bird represents a bird because of the physical resemblance between the two. However, there is no necessary connection between the sounds /b/, /ir/, and /d/ in the word *bird* and a physical bird itself.

However, serious drawbacks affect pictorial communication as well. First, it depends on having some skill at drawing. If your drawing ability is as poor as mine, then a receiver might have a hard time deciphering what a picture actually shows, let alone interpreting its meaning. Second, the meaning of the picture is ambiguous: the picture is open to more interpretations than a corresponding text would be. For example, when you were told that the lines connecting the eyes signal harmony, you probably thought that it was quite plausible, but did you realize that was what the lines meant before you read the explanation? A person viewing the picture might have thought that the lines signify that all the participants in the picture see each other. Or perhaps they are all tied together in some way as prisoners. Or maybe the lines signal some kind of intention—perhaps they all want to see each other or be in harmony with each other. Here is where we run into difficulty. How would you draw two pictures to signify the difference between "we are in harmony" and "we want to be in harmony"? How could you distinguish between "we see each other," "we want to see each other," and "we doubt we can see each other"? In fact, as you begin to think about different ideas you convey in English, you can quickly see how difficult it would be to draw pictures to convey all those ideas.

Writing solves all of these problems. First, symbols used for writing are stylized and simplified, and this puts less of a premium on being a skilled artist and opens the use of symbols up to a larger audience. Second, all of the ideas that would be difficult to convey simply with pictures are easy to convey with writing. Third, though we often complain about ambiguity in writing, pictures are even harder to interpret. As you write carefully, you can eliminate a lot of ambiguity. Much of what we will talk about in this book with regard to grammar will relate to reducing ambiguity.

Writing vs. Speech

We all can speak (or sign), in fact, quite well. Some of us may be shy, and most of us dread standing in front of an audience, but all of us can convey subtle emotions and a wealth of information in our conversations. What then is the

Frank and Ernest

©1980 Thaves. Reprinted with permission. Newspaper dist. by NEA, Inc.

relationship between writing and speech? They might seem quite similar, but in fact they are very different in a number of ways that are especially important to good writing. Before we get to the differences, let's single out one similarity that sheds light on what writers need to know.

Sender's Efficiency vs. Receiver's Understanding

There is a continual tradeoff in communication between the two parties involved: the sender and the receiver. The sender needs to make her job of production easy, and the receiver needs the message sent as clearly as possible. This is where the need for balance comes in. Consider if speech situations always favored the sender. Making a message as efficient as possible consists in making sounds less dissimilar. "Going to," for example, takes a little more time and effort to utter than "gonna." A speaker might rush even more and simply say "gon." If this process were carried out to its extreme, the message would come out with indistinguishable sounds, and the person hearing, or receiving, it would not be able to understand what was being communicated. A scenario that highly favors the speaker shortchanges the hearer.

Consider now how the world would look if speech situations always favored the hearer. Maximum intelligibility requires clear distinctions between sounds, but these in turn require more effort on the part of the speaker. The speaker would be forced to slow down, potentially to the point that she would be unwilling to communicate or maybe unable to communicate when the pressures of the situation call for quick speech. For example, if a parent had to call out to a child,

> "Do [pause] not [pause] touch [pause] the [pause] stove, [pause] John [pause] Francis."

rather than

> "Dontuchdastove, Johnnie."

the added burden of distinguishing sounds might result in a couple of burned fingers for little John Francis.

This same kind of tradeoff holds true for written communication as well. As texts are made easier for readers to read, they are made more difficult for writers to write. Conversely, as we lessen the difficulties for writers, the text becomes more difficult to read. We will see, though, in the pages to come that written language should be produced so that it favors the reader, and this means that the writer will have a greater burden in composing her text.

Let's consider what a text might look like as we increase the writer's burden of producing a composition. The original version doesn't even require word spaces:

Version 1

WHATISEXTRAORDINARYFROMOURPOINTOFVIEWISHOWWEL
LITTURNEDOUTFORUSIFTHEUNIVERSEHADFORMEDJUSTATIN
YBITDIFFERENTLYIFGRAVITYWEREFRACTIONALLYSTRONGE
RORWEAKERIFTHEEXPANSIONHADPROCEEDEDJUSTALITTLE
MORESLOWLYORSWIFTLYTHENTHEREMIGHTNEVERHAVEBEE
NSTABLEELEMENTSTOMAKEYOUANDMEANDTHEGROUNDWE
STANDONHADGRAVITYBEENATRIFLESTRONGERTHEUNIVERS
EITSELFMIGHTHAVECOLLAPSEDLIKEABADLYERECTEDTENT
WITHOUTPRECISELYTHERIGHTVALUESTOGIVEITTHERIGHTDI
MENSIONSANDDENSITYANDCOMPONENTPARTSHADITBEENW
EAKERHOWEVERNOTHINGWOULDHAVECOALESCEDTHEUNIV
ERSEWOULDHAVEREMAINEDFOREVERADULLSCATTEREDVOI
D

(adapted from Bill Bryson, *A Short History of Nearly Everything*)

At one time, texts were written like this. Words were not separated. There was no distinction between upper- and lowercase. If a scribe ran out of space before he finished a word, it was continued on the next line. We who have already been taught how to write would probably find this style harder to produce, but imagine how easy it would be for people learning how to write for the first time. They would only have to learn one form for every letter. They wouldn't need to be bothered with any rules for punctuation. They could jot down letters as the words came to their mind without worrying where one ended and one began. However, there is no doubt that this text, which carries little burden for the writer who pens it, greatly worsens the burden on the reader. Imagine trying to read an entire book written like the paragraph above. I doubt many readers today would make it past a few lines. We'd all wait for the movie.

A text like this shows us graphically how important something as simple as punctuation is. (Of course, it is easy to forget that putting spaces between words to mark word boundaries is a piece of punctuation, too.)

Let's take our sample paragraph above and add consistent word boundaries by using spaces. This gives us the following text:

Version 2

WHAT IS EXTRAORDINARY FROM OUR POINT OF VIEW IS HOW
WELL IT TURNED OUT FOR US IF THE UNIVERSE HAD FORMED
JUST A TINY BIT DIFFERENTLY IF GRAVITY WERE FRACTIONALLY

STRONGER OR WEAKER IF THE EXPANSION HAD PROCEEDED JUST
A LITTLE MORE SLOWLY OR SWIFTLY THEN THERE MIGHT NEVER
HAVE BEEN STABLE ELEMENTS TO MAKE YOU AND ME AND THE
GROUND WE STAND ON HAD GRAVITY BEEN A TRIFLE STRONGER
THE UNIVERSE ITSELF MIGHT HAVE COLLAPSED LIKE A BADLY
ERECTED TENT WITHOUT PRECISELY THE RIGHT VALUES TO GIVE
IT THE RIGHT DIMENSIONS AND DENSITY AND COMPONENT
PARTS HAD IT BEEN WEAKER HOWEVER NOTHING WOULD HAVE
COALESCED THE UNIVERSE WOULD HAVE REMAINED FOREVER A
DULL SCATTERED VOID

The simple act of adding spaces goes a long way toward making the text readable. In particular, we eliminate any ambiguity with respect to word boundaries. Nonetheless, the reader must still spend time in deciphering sentence boundaries. For example, the reader must decide whether the first sentence ends with the word *us* or continues on. The word *if* could be a part of the preceding sentence or begin a new sentence. A reader might try to combine the following words:

WHAT IS EXTRAORDINARY FROM OUR POINT OF VIEW IS HOW WELL
IT TURNED OUT FOR US IF THE UNIVERSE HAD FORMED JUST A
TINY BIT DIFFERENTLY

Thus, we have a true ambiguity that could easily be made clear by punctuation.

We could continue to add to the readability of the paragraph by marking the ends of sentences with a period. That would give us the paragraph below:

Version 3

WHAT IS EXTRAORDINARY FROM OUR POINT OF VIEW IS HOW
WELL IT TURNED OUT FOR US. IF THE UNIVERSE HAD FORMED
JUST A TINY BIT DIFFERENTLY IF GRAVITY WERE FRACTIONALLY
STRONGER OR WEAKER IF THE EXPANSION HAD PROCEEDED JUST
A LITTLE MORE SLOWLY OR SWIFTLY THEN THERE MIGHT NEVER
HAVE BEEN STABLE ELEMENTS TO MAKE YOU AND ME AND THE
GROUND WE STAND ON. HAD GRAVITY BEEN A TRIFLE STRONGER
THE UNIVERSE ITSELF MIGHT HAVE COLLAPSED LIKE A BADLY
ERECTED TENT WITHOUT PRECISELY THE RIGHT VALUES TO GIVE
IT THE RIGHT DIMENSIONS AND DENSITY AND COMPONENT
PARTS. HAD IT BEEN WEAKER HOWEVER NOTHING WOULD HAVE
COALESCED. THE UNIVERSE WOULD HAVE REMAINED FOREVER A
DULL SCATTERED VOID.

What makes this paragraph interesting is that while the addition of periods provides unambiguous sentence boundaries, the paragraph is still not easy to read because everything is in capital letters. The ends of sentences are explicitly marked but not the beginnings; surprisingly, we need to mark both the beginnings and ends of sentences to help the reader efficiently process the text. One indicator of sentence boundaries is not enough. Upper- and lowercase letters are part of our system of punctuation, too, and adding them dramatically improves the readability of the text, as seen below.

Version 4

What is extraordinary from our point of view is how well it turned out for us. If the universe had formed just a tiny bit differently if gravity were fractionally stronger or weaker if the expansion had proceeded just a little more slowly or swiftly then there might never have been stable elements to make you and me and the ground we stand on. Had gravity been a trifle stronger the universe itself might have collapsed like a badly erected tent without precisely the right values to give it the right dimensions and density and component parts. Had it been weaker however nothing would have coalesced. The universe would have remained forever a dull scattered void.

The above paragraph is still missing sentence-internal punctuation that would aid our processing of the text, but it has become much easier to read with the addition of a few basic punctuation conventions. Altogether, these four versions of the same paragraph illustrate something very basic about punctuation. Strictly speaking, it is often largely **redundant.** It contributes information that could be predicted from the text via other means. For example, the first four letters in the sequence ISEXTRAORDINARY from the first line of version 1 could be separated as *I sex* or *is extraordinary*. The reader knows that the first division is not possible because *traordinary* is not a word in English, and *I sex* is not a grammatical sequence. Hence, the space between *is* and *extraordinary* in versions 2–4 does not add new information to the text.

This phenomenon raises an intriguing question: why punctuate? The simple answer is that language works on the basis of redundancy. Multiple factors in a communication situation contribute information, and this multiplicity increases the probability for successful communication. For example, readers can figure out that the sequence *is extraordinary* consists of the words *is* and *extraordinary* based on (1) their knowledge of English spelling (there is no other way to break this sequence into complete words) and (2) the space between *is* and *extraordinary*. Communication is always subject to the plague of noise. Noise is anything that might hinder the message from going through. It could be actual sound that overpowers speech or it could be a smudge on a handwritten note. Redundancy helps combat noise as well as improve the readability of a sentence even in optimal conditions. Punctuation and other grammatical conventions in writing are some of the key redundancies we need in a text to make it efficient to read. Some people think that the formalities and conventions of writing are becoming outdated and someday will no longer be needed. Nothing could be further from the truth.

The Differences between Speaking and Writing

Texts need redundancy in the form of punctuation to make them readable. In addition, there are a number of differences between speech and writing that highlight the need for the conventions of written English. It is becoming increasingly important for teachers to be familiar with these aspects of language and communication. Many students struggle with writing because they lack sufficient exposure to language on the printed page. They take in information primarily through oral language rather than written language, and so they approach writing as if it were merely speaking on paper. The more we understand how speaking and writing differ, the better equipped we can be as writers and as teachers to instruct such students.

Let's examine eight differences between speaking and writing:

1. Spoken language is full of **paralinguistic cues,** cues that are outside of the language system, such as voice quality, facial expression, posture, and gestures. Written language lacks these signals. A lot of the message in a speaking context is gotten across by paralinguistic cues. In particular, they are used to signal the sender's rhetorical purpose—humor, entertainment, warning, and so forth. I might make a funny expression with my face, or perhaps my voice will be full of sternness or fear. In either case, I alert my listener to how he should interpret my words.

Paralinguistic cues can also override the actual meaning of the words themselves. We see this in the difference between a normal utterance of "You got an *A*," versus a sarcastic utterance of "Yeah, you got an *A*," where the speaker intends the exact opposite of her words. One reason that sarcasm is harder to convey in writing than in speech is because paralinguistic cues are often used to convey such meanings.

2. Similar to the point above, spoken language also has **intonation** and rhythm. Unlike paralinguistic cues, these resources are inside the language system itself. In science fiction movies, one can hear computers speaking with flat voices, but our human voices rise and fall throughout a sentence. This "music" that speaking produces not only is pleasant to listen to but also carries valuable information that hearers use to make sense of the speaker's words.

Like paralinguistic cues, intonational and rhythmic cues are used to signal the speaker's rhetorical purpose. For example, statements in English end with a falling intonation. *Yes/no* questions end with a rising intonation. Thus, our intonation distinguishes between the statement "You got an *A*," and the question "You got an *A*?"

These two differences between speaking and writing highlight a particular challenge for writing. Speakers use paralinguistic and intonational cues to communicate their purposes for communication. Unfortunately, writing lacks both of these powerful resources. It should come as no surprise that we often struggle with making our rhetorical purpose clear in our text, because we have been used to conveying rhetorical purpose through means that are unavailable in writing. Our listeners usually understand our purposes when we speak because they discern them in our tone of voice and our posture and intonation. We don't have to work hard at those cues because they come naturally to us. However, we then assume that our reader can follow what we are trying to do in a text just as easily, but that won't be true unless we have signaled our purposes through the specific resources that writing offers.

3. A third difference between writing and speaking is that spoken language often has the advantage of **situational transparency.** The context of the spoken utterance contributes information useful to understanding, but when we read, we don't have access to the place and time that the message of the text is set in or access to the place and time that the text was composed in. For example, if you ask me, "What's the temperature?" as I peer into an oven on Thanksgiving Day, I will interpret your words as a question about the internal temperature of the turkey as it roasts. Yet if you ask me, "What's the temperature?" when I am standing outside on a winter day, I will interpret your words as a question about the outdoor air temperature. You don't need to specify in the first context that you want to know the turkey's temperature or in the second context that you want to know the air temperature. Your question can be less informative because the situation fills in the missing information for me. On the other hand, you can read a text in a variety of places that will not necessarily add anything useful to its understanding—a dorm room, the bathroom, almost anywhere. Likewise, you can read a text at any time, not necessarily some particular time that adds to your understanding it.

This puts an added burden on writing: the writer needs to make the words themselves say or imply everything because the reader does not have recourse to the time and place of the text. Therefore, we can be looser in our speech. We can be more vague, less specific, because the context will often supply information that is missing from the words themselves. When the writer writes, "I can see the bank," for example, she must make clear in her text whether she is at the river or in the middle of town if she wants the reader to know clearly what she is talking about. In most spoken contexts, the hearer will know quickly what the speaker of "I see the bank" intends to convey.

4. A fourth difference is that spoken language can be modified on the spot by the speaker as she processes feedback from the hearer. However, writing has no access to immediate feedback and so cannot self-correct. Self-correction comes in handy for speech. We engage a friend in conversation, and when we see a puzzled looked on his face, we amend what we have said. Furthermore, our hearers can ask questions and seek clarification when our communication does not go through successfully. Unfortunately, when our readers don't understand our prose, that's too bad. We are not there to amend what they didn't understand.

5. A fifth difference is that spoken language is primarily disposable, intended for one-time use. Written language, however, has an important storage function. It can be read multiple times and is often meant to be reread. Writing is what makes study possible, allowing us to concentrate on the words that convey someone's meaning. This means that breakdowns in communication are often more serious on the written page. A mistake there is a mistake that can last forever. When we speak, we often make little mistakes—we slur our words, we leave out words, we mispronounce words. Typically, our hearers don't remember these slips, and so they don't interfere with successful communication. When we write, we can make little mistakes too, but now they are preserved and so are always there to interfere with the reading of the text.

Another relevant consideration is that one writer often writes to numerous readers. This can lead to the following scenario: weaknesses that might be ignored or unnoticed by our first nine readers still might be noticed by that tenth reader and so hinder his comprehension of the text. Furthermore, another reader might read the text twice without a problem but then notice the error on a third reading, and so the mistake still comes back to haunt the communication situation. This is because comprehension proceeds at different speeds in speaking and writing. In speech, a hearer is compelled to comprehend at the speed the language is produced. If the hearer misses something that the speaker says, then the hearer simply misses out on that part of the message. In reading, however, a reader can slow down the comprehension process. He can read and reread as many times as he likes.

For example, perhaps nine out of ten readers might read the following sentence,

I only have eyes for you.

and experience nothing but warm sentiment at the fond affection expressed by the line. A tenth, though, might read the sentence more carefully and then stumble over the meaning by asking, "Did the writer mean 'only have' as in

> I only HAVE eyes for you (I don't <u>need</u> eyes for you);

did the writer mean 'only eyes' as in

> I have only EYES for you (I don't have <u>arms</u> for you);

or did the writer mean 'only you' as in

> I have eyes only for YOU (I don't have eyes for <u>other people</u>)?"

Because of the enduring nature of writing, such difficulties are more serious than they are in the fleeting nature of speech.

6. A sixth difference is that spoken language is used predominantly for **interactional** purposes, the maintenance of human relationships. Written language is more often used for **transactional** purposes, the exchange of information. This means that written language has a greater need for accuracy, for making the meaning clear. In interactional situations, we convey information that is already in some way familiar to our hearers, which makes it simpler to encode it in language. However, in a transactional setting, the sender transmits novel information. Novel information is harder to understand, and as the content becomes more novel or complex, the reader's task becomes more difficult.

7. A seventh difference is that spoken language relies on a relatively simple syntax or sentence structure, whereas written language uses a more complex syntax. Both speaking and writing have a grammar, a system of rules that characterizes which word orders are well formed. However, when we reflect on a typical conversation, we know our speech contains many incomplete sentences. Sometimes it consists of little more than sequences of phrases. Written language cannot get away with this. Even when human conversation is included in a creative work, it tends to be smoothed out and adapted to the rigors of writing.

An example of this difference in complexity is that spoken language tends to use coordination rather than subordination. If sentences and clauses are linked together at all, it is with coordinate conjunctions such as *and,* which is the simplest of connective devices. The conjunction *and* simply tells the hearer to add new information to the preceding information, without specifying any further relationship between the two pieces of information.

Written language, however, uses subordination much more frequently. Consider the two sentences below:

> The student handed in her paper *because* her instructor threatened her with an *F.* [subordination]

The instructor threatened the student with an *F, and* the student handed in her paper. [coordination]

Both sentences convey almost the same information, but the first is more likely to show up in writing and the second in speaking. If we compare the two sentences, we see two things. First, the structure of the first sentence is more complex than the second. In the second sentence, the conjunction *and* is redundant. We could remove it and make the utterance consist of two separate sentences. However, in the first sentence, the word *because* does not stand outside of its clause but is directly connected to it, changing the relationship of the two clauses.

The issue of complexity helps us see why the second sentence is preferred in speech. Because we produce speech spontaneously and fluently, without concentrating on the words we speak, we must use simpler structures. Complexity, however, is not a drawback for writing, because writing can be produced at a more leisurely pace. With few exceptions, people don't read what we write as we write it; they read it afterward, no matter how long we have spent writing and refining and polishing our words.

Clearly, the first sentence is more precise: the conjunction *because* is more informative than the conjunction *and*. The conjunction *because* tells us the exact relationship between the content of both clauses: the two stand in a cause-effect relationship. The conjunction *and* by itself gives us a less precise account of how the two clauses are related; it tells us that both clauses are true, but nothing beyond that. That is why *and* can be used when a number of different logical relationships hold between clauses, such as

ADDITION: Joan plays the guitar, and Kyle plays the piano.

TEMPORAL: The alarm clock rang, and Stacy got out of bed.

REPETITION: They knocked, and they knocked.

CONTRAST: Carl is nosy, and Fred minds his own business.

COMMENT: The party was a flop, and that's no lie!

CONDITION: Give me $5, and I'll pay you back tomorrow.

Because of its capacity to express more thought in fewer words, subordination is used more in writing. Writing holds a premium on conveying complexity, so the added information contained in subordinate conjunctions as compared to coordinate conjunctions comes in handy. However, this kind of complexity is not as necessary when a speaker is engaged in transactional purposes. These considerations about subordination and coordination are relevant to our next point as well.

8. An eighth difference is that spoken language contains less information per sentence than written language does. That is, each sentence tends to say less. Spoken language contains much repetition. Written language has a higher level of information content per sentence. We tend to pack more new information in each sentence. The diluted information of speech again serves two purposes. It eases the task of the speaker, who must produce speech in real time, and it eases the burden on the hearer, who must process and comprehend language in real time. Stretches of spontaneous speech tend to look like the following:

> I entered the classroom + and I looked towards the teacher + I looked at what she had on the board + I looked at the pile of books on her desk + were they thick + were they hardcover

In writing, however, content isn't diluted. It seems possible that our writing could also be made to incorporate less content in each sentence and thereby make it easier for readers to comprehend. Surprisingly, this doesn't work. Redundancy in writing on the same scale as we have it in speech is boring. Furthermore, it distracts readers and makes writing harder to comprehend. Writing needs a sufficient amount of novel content in each succeeding sentence to keep the discourse going.

Why Writing Is Harder than Speaking

The upshot of all of this is that writing and speech are different enough to warrant looking at them individually, and this gives us a basis for considering this thing called grammar and the conventions that are based on grammar, such as punctuation. Spoken and written English have different purposes and face different demands. In particular, written English involves the very difficult task of communicating large amounts of complex material in a compact manner.

In a context where spoken English is used, receivers can rely on that context—the place and time of the speaking—and so can generally depend less on getting right all the lower-level details of the linguistic medium. However, if the details are necessary, spoken English has more of them—in particular, the intonation and rhythm of language, which carry a tremendous amount of information. Written English relies on word order and punctuation in their place. However, punctuation does not carry as much information as intonation and rhythm, and this places a greater burden on the accuracy of punctuation.

Taken all together, these differences between written and spoken language show that writing is a much more difficult form of communication than speaking, and there are particular challenges inherent in the encoding of written language. It is called upon to convey new and complex material, yet it has fewer resources at its disposal than does speech. Once a text is completed and placed before the reader, it cannot be corrected. Furthermore, writing is the medium of choice for permanently storing language. Consequently, the few resources writing has—word order, word choice, and punctuation—carry a greater burden for a more difficult task. The accurate and most effective use of these resources is crucial, and errors or weaknesses in these areas have serious consequences. Teachers and writers need to know the differences between writing and speaking to understand what role grammar plays in writing, a medium that requires greater accuracy and precision than speaking. All of these eight distinctions between writing and speaking provide compelling reasons for studying grammar, because, as this book will show, grammar is the basis for punctuation and the other conventions of writing.

EXERCISE 1

Draw a picture that is elaborate enough to convey a meaning as complex as that conveyed by the picture on page 5. Write down on a separate page what the meaning of that picture is. Then exchange your picture with a classmate. Write down in a short paragraph what you think your classmate's picture means. Then compare your interpretation with the artist's intended interpretation. Discuss where and why the communication was and was not successful.

EXERCISE 2

Write a paragraph completely in capital letters with no punctuation and no spaces between words or sentences. Then exchange it with a classmate and discuss where it becomes especially hard to figure out the boundaries of words and sentences.

EXERCISE 3

A new form of communication has emerged in which people write in real time. Take a look at an online chat room or some instant-messaging text. How does such language compare to spontaneous speech? How does the language compare to published writing? In light of the eight differences between speech and writing listed above, how is real-time writing similar to and different from speech?

COMPREHENSION QUESTIONS

1. What is the most important technology in our world today? Why?

2. How does writing differ from speaking with respect to how we learn it?

3. What are conventions? How does writing compare to computers with respect to conventions?

4. What advantages does writing have over communicating with pictures?

5. What tradeoff takes place between the sender and the recipient in every speech situation? How is this tradeoff pertinent to the writing situation?

6. How does language depend on redundancy? How does punctuation relate to redundancy?

7. What are eight differences between speech and writing? Describe each one in detail.

8. In light of the differences between speech and writing, what unique difficulties does writing face?

The Major Parts of Speech

PREVIEW *This chapter concentrates on the four largest word classes in English: nouns, verbs, adjectives, and adverbs. Nouns are distinguished from proper nouns and pronouns. Various tests are given for identifying these classes so that you can explain to yourself and others why a word belongs to a particular part of speech. Attention is drawn to homonyms so that you can be aware of words that belong to more than one word class.*

To write well, we need to know many different things, one of which is how to revise and correct what we write. Imagine you are in a class and your teacher is reading a draft of your essay. She notices various sentences where your style could be improved, so she says to you, "Your nouns in this paragraph should be made more vivid and concrete." Would you know which words she is referring to? This chapter will discuss the names that we give word categories in English, both so that we can understand when other people talk about them and also so that we can talk about them ourselves. We need to be clear about these terms so that we can use them in determining the overall structure of our sentences, all for the ultimate goal of making our language serve our purposes in writing. This chapter and the next three will elucidate the technical side of this technology called writing. You may legitimately wonder, as many people do, what IS the point of grammar. As a matter of fact, when you read through Chapters 2 through 5, I would like you to speculate about how this material might relate to the practical concerns of writing. I will give you one little suggestion about why knowing grammar will improve your life. It will allow you, as you write or deal with other people's writing, to turn problems that are vague into problems that are specific and concrete.

One of the greatest hindrances to solving problems is not being clear about what you are trying to solve in the first place. Vague problems are notoriously difficult to solve. "My car doesn't run," I say to myself. So what do I do? My vague assessment doesn't give me any help in getting my old clunker up on the highway again. Should I replace a dead battery or get a tune-up? I don't know what I should do about a car that doesn't run. What I need at this point is some technical knowledge.

What is more complex than a car engine? Writing. So often, we read a passage and intuitively recognize that something is wrong without being able to say any more about it than "My essay doesn't run." At this point we need many different kinds of knowledge to pinpoint what exactly doesn't work. With knowledge of the technical details of language, we can distinguish dangling modifiers from comma splices, subject-verb agreement from tense problems, and mechanical problems from higher-level organization and content problems.

What's a Part of Speech?

The biblical book of Genesis records how God brought the animals to Adam for him to name: "He brought them to the man to see what he would name them; and whatever the man called each living creature, that was its name." Adam did all the work here of naming, but in doing so he also increased his knowledge. Before this event, Adam perhaps would have had a single word, something like *animal,* to talk about tigers and elephants and monkeys and hawks and so forth. Using only one word puts all these creatures into a vast, undifferentiated category. However, when Adam started to give these animals individual names, it became necessary for him to differentiate them and to understand them.

Names do that for us. They help us to systematize our knowledge and to make decisions about whether two things are the same or different. We need names to talk about language as well, and without the ability to identify its machinery, so to speak, we are severely limited in talking about language. We can read a sentence and perhaps sense that something is wrong with it, but we will probably be vague about the specific problem and therefore less likely to know how to fix it.

Traditionally, these names have been called **parts of speech:** those basic categories such as noun, verb, adjective, and the rest. These categories are also known as *word classes,* and I will use these two terms interchangeably. The great thing about these categories is that you already know them in your head, even if you don't consciously know how to match a word-class label to a given word in a sentence. The fact that you understand when other people speak and that other people understand you when you speak shows that you have an unconscious mastery of these categories.

One of the best ways for you to start this chapter is to get some informal practice in identifying the category of some specific words. Put aside this textbook for a moment and look at some sentences, any sentences, perhaps from a newspaper or magazine or book that you like. Observe each word and ask yourself, "Which words have similar characteristics?" When we find words that have similar characteristics, we may find that these words form a group that is determined by the characteristics we have identified.

What might count as similar characteristics? One consideration that might count is that you find similarities with regard to the kind of meaning they have. For example, if you look at the following two sentences,

> Fifi hugged the cat.

> Gus caught the baseball.

you might notice that *hugged* and *caught* both seem to designate some kind of action. The next logical step would then be to ask whether *hugged* and *caught* belong to the same word class. If they do, it suggests that there is a word class that is defined (at least partly) by this similarity in meaning.

Another kind of similarity might be a similarity of position within a sentence. We might find that certain kinds of words occur in certain places, perhaps before or after a particular word. For example, in the above two examples, we see that both *cat* and *baseball* occur after the word *the*. This raises the possibility that there exists a category that is defined by the characteristic that its members may occur after the word *the*.

Let's brainstorm a minute to ask ourselves what we should consider when we set up these classes of words. We have already noted that we want each class to have a set of characteristics that all of its members share. We should add that we want nonmembers, those words outside the class, to lack these characteristics. Another thing that we want is for the members of the class to be interchangeable. If we find a member of the class in a certain sentence, then we should be able to put any other member of the class in that same sentence in place of its fellow member. In the above two examples, if we treated *cat* and *baseball* as members of the same class, interchangeability would allow us to make the following two sentences:

> Fifi hugged the baseball.

> Gus caught the cat.

Because *cat* and *baseball* are interchangeable, they may be members of the same word class.

Content Words

When you look at a text, you can find a number of different words, some of which give us content about the world and some of which act like a kind of glue that connects words to one another. English is always adding new examples of content words to the language. For example, in my great-grandparents' day the words *cell phone* or *Internet* would never have been used, but you probably use these terms every day. Hence, we call categories that include these content words **open classes,** because they are open to new members.

There is another set of words we call **closed classes:** these classes rarely add new members and so are closed to membership. I will talk about closed classes in the next chapter. The open classes are very large, in fact so large that no one person would know every word that belongs in each open class. The closed classes are smaller. It is possible for someone to simply memorize all the members of a closed class. However, we can't simply memorize what belongs in all the open classes because they are always expanding; we need some other way of identifying words that belong in these classes. We could just guess or use our intuition, but we really require a more productive method of identifying words.

Tests for Identification

If we move beyond guessing, we need to replace it with something concrete, something specific that we can apply when we analyze a sentence. Hence, this section lists a number of tests that will help us look for specific characteristics of words that can help us identify the categories to which they belong. We unconsciously know the criteria that will be described in this section, but using these tests gives us a way of making our unconscious knowledge conscious so that we can knowingly manipulate it and use it as we work with language.

There are two different kinds of tests for determining parts of speech: **structure tests** and **meaning tests.** As you master the application of both kinds of tests, you will be better equipped to diagnose what is going on in a sentence. Structure tests are tests that identify parts of speech on the basis of their structural properties, in particular, where they occur in the sentence relative to other words or categories of words. Other structure tests identify words based on the kinds of forms they can take. Meaning tests base their identifications on the meanings of words. Generally, structure tests are the more accurate tests in determining grammatical categories, but this need not be a reason for eliminating meaning tests from our repertoire of grammatical tools.

Here, then, are structure and meaning tests that can identify the four parts of speech that are open classes: nouns, adjectives, verbs, and adverbs.

NOUNS

MEANING TEST

■ A noun is a person, place, or thing.

STRUCTURE TESTS

■ A noun can occur in the following positions:

the _____, a/an _____

the (adjective) _____, a/an (adjective) _____

■ A noun can have a plural marker added to it.

■ A noun can have a possessive marker added to it.

The meaning test is the test that probably first comes to mind when trying to identify the **nouns** in a sentence. It allows us to use the word meanings we have stored in our heads. Also, in the great majority of cases, it will give the right results for grammatical analysis, though there are important exceptions to the meaning test. In particular, we sometimes encounter nouns that have a verblike meaning, such as the word *destruction* in the following sentence:

The destruction was horrendous because of the bombing.

We know that the word *destruction* does not designate a person or a place. Neither is it a thing in any tangible sense. If we were pressed to put this word into a category, we might call it an event, but events are items that seem to correspond better to verbs than to nouns. These kinds of nouns show us that we need another kind of test besides the meaning test.

A meaning test will also be of limited help when a truly novel noun is encountered for the first time, such as the word *syzygy:*

The scientist could not calculate the next syzygy for that distant moon without more information.

The American Heritage Dictionary defines *syzygy* as "either of two points in the orbit of a celestial body . . . where the body is in opposition to or in conjunction with the sun," but chances are that many of us don't know the meaning or would even have a reasonable guess if the word was given in an opaque context where the surrounding words didn't give us enough information to figure out the meaning. This is where structure tests become useful.

The structure tests identify that nouns directly follow words like *the* or *a/an,* or they follow those words plus an adjective. (We haven't explained yet what adjectives are, so let's identify them for the present by giving examples of them — they include words like *big, old, happy, blue,* and *fast.*) Other parts of speech are excluded from such positions, which makes this a good test for one of the two most important parts of speech.

Now we need to be aware of a wrinkle involving adjectives that arises for the structure test. It is stated as if only a single adjective can precede the noun, but actually a number of adjectives can go before the noun, as in the following phrases:

>   the <u>big</u> dog
>
>   the <u>big</u> <u>red</u> dog
>
>   the <u>big</u> <u>red</u> <u>nervous</u> dog

In addition to noting the positions where a noun is found to the exclusion of other categories, we notice that nouns are the only category in English that can take a plural marker, usually that simple little *-s* or *-es,* or a possessive ending, the *'s* for singular nouns and the *s'* for plural nouns. Thus, when we look at a sentence, we can check and see which words can take one of these endings to make them plural or possessive and which cannot. In the example below,

>   The student attended the class.

we see that the words *student* and *class* can take the *-s* and *-es* plural, respectively, but the words *the* and *attended* cannot.

All of the tests given in this chapter are general rules of thumb. However, they do have exceptions that grammar students need to be aware of. For example, the structure test for nouns involving the ability to take a plural ending is a test that works only when it shows up. That is, the fact that a plural marker can be added confirms that a word in question is a noun, but the fact that a plural marker cannot be added does not confirm that a word is not a noun. Some nouns simply don't take plural markers. In English, we don't use the word *destruction* in the plural, but the other tests will still show *destruction* to be a noun. This is why it is important to learn all the identification tests for each category, so that you can compensate for exceptions when they arise.

ADJECTIVES

MEANING TEST

■ An adjective describes, modifies, or qualifies the meaning of a noun.

STRUCTURE TESTS

■ An adjective can occur in the following positions:

the _____ (noun)

very _____

■ An adjective can have the comparative marker *-er* or the superlative marker *-est* added to it.

The meaning test is normally the first one we are taught and the first one that consequently comes to our mind. Thus, in the phrase *the big chair,* the adjective *big* describes the size of the chair. In the phrase *the smart student,* the adjective *smart* describes the intelligence of the student. This is a helpful test to keep in your arsenal of diagnostic tools for adjectives.

It is useful to apply the position test for nouns and the position test for **adjectives** together, as these tests depend on one another. Looking at the first structure test, we see that adjectives may appear between words like *the* or *a/an* and nouns. (Jumping ahead a bit, the words *the* and *a/an* belong to a category called determiners.) Nouns follow the determiner and perhaps an adjective as well. Hence, one of the common patterns that we find in language is the determiner + adjective + noun pattern, as in the following examples:

the silly song

a hard book

the quick hare

The second structure test looks to see if the word in question can follow *very*. In the above three examples, we see that *very* can precede each of the adjectives:

the very silly song

a very hard book

the very quick hare

The final structure test notes that adjectives take two forms that no other word class takes: the comparative form and the superlative form:

> the sillier song

> a harder book

> the quickest hare

Note that some adjectives form their comparative and superlative forms by adding *more* or *most:*

> more intelligent   (not *intelligenter*)

> most intelligent   (not *intelligentest*)

As with all tests, there are exceptions. Most adjectives describe characteristics that can be true in degree. For example, a song can be more silly or less silly. A book can be more hard or less hard. A hare can be more quick or less quick. However, there are also adjectives that don't admit degrees, as in the following phrases:

> a <u>financial</u> decision

> the <u>main</u> point

We cannot say *a very financial decision* or *the very main point,* yet *financial* and *main* are still adjectives.

The following exercise gives you the opportunity to apply the identification tests for nouns and adjectives.

EXERCISE 1

Identify the nouns and adjectives in the following paragraph.

> A thoughtful president in very pretty clothes should consider the largest number of greasy sandwiches a counselor could eat. Her deliberate decision could prompt an intelligent doctor to fire some deadbeat employees. Many medical personnel may also choose to dine out because of the interesting challenges of lean cuisine.

EXERCISE—APPLY YOUR KNOWLEDGE

Why isn't the following a good rule for identifying adjectives?

> Adjectives follow the words *more* and *most.*

NOUNS VS. ADJECTIVES A difficulty can arise when you need to distinguish between certain nouns and adjectives. Compare the following two phrases and identify the nouns and adjectives:

> a tasty pizza   a pepperoni pizza

The word *pizza* is a noun. In the first phrase, we can put the word *very* before the word *tasty,* indicating that *tasty* is an adjective. However, we can't put *very* before *pepperoni*. Still, the word *pepperoni* appears between the determiner *a* and its following noun. That is, *pepperoni* in this phrase meets one of the tests for being an adjective but also fails a test for being an adjective.

We are left with a few choices as to what to conclude. We might say that the tests don't work or that we have encountered exceptional cases here. Fortunately, there is a simple way out of this problem. Our test as given above suggests that if a single word appears between *the* and a noun, it must be an adjective, but it turns out that in addition to *the* + adjective + noun sequences, we also find *the* + noun + noun sequences. What we have then in *pepperoni pizza* is a unit consisting of a noun plus a noun—in other words, a noun compound. Hence, it is not really an exception to the tests given above. Notice that a noun compound can have an adjective appear in front of it, as in the phrase *a tasty pepperoni pizza.*

You might have noticed that nouns and adjectives seem to have a fair amount in common when it comes to their language properties. The structure tests have already shown that both can be used to modify nouns. There are also common positions in which they both occur, such as following *be*-verbs, as in the following examples:

> Kim is president.
>
> Kim is happy.
>
> Kim is asleep.

The three examples show how this position after a *be*-verb takes either nouns or adjectives and also that nouns and adjectives are related categories. In addition, the examples show us that there is a kind of adjective that cannot occur between a determiner and a noun but that can follow a *be*-verb. The adjective *asleep* is an example. While we can say, "Kim is asleep," we can't say the following (the * signals that the sentence is ill formed in some way):

> *The asleep dog was a motel for fleas.

An observant reader might notice that the word *asleep* also cannot be modified by *very* or occur in the comparative or superlative form:

> *Kim is very asleep.

> *Kim is more asleep.

> *Kim is most asleep.

This adjective appears to fail all our structure tests for adjectives. How do we know then that the word *asleep* is an adjective? Other words similar to *very* can modify *asleep:*

> Kim is quite asleep.

> Kim is really asleep.

VERBS

MEANING TEST

■ A verb carries the meaning of an action or a state.

STRUCTURE TESTS

■ A verb can occur with

tense

third-person-present suffix

■ A verb can occur in the following position:

(please) _____.

The meaning test for **verbs** is a useful rule of thumb for a majority of cases again, but it runs into problems with verbs like *be,* as in the following sentence:

> John is tired.

If we ask which word tells us the state or condition John is in, we would say that the adjective *tired* rather than the verb *is* gives us this information. The verb *is* appears to contribute very little meaning to the sentence. Nonetheless, the meaning test will be helpful in many cases, especially when the verbs in question denote physical actions.

The structure tests for verbs consist mainly of what are called morphological tests, tests about how to put together words. In this case, we are looking at what kind of suffix can combine with the individual verbs. The first structure test depends on manipulating tense. **Tense** is that feature of the verb that conveys

Frank and Ernest

© 2003 Thaves. Reprinted with permission. Newspaper dist. by NEA, Inc.

the time of the sentence relative to past, present, and future. In English, there are only two tenses that are marked on the verb itself—past and present. When you find a past or present sentence in a text, locate the word that makes the sentence past or present to find the verb. If you are not sure which word it is, change a past-tense sentence into present tense or a present-tense sentence into past. The word that changes form is the one that is the verb. In the following sentence,

> This information shows the importance of the idea of citizenship.

your understanding of the sentence would allow you to identify *shows* as the word that determines the tense of the sentence. If you weren't sure, you could transform the sentence into past tense,

> This information showed the importance of the idea of citizenship.

and see that *shows* turns into *showed,* identifying that word as the verb.

In the majority of cases, we can identify a verb in past tense by looking for the suffix *-ed,* the regular past-tense ending. However, this structure test will not suffice by itself because of irregular verbs like *cut,* which do not change their form in the past tense, as the following shows:

> Yesterday, Gus cut the rope.   [past tense]

Another morphological test would be to identify the word that takes the suffix *-s* in a present-tense sentence with a third-person-singular subject, as in the following sentence (we'll talk about how to identify subjects in Chapter 5):

> Gus <u>cuts</u> the rope. *vs.* The soldiers <u>cut</u> the rope.

Be careful to distinguish between the suffix *-s* that appears on present-tense verbs and the plural suffix *-s* that appears on nouns. If you encounter a sentence where you are not sure whether a word with an *-s* suffix is a noun or a verb, you can test it by placing a number larger than one in front of the word in question. Numbers can be placed before nouns but not before verbs, as the following sentences show:

> Andrea brought the pizzas.

> ☻

> Andrea brought the five pizzas.

Therefore, the word *pizzas* must be a noun:

> Andrea cuts the rope.

> ☻

> *Andrea five cuts the rope.

Therefore, the word *cuts* must be a verb.

The last test is to try to insert the word you suppose to be the verb into a sentence that issues a command. You can add the word *please* in front of it to make it an unambiguous command. This will work for the majority of cases. Taking the sentence above, if I suppose the word *cut* to be the verb, I can make a new sentence like

> Please cut the bread.

Here again, there will be exceptions like the verb *resemble,* which does not lend itself to commands. Thus, though *resemble* is the verb in the following sentence,

> Your sister resembles Aunt May.

it does not make a good command:

> *Resemble your Aunt May.

This sort of discrepancy explains why we use multiple tests.

ADVERBS

MEANING TEST

■ Adverbs modify or qualify the meaning of a verb.

STRUCTURE TESTS

■ Adverbs are formed by adding an *-ly* suffix to an adjective.

Adverbs are a class that requires us to learn multiple tests, because they can be slippery to identify. We traditionally think of adverbs as contributing information that modifies the meaning of the verb. In the following sentence,

> Gail walked slowly.

the adverb *slowly* tells how the walking took place. These are the easiest examples to pick out. However, there are many exceptions to the meaning test. In the next example,

> Honestly, I did my homework, Teacher.

the adverb *honestly* doesn't tell how the homework was done but rather is an assertion by the speaker of the sentence of how she is addressing her teacher. This alerts us to the fact that meaning tests for identifying adverbs are of limited use and that structure tests must be relied on more heavily. Fortunately, the majority of adverbs in English are formed by adding the suffix *-ly* to an adjective, and this simple test makes the category easy for us to pick out of a sentence.

EXERCISE—APPLY YOUR KNOWLEDGE

Not all adverbs in English end in *-ly*. Find two manner adverbs (adverbs that modify or qualify the meaning of a verb) that don't end in *-ly*. Give a sentence for each word that demonstrates its use as an adverb.

PROPER NOUNS AND PRONOUNS   There are two word classes that are similar to nouns: **proper nouns** and **pronouns.** Proper nouns, another open class, are words that give a specific name to something. They are typically capitalized in written English, which makes them easier to identify. The following sentence gives an example with the proper noun *Sandy:*

> The monster was no match for Sandy.

The crucial issue for us is that proper nouns are a distinct word class from (common) nouns; they appear in different places in the structure of the sentence. Consider for a moment why we simply can't call the word *Sandy* a noun. If we did, it should conform to our previous tests for identifying nouns. So, for example, I should be able to put the word *the* before the proper noun *Sandy:*

> *The monster was no match for the Sandy.

However, I can't do this when I am using the word *Sandy* to actually name a person. Likewise, I can't put a plural marker on the word *Sandy* when it is being used as a proper noun:

> *The monster was no match for Sandys.

Observe, though, that proper nouns like *Sandy* can be used as common nouns, just as all other parts of speech can be used as common nouns. The following sentence gives an example of the name *Sandy* being used as a common noun:

There are three Sandys on this list.

In this sentence, the word *Sandy* is not being used as a name that picks out one particular individual.

Hence, while proper nouns are similar to nouns, their structural properties necessitate putting them in their own word class.

The same issue arises for the personal pronouns, a closed class consisting of the following words: *I, you, he, she, it, we, they, me, him, her, them, my, mine, your, his, its,* and *their*. Personal pronouns also are similar to nouns, but we can't simply treat them as nouns, because they also cannot be preceded by words like *the*. Thus, we can say:

You met your match when you faced the monster.

but not:

*The you met your match when you faced the monster.

Hence, pronouns will go in their own word class.

The following exercises will give you practice in recognizing all of the open-class parts of speech in a sentence.

EXERCISE 2

Identify all of the nouns, verbs, adjectives, and adverbs as well as proper nouns and pronouns in the following sentences. Cross out all other words that do not belong to these categories.

1. Slowly but surely ants devoured the delicious pizza pie.

2. The committee will meet for an appropriate amount of time before coming to a decision.

3. "Run to your clubhouse quickly, you naughty child!" yelled the flustered babysitter.

4. If chocolate grew on trees, then possibly the nursery could give me a bon-bon.

5. I am definitely not a god, and my name is not famous.

6. After the curious manager e-mailed the bill to the customer, her secretary composed a brief letter to the weekend supervisor.

7. Spud wanted to write an adjective, but all he could think of was the word *deleterious.*

8. Help me at the booth next week.

9. The administration building was carried away by giant eagles in the sky.

10. When Patrice arrived, we all came out of our hiding places.

11. Andy and Barney patrolled Mayberry, North Carolina.

12. Ringo Starr replaced Pete Best in a famous band named after bugs.

13. The earth weighs 6,600 billion billion tons.

14. A monophobe fears solitude.

15. The rodeo clown bravely saved the life of the star cowboy, his rival in love.

EXERCISE 3

Compose your own sentences that have exactly the number of parts of speech listed. You may add any other parts of speech you need to complete the sentence.

> EXAMPLE: A sentence with 2 nouns and 1 verb
>
> The rabbit sat on the bank.
>   N   V   N

1. A sentence with 3 nouns and 1 verb

2. A sentence with 2 nouns, 2 verbs, and 4 adjectives

3. A sentence with 3 nouns, 2 verbs, 3 adjectives, and 2 adverbs

4. A sentence with 5 nouns, 2 verbs, 1 adjective, and 1 adverb

Difficult Cases

As with all aspects of language, there are difficult cases that arise in identifying parts of speech. One case that we need to be alert to is **homonyms**—words with different meanings that sound alike and sometimes are spelled alike. The word *can* is an example in the following three sentences:

(1)   Judy can take the test.

(2)   Judy will can the peaches tomorrow.

(3)   Judy will fill the can.

We haven't talked yet about the part of speech *can* occupies in (1). It is a modal, a category to be introduced in the next chapter. If you apply the tests you have learned, you will identify *can* in (2) as a verb and *can* in (3) as a noun. Likewise, English is full of words whose forms double as both noun and verb, such as *ski, table, battle*, and so forth. Homonyms show us that we need to consider parts of speech in the context of a specific sentence. Language is so flexible that words can often function in a number of different word classes.

The following exercise will give you some practice at recognizing the different uses of a common homonym in English.

EXERCISE 4

Identify the part of speech for the word down *in each of the following sentences. (Note that one category needed below will be introduced in the next chapter.)*

1. Custer downed a quick meal before he rode to the river.

2. We'll drive down the road to a fast-food joint.

3. Zelda traded her swimsuit for a down jacket.

4. The team seemed down after the crushing defeat to the Sockers.

5. After ten minutes of vigorous dancing, the bride and groom sat down at their table.

Exercise 5 will give you a different kind of practice with word classes. The ability to comfortably handle errors is a sign of robust understanding.

EXERCISE 5

Nouns, verbs, adjectives, adverbs, proper nouns, and pronouns are identified in the following sentences. However, one or more words in each sentence may be identified incorrectly. Find the word(s) that are misidentified, give them their correct part-of-speech label, and explain on the basis of identification tests why their former label was wrong. Some sentences may have no errors.

1. The skis sold for forty-five dollars.
      V V   N

2. This good shepherd protects his sheep from predators.
      N   N   V   Pron N   N

3. While Jessie mowed the grass, Bobbie took them to the clinic.
     Pron   V   N Pron   V   N   N   N

4. Speak softly and carry a lawyer's phone number.
    N   V   V   N   N   N

5. Alfred Binet was a French doctor who invented the IQ test.
    Prop N   V   Prop N   N   V   N N

6. In 1902, flirting in public was banned in New York City.
    Prop N   N   N   V   V   Prop N

7. In 1972, an ex-nun became the first woman FBI agent.
    Prop N   Adj   V   Adj   N   Prop N N

8. I will fully rely on frogs.
  Pron   Adv Adv   N

9. Blue keys stay in that bag.
    N   N   V   V

10. Olga ran too fast for Serge to follow.
    Prop N V   Adj   Prop N   N

 # Application to Writing

This text will build on your knowledge of parts of speech, but there are things you can do right now with a basic knowledge of nouns, verbs, adjectives, and adverbs. One particular aspect you might focus on is to consider how much of your content you express in verbs instead of nouns. Compare the following two paragraphs:

> The city beautified the park and surprised many residents. The Department of Public Works really exerted themselves. They scoured the fountains for a whole week. Workers pruned the trees and bushes and scrubbed the pavements. Many residents volunteered their time, and so the whole operation cost the city only $20,000.

> The city's beautification of the park was a surprise to the residents. It was an intense effort for the Department of Public Works. The scouring of the fountains took a whole week. There was tree and bush pruning and scrubbing of pavements by the workers. Many residents were volunteers, and so the total cost of the operation was only $20,000.

One of the major differences between the two paragraphs is that the first one uses verbs to express ideas where the second one uses nouns, as the underlined words demonstrate:

> The city <u>beautified</u> the park and <u>surprised</u> many residents.   verbs
> The city's <u>beautification</u> of the park was a <u>surprise</u> to the residents.   nouns

The Department of Public Works really <u>exerted</u> themselves.	verb
It was an intense <u>effort</u> for the Department of Public Works.	noun
They <u>scoured</u> the fountains for a whole week.	verb
The <u>scouring</u> of the fountains took a whole week.	noun
Workers <u>pruned</u> the trees and bushes and <u>scrubbed</u> the pavements.	verbs
There was tree and bush <u>pruning</u> and <u>scrubbing</u> of pavements by the workers.	nouns
Many residents <u>volunteered</u> their time, and so the whole operation <u>cost</u> the city $20,000.	verbs
Many residents were <u>volunteers</u>, and so the total <u>cost</u> of the operation was $20,000.	nouns

When we use nouns instead of verbs, our sentences require more words and so tend to be longer. This also can make your prose more abstract and harder to read. For example, the noun *beautification* is not as reader-friendly as the verb *beautified*. Often your own writing will be more direct and vivid if you use the verb form of a word rather than the noun form to convey your ideas.

Are there ever situations in which the noun form is preferred to the verb form? There are. Verbs convey the idea of impermanence, something that does not last. Nouns, on the other hand convey a sense of permanence, something that continues over time. We can illustrate this by comparing why a writer might use a verb like *destroy* instead of the noun *destruction*. If the writer wanted to communicate the intensity of action, then she could aptly use the verb *destroy*, as in the following sentence:

The Vikings destroyed the monastery at Lindisfarne.

If, however, the writer wanted to portray the long-lasting effects of the Viking attack, she would probably use the noun *destruction*, as in the following sentence:

The destruction of the monastery at Lindisfarne was evident on the island for centuries.

EXERCISE 6

Rewrite the following paragraph by turning as many of its verbs into the corresponding noun forms as possible. Then compare the two paragraphs for their effectiveness in conveying ideas.

The edges of his mouth were turning blue. Yossarian was petrified. He wondered whether to pull the rip cord of Snowden's parachute and cover him with the nylon folds. It was very warm in the plane. Glancing up unexpectedly, Snowden gave him a wan, cooperative smile and shifted the position of his hips a bit so that Yossarian could begin salting the wound with sulfanilamide. Yossarian worked with renewed confidence and optimism. The plane bounced hard inside an air pocket, and he remembered with a start that he had left his own parachute up front in the nose. There was nothing to be done about that.

(from Joseph Heller, *Catch-22*)

EXERCISE 7

Rewrite the following paragraph by turning as many of its nouns into the corresponding verb forms as possible. Then compare the two paragraphs for their effectiveness in conveying ideas.

However, there are critical areas within the Johnson Space Center facilities where the occurrence of an emergency such as a fire or other related mishap (flammable liquid spill, etc.) would demand a unique response from workers in the area, the safety organization, the security force, and responding firefighters or emergency medical service personnel. Consequently, comprehensive planning should be undertaken after a thorough analysis of the potential hazard has been completed. While even office-type facilities require a basic emergency action plan, the following target areas may require more extensive preplanning consideration.

(adapted from the *Johnson Space Center Handbook*, Section 207.6.1)

COMPREHENSION QUESTIONS

1. What benefit comes from having names for things?

2. What are parts of speech? What is a word class?

3. What characteristics should a word class have?

4. What are open-class parts of speech?

5. What are two different *kinds* of tests that can be used to identify parts of speech? Which test is generally more accurate?

6. List the tests that can identify each part of speech and explain in your own words how they work.

7. What are homonyms? How can these words complicate the determination of parts of speech?

8. How are proper nouns and pronouns different from common nouns?

The Minor Parts of Speech

PREVIEW *This chapter presents the smaller word classes in English that are used to weave together the open-class parts of speech (presented in Chapter 2) into a coherent piece of writing or speech. Function and structure tests are given so that you can both recognize these words and understand how they work in language.*

Literacy, the ability to read and write, opens up for literates a world of abstraction. Without writing, it is not possible for humans to engage in the complex analysis of ideas and concepts. It is much easier, though, for us to think about concrete objects. As I write this, I am sitting in a very physical chair. If I push against the computer table in front of me, I will move my chair back from the table. The chair, the table, the action of pushing—they all seem very real, and the relationships between them operate according to my commonsense view of the world.

However, the moment I bring language in to describe the preceding scenario, I must introduce abstractions, things that are not concrete objects. I can't restrict myself to using only open-class parts of speech and simply say,

> Man sit chair push table move chair.

It is not completely clear what the above string of words means. The relationships between the concepts conveyed by the open-class parts of speech have not been spelled out. Does the pushing of the table cause the table to move the chair, or does the man move the chair? We can't be sure. Instead, if I want to describe my situation, I would have to write something like the following:

> A man sat *in a* chair. He pushed *against the* table *in front of* him *and as a* result moved his chair *away from the* table.

I have ended up introducing a number of words into these sentences that make clear the relationships between the open-class parts of speech.

These are the kinds of words this chapter will briefly present. I will present them as a group so that when you look at a text you will be able to place the words you encounter into their appropriate categories.

In Chapter 2, we looked at the open-class parts of speech, those that provide the content of a piece of writing: nouns, verbs, adjectives, and adverbs. Chapter 2 also presented proper nouns, a word class that is related to common nouns but has slightly different characteristics from common nouns, and pronouns, a word class that is closed but is similar to nouns and proper nouns. That still leaves a number of other categories to be accounted for. These other parts of speech can be troublesome to identify, but it is important to become familiar with these categories so that sentences do not seem like alien beings when we try to understand their structure.

Selected Closed Classes

The word classes presented in Chapter 2 make up the content words of English. These words link up with what the text is about, the content that is outside of the text. For example, if I am reading a story and come across a sentence like

(1)   The dog chased the cat through the park.

I would link the noun *dog* to some dog in the real world or in the fictional world that the story creates. Likewise, the noun *cat* would be linked to a feline animal outside the story, and the noun *park* would be linked to a physical park outside it. In a similar vein, the verb *chased* would be linked to the physical action taking place between the dog and cat as the dog ran after the cat.

However, not all the words in the above sentence can be linked so easily to something outside of the text. For example, the word *the* before any of the nouns does not link up with an object or place or thing outside it. Instead, the word *the* appears to give us information that is internal to the text. The word *the* before the noun *dog* identifies a particular dog that perhaps was mentioned previously in the text.

This kind of word belongs to the closed-class parts of speech. Let's look at some of the characteristics that distinguish these from the open-class parts of speech we looked at earlier.

First, closed classes do not easily add or lose new members. Previously we saw that the class of nouns in English is constantly adding new members, such as the word *Internet*. However, the closed classes are relatively constant.

Second, the closed classes are much smaller classes than the open classes. It would be virtually impossible to count all the nouns that exist in the English language today. However, we can count the number of prepositions or conjunctions that English has.

Third, almost all closed-class items have a single form. They don't take prefixes or suffixes as open classes do. For example, we can add the plural ending *-s* to most nouns and the past tense ending *-ed* to most verbs, but we can't add such endings to words like *the* and *or* when they are being used as closed-class words.

Fourth, closed-class items tend to have a more abstract meaning than open-class items. It is much easier for speakers to explain what the noun *dog* means compared to a closed-class item like *the*. When you look at all the different ways the word *the* is used, you can see why meaning is hard to pin down for closed-class items.

Let's turn our attention now to a number of closed-class parts of speech. Earlier, we used structure tests and meaning tests to identify the open-class parts of speech. Because meaning is more abstract when it comes to closed classes, we will talk about structure tests and **function tests** for the closed-class items. That is, we will talk about the ways in which closed-class parts of speech function in a sentence.

DETERMINERS   Determiners name a category of words that appear before and modify nouns. They include a number of more specific categories such as articles, demonstratives, quantifiers, numbers, and possessive pronouns.

Articles in English consist of a very small and specific list: *the, a,* and *an,* that is, a list that you can easily memorize. We can give one function test and one structure test for articles, which I will label *determiners* in this book.

FUNCTION TEST
- Articles modify nouns.

STRUCTURE TEST
- Articles can appear in the following positions.

_____ N

_____ Adj N

Articles determine the relationship of a noun to the text it is in. If you opened the middle of a book to a random sentence, consider what difference the determiners would make in the following sentences:

(2)   **A** customer walked up to the cosmetics counter.

(3)   **The** customer walked up to the cosmetics counter.

In the first sentence, the author does not identify the customer for the reader. Writers often use the article *a* before a noun when the noun introduces someone or something for the first time into the text. In the second sentence, the author does identify the customer. The use of the article *the* signals to the reader that he can identify whatever the noun phrase refers to. The customer in sentence (3) most likely has been introduced in the story at some time previous to this sentence.

Another kind of determiner is **demonstratives:** the words *this, that, these,* and *those.* Their function and structure tests are the same as those that identify articles. Demonstratives also describe the relationship between a noun and its text, but they do this by conveying how close (physically or metaphorically) an object is to the speaker. Sentence (4) demonstrates this:

(4)   **This** tree is a pine, but **that** tree is an oak.

The choice of demonstratives in sentence (4) tells us that the pine tree is closer to the speaker than the oak tree.

Quantifiers are words that convey how much or how many. They include words like the following:

all   any   every   few   many   much   none   several   some

We can give a function test and a structure test to identify quantifiers:

FUNCTION TEST

■ Quantifiers modify nouns by conveying how much or how many.

STRUCTURE TEST

■ Quantifiers appear in the following position:

_____ N

_____ Adj N

Most quantifiers can appear in the same positions as noun phrases (NP). We haven't yet defined what a noun phrase is, but a quick and dirty definition is that a noun phrase is a noun plus the words that directly modify it:

(5)   **The players** can participate.
      NP

(6)   **All** can participate.
      NP

Quantifiers, like **numbers** (*one, two, three,* etc.), tell us the number or quantity of whatever a noun refers to. Articles and demonstratives contribute a different kind of information to the sentence than do quantifiers and numbers, and so noun phrases can consist of both parts of speech:

(7)   **Those three** guys are the bouncers.

(8)   **The many** players who win get a free jacket.

Possessive pronouns include the following words:

> my   your   his   her   its   our   their

These too occur before and modify nouns in English:

(9)   **Her** insight is legendary.

(10)   **Our** house is falling apart.

It is important to distinguish between the personal pronouns given in Chapter 2 and possessive pronouns, because they occur in different positions in the sentence. The personal pronouns cannot occur in the place of the possessive pronouns in (9) and (10). (I will put an asterisk in front of any sentence that has something wrong with its structure.)

(9a)   *She insight is legendary.

(10a)   *We house is falling apart.

Neither can the possessive pronouns occur in the position of personal pronouns.

(11)   You have a sunny smile.

(11a)   *Your have a sunny smile.

However, there is also a set of possessive pronouns that can stand alone:

> mine   yours   his   hers   ours   theirs

The sentence in (12) gives an example.

(12)   Theirs is the green house on the corner.

PREPOSITIONS Prepositions are a class of words that appear before noun phrases. The following list gives the twenty **prepositions** most commonly used in English:

of	as	out	before
to	on	up	through
in	at	about	down
for	by	into	between
with	from	after	under

We can give a function test and a structure test to identify prepositions:

FUNCTION TEST

■ Prepositions link a noun phrase to another word or phrase.

STRUCTURE TEST

■ Prepositions appear in the following position:

_____ NP

Because noun phrases won't be defined until we get to the next chapter, I will give some examples instead. A typical noun phrase consists of a determiner plus a noun, as in *my slippers, the dog, a sunset*. Prepositions precede these kinds of phrases.

Prepositions link noun phrases to other elements in the sentence. Sometimes the preposition links a noun phrase to a verb, as in sentence (13), and sometimes to a noun, as in sentence (14):

(13)   Josie drove **to** Ely.
        [the preposition connects *Ely* to the verb *drove*]

(14)   The title **of** the book was forgotten.
        [the preposition connects *the book* to the noun *title*]

QUALIFIERS Qualifiers are a class of words that modify the meaning of adjectives and adverbs. They include words like the following:

very really quite fairly rather pretty (informal) awfully mighty too

Frank and Ernest

©1999 Thaves. Reprinted with permission. Newspaper dist. by NEA, Inc.

We can give a function test and a structure test to identify them:

FUNCTION TEST

■ Qualifiers modify adjectives and adverbs.

STRUCTURE TEST

■ Qualifiers can appear in the following positions:

_____ Adj

_____ Adv

If adjectives and adverbs communicate an attribute of some object or event, qualifiers give the degree to which that attribute holds. Are you tired, *fairly* tired, *very* tired, or *too* tired? I hope none of the above, but a **qualifier** comes in handy when you want to comment on the degree of an attribute. Note that these words have traditionally been classified as adverbs. However, the traditional label is misleading because qualifiers like *very* have different properties than content adverbs such as *slowly*.

COORDINATE CONJUNCTIONS Conjunctions are words that connect other words or phrases together. Coordinate conjunctions connect equal units together. That is, the units connected must be grammatically the same. There are seven coordinate conjunctions in English:

and   or   but   yet   nor   for   so

We can give a function test and a structure test to identify coordinate conjunctions:

FUNCTION TEST

■ Coordinate conjunctions connect units in an equal grammatical structure.

STRUCTURE TEST

■ Coordinate conjunctions appear in the following position:

X _____ X (where *X* stands for the same kind of unit on either side)

This last test specifies that words like *and* must appear between identical grammatical units. For example, if the conjunction *and* combines two sequences of words and the first sequence is a complete sentence, then the second sequence must be a complete sentence as well.

Coordinate conjunctions will be discussed in more detail in Chapter 9.

SUBORDINATE CONJUNCTIONS A second type of conjunction is the subordinate conjunction. Unlike coordinate conjunctions, subordinate conjunctions combine grammatical units in an unequal manner. Far more numerous than coordinate conjunctions, they include the following examples:

after	although	as	as if	as though
because	before	even if	even though	if
if only	in order that	now that	once provided	rather than
since	so that	than	that	though
till	unless	until	when	whenever
where	whereas	wherever	whether	while

Here is a function test and a structure test to identify subordinate conjunctions:

FUNCTION TEST

■ Subordinate conjunctions connect units in an unequal manner.

STRUCTURE TEST

■ Subordinate conjunctions appear in the following position

_____ clause

(A clause is a group of words that has a subject and a verb.)

Subordinate conjunctions will be discussed in more detail in Chapter 9.

MODALS Modals, sometimes called *modal auxiliaries,* are words that add information to the predicate. In a statement, they normally appear before the main verb of the sentence. This category includes the following words:

can could may might must ought shall should will would

The function of **modals** is a complex matter, so we will limit ourselves to structure tests to characterize them. Modals are sometimes confused with verbs; hence, our structure tests will be geared to distinguishing these two categories:

STRUCTURE TESTS

■ Modals appear in the following position in a declarative sentence:

_____ V[base]

■ Modals have a single form. Unlike verbs, they do not take suffixes.

■ Modals cannot be preceded by the negative *not*.

The first test tells us to look for modals before the base form of the verb, which is that form that we will find in the dictionary entry for the verb:

(15)   Emmy   **must**   **finish**   her homework.
                    Modal   V[base]

(16)   Oliver   **could**   **drop**   that class.
                   Modal   V[base]

The second test shows us that modals don't change form, unlike verbs:

(17)   *Mary shoulds know better than to buy that car.

The third test can be applied to distinguish the modal from the verb in the same sentence. For example, negation can precede the verb *yield* as in (19) but not the modal *will* as in (20):

(18)   An experienced driver **will yield** the right of way in that situation.

(19)   An experienced driver will **not yield** the right of way in that situation.

(20)   *An experienced driver **not will** yield the right of way in that situation.

Modals are rich words that convey many subtle shades of meaning. We use them to make moral and value judgments (21) and to make statements related to necessity and probability (22):

(21)   Nolan **should** not smoke because it is bad for his health.

(22)   We **might** have a test tomorrow if the professor returns in time from that conference on alien life forms.

In general, a modal allows a writer to introduce an attitude into a sentence that otherwise would not be conveyed.

INFINITIVE MARKER The category **infinitive marker** is unusual because it has only one member, the word *to*. Its sole purpose it to precede the base form of the verb in infinitive-verb constructions. It can be distinguished from the

TABLE 3.1   Closed-Class Parts of Speech

CATEGORY	EXAMPLES	SENTENCE POSITION	SAMPLE SENTENCES
Determiners:			
Articles	*the, a, an*	_____ N	The end is not near.
		_____ Adj N	I saw an empty bucket.
Demonstratives	*this, that,*	_____ N	Jerry needs these skates.
	these, those	_____ Adj N	That funny movie was a scream.
Quantifiers	*every, many, some*	_____ N	Every donkey belongs to a farmer.
		_____ Adj N	Auntie bought some fluffy pillows.
Numbers	*one, two, three*	_____ N	Forty-five bottles were broken on the trip.
		_____ Adj N	A frippy contains three large spoons of fruit.
Possessive Pronouns	*my, your, their*	_____ N	The coach saw her team play superbly.
		_____ Adj N	His inner child is on display.
Prepositions	*of, to, in, at*	_____ NP	At the kitchen table is an important letter.
			Fly me to the moon.
Qualifiers	*very, really, quite*	_____ Adj	Really tall people play basketball.
		_____ Adv	Pibbs threw the ball quite quickly.
Coordinate Conjuctions	*and, or, but*	X _____ X	The restaurant on the corner is tasty but cheap.
			We can fly to Rio or drive to Philly.
Subordinate Conjunctions	*if, because, though*	_____ clause	Though the mountains are high, the path is a joy.
			Eleanor competed, because she could.
Modals	*can, may, must*	_____ V [base]	We must find a well.
			You may have been mistaken.
Infinitive Marker	*to*	_____ V [base]	Nguyen wants to meet us.
Negation Marker	*not*	_____ (V det + N, Adj, Adv)	Constance does not read Greek.

preposition *to* by what follows. If the word *to* is followed by a noun phrase, it is a preposition. If the word *to* is followed by the base form of the verb, it is an infinitive marker. The sentences below demonstrate these uses:

(23)   Casey went **to** the store.   [*to* is a preposition]
       _{NP}

(24)   Casey went **to** study.   [*to* is an infinitive marker]
       _{V[base]}

We will see in Chapter 5 that infinitive-verb phrases are units of grammar that primarily occur inside other verb phrases.

NEGATION MARKER In this textbook, I will give the word *not* its own label and classify it as a **negation marker** (neg). It can be used to negate many different kinds of categories.

(25)   Sami did not *see* the lightning bolt.   [verb]

(26)   Murnia saw the lightning bolt, not *the tornado*.   [noun phrase]

(27)   Janna was not *cautious* about spreading the news.   [adjective]

(28)   Ernst finished not *hastily* but efficiently.   [adverb]

Table 3.1 has an overview of the closed-class items in this chapter.

The following two exercises will give you an opportunity to apply the tests given earlier.

EXERCISE 1

Identify all closed-class items (including pronouns) in the following sentences. Cross out all nouns, verbs, adjectives, and adverbs.

1. The red rock glistened with drops of dew.

2. Very tired campers slept in the van.

3. Every professor attended the council, yet some progress was made.

4. His boss wants to buy a large yellow convertible with chrome wheels.

5. Did Isaac leave for the cabin for two weeks?

6. Until last year, Madeleine rarely ran around the track.

7. When you come to visit us, turn before the purple gas station.

8. Vince was too sleepy for the inspector's visit to be a success.

9. I come to this grove for the love of you.

10. Greta or Wilfred should win the prize, though my boss thinks Octavia is more deserving.

11. Lou Gehrig was known as the "Iron Horse."

12. Before Jeeves saved the day, Bertie Wooster was in a pickle.

13. If Hamlet were not Danish, then I would read the play very differently.

14. Tibetans revere Mount Everest as Goddess Mother of the Earth.

15. She needs to find her courage or withdraw from the race.

EXERCISE 2

Bring a paragraph from a favorite story or other piece of writing and identify the parts of speech for each word. If you come across a word that doesn't belong to any of the word classes discussed in this chapter, circle it and discuss what you think it might be. Try to write your own tests for identifying that new word class.

Application to Writing

The following two exercises will ask you to write without the benefit of using closed-class word classes. This will give you the chance to experience (by their absence!) what contribution these words make to a text.

EXERCISE 3

Write a paragraph (or a poem) that consists of entirely open-class parts of speech: nouns (and proper nouns), verbs, adjectives, and adverbs. What effect does your paragraph have on a reader when it lacks closed-class parts of speech? Is it possible to write a paragraph that has no open-class part of speech items? Why or why not?

EXERCISE 4

Write a paragraph (or a poem) that consist of only open-class parts of speech and one of the following classes:

1. prepositions

2. determiners

3. qualifiers

4. quantifiers

5. coordinate conjunctions

6. subordinate conjunctions

7. modals

Discuss what kinds of ideas it is difficult to express because of the restrictions on your writing.

COMPREHENSION QUESTIONS

1. What are closed classes? How do they differ from open-class parts of speech?

2. Name the closed-class parts of speech listed in this chapter.

3. What function tests and structure tests identify each closed-class part of speech?

4. What kinds of meaning do the various closed-class parts of speech convey?

Phrases: The Art of Chunking

PREVIEW *This chapter will introduce you to the structure of English sentences by asking you to identify phrases and clauses within sentences.*

I know. You're still asking, "So what?" Now you can identify the word classes of most words in actual sentences. Yet you're still wondering what difference this will make to your teaching or writing. Please bear with me. If you want to know how to use the technology of writing to its fullest, you need to understand how the technology works. Understanding word classes is a preliminary to studying the heart of the technology—the units that individual words form.

What Are Phrases?

All languages have rules that describe those sentences in the language that are well formed, and English is no exception. One of the questions that linguists, who study language, like to ask is this: Could the rules be different? Could it be possible for English to have sentences like those in (b) rather than their counterparts in (a)? (The asterisk in front of any sentence signals that there is something wrong with its structure.)

(1a) The cat came back.

(1b) *The came back cat.

(2a) I depend on the kindness of strangers.

(2b) *On I depend the kindness of strangers.

(3a) The tender night calls me home.

(3b) *The night calls tender me home.

The answer appears to be a qualified no. While there is some variation allowed in the order of words, it does not appear that any and every order is possible. In (1), we see that the determiner *the* cannot be separated from its noun by the verb. In (2), we see that the preposition *on* cannot be separated from its following noun phrase by a pronoun and a verb. In (3), a single adjective, which usually goes between the determiner and the noun, cannot appear outside of those two and after the verb.

These examples show that certain words have an affinity for one another, a stronger connection to each other than they do to the words that appear elsewhere in the sentence. We call sets of adjacent words that adhere strongly together **phrases.** Once parts of speech are mastered, you should become proficient at identifying phrases, that is, showing how words chunk together in a sentence. Again, the unconscious grammar in our heads allows us to do this naturally in speech. Learning about grammar allows you to consciously identify what words go together in a sentence. Here, as in other places, we will depend on our innate linguistic ability. If I give you a random sentence in English, you will find that you have intuitions about which words are especially closely linked in terms of meaning. For example, in the following sentence,

(4)   Marty chased the cat.

you can ask yourself about the affinities of the determiner *the*. In particular, does the word *the* have a closer relationship to the word before it, *chased*, or the word that follows, *cat*? You probably have the intuition that *the* has a stronger connection to the word *cat*, which follows it, and your intuition is correct.

Structure and meaning are two important aspects of phrases. Structurally, they consist of words that are all adjacent to one another. (It is possible for phrases to have nonadjacent parts, but for the most part we will not worry about such phrases in this book.) For example, in the sentence above, we saw that the words *the* and *cat* were a phrase, and the two words were adjacent to one another. If we tried to put any of the other words in the sentence between *the* and *cat*, we would end up with an ill-formed sentence:

(5)   *Marty the chased cat.

(6)   *Chased the Marty cat.

Therefore, there must be something about the nature of phrases that requires their members to stay together.

The adjacent words of a phrase are also closely connected in terms of meaning. If we apply this concept to our sentence above, it means that the meaning of *the* has a closer connection to the meaning of *cat* than to the meaning of *chased*. Now talking about the meaning of *the* is no easy task, but for our purposes let's just treat it as a word that picks out a particular item. In sentence (4), we know that the meaning is that Marty chased a particular cat, and this is a good indication that the meaning of *the* combines with the meaning of *cat*.

So far, we have operated on the basis of intuition, but if we don't make our knowledge explicit, we are likely to make mistakes as we try to identify all the phrases in a given sentence. Therefore, it will be helpful if we can have some operating procedures to guide us in our identification of phrases. Let's look at three rules that can be used for identifying phrases when intuition lets us down: substitution by pro-forms, movement, and ability to stand alone.

SUBSTITUTION BY PRO-FORMS Rule number one is this: Phrases can be replaced by **pro-forms.** Pro-forms are those words that "stand in" for a phrase, the most-familiar examples being pronouns. A pronoun like *it* can take the place of the phrase *the cat* in sentence (4) to give us a sentence that could have the same meaning:

(7)   Marty chased it.

Likewise, the pronoun *he* can take the place of the word *Marty* to give us a possible sentence:

(8)   He chased the cat.

Both of these pronoun substitutions show us that the word *Marty* is a phrase by itself and the words *the cat* are a phrase.

However, in addition to pronouns, there are other pro-forms as well. For example, the word *do* and its various forms are pro-verbs. They can take the place of a different kind of phrase than pronouns replace. In the following sentence,

(9)   Yesterday, Cory raked the yard.

the pro-form *did* can take the place of the words *raked the yard* to give us (10b), which could be the answer to the question in (10a):

(10a)   Who raked the yard?

(10b)   Yesterday, Cory did.

This substitution by a pro-verb shows us that *raked the yard* is a phrase.

The various forms of *be* can also function as a pro-verb. In the next sentence,

(11)   The novice cook was frustrated by the burnt cake.

was can take the place of *was frustrated by the burnt cake* to produce the sentence in (12b), which could be the answer to the question in (12a).

(12a)   Who was frustrated by the burnt cake?

(12b)   The novice cook was.

Thus, both *do* and *be* can function as pro-verbs.

Another kind of pro-form is the word *such*. In the following sentence,

(13)   Candy likes very scary movies.

such can be substituted for *very scary* to give us the following sentence:

(14)   Candy likes such movies.

This substitution shows us that *very scary* is a phrase.

Finally, there are pro-locatives, such as the word *there*. A **locative** is a kind of phrase that designates a location. Thus, we find that the pro-locative *there* can replace location phrases. For example, the words *at the courthouse* can be replaced by *there*, as the following sentences show:

(15)   I'll meet you at the courthouse.

(16)   I'll meet you there.

Hence, *at the courthouse* must be a phrase as well.

Pro-forms do not pick out unconnected words in a sentence. In the example

(17)   Fay went to the store.

the attempt to replace the sequence *went to the* by a pro-form shows that these three words are not a phrase by themselves, because the sentence in (18) is ill formed.

(18)   *Fay did store.   [*did* replaces *went to the*]

However, the pronoun *it* could replace the words *the store*, the pronoun *she* could replace *Fay*, the pro-form *there* could replace *to the store*, and the pro-form *did* could replace *went to the store*, showing that all of these sequences are phrases:

(19)   Fay went to it.   [*it* replaces *the store*]

(20)   She went to the store.   [*she* replaces *Fay*]

(21)   Fay went there.   [*there* replaces *to the store*]

(22)   Fay did.   [*did* replaces *went to the store*]

The tests also show that a phrase could consist of a single word, as in the case of *Fay*.

Pro-forms also must pick out an entire phrase, not a partial phrase. Thus, in the following sentence,

(23)   Marty chased the striped cat.

a pronoun could not replace only the two words *striped cat* and exclude the determiner *the,* which would give us an ill-formed sentence:

(24)   *Marty chased the it.   [*it* replaces *striped cat*]

The pronoun could only stand in for all three words *the striped cat.* This shows us that in this sentence, *striped cat* is not a phrase by itself, but *the striped cat* is.

MOVEMENT Rule number two for identifying phrases is that they can be moved around in a sentence—that is, it may show up in different positions. As an example, consider the following:

(25)   Teenagers enjoy very scary movies.

The sequence *very scary movies* is a phrase, and this is demonstrated by its ability to appear in other places in the sentence:

(26)   Very scary movies are what teenagers enjoy.

(27)   Very scary movies are enjoyed by teenagers.

If we try to move less than the entire phrase—for example, the words *scary movies* or the words *very scary*—we get an ill-formed sentence:

(28)   *Scary movies is what teenagers enjoy very _____.

(29)   *Very scary is what teenagers enjoy _____ movies.

If you try to apply this test to identify phrases in a sentence you are analyzing, it is important to note some of the wrinkles that can arise. The English language has a number of alternate word orders, but less-common orders often need the addition of certain words and phrases to make them sound more natural. Sometimes, for example, a phrase following the verb can be directly moved to the front of the sentence with no other change in the structure. The sentence

(30)   I hate peas.

could also assume the following word order:

(31)   Peas I hate.

If you read the above sentence in isolation, *Peas, I hate* may sound unnatural to you. However, the sentence can be improved by adding adverbs like *really:*

(32)   Peas I really, really hate.

One of the best things you can do as a student of grammar is to pay attention to the various word-order patterns you encounter as you read. After a while, you will become familiar with the kinds of phrases that can move in a sentence.

STANDING ALONE Rule number three for identifying phrases is that they can stand alone as the answer to a question, but nonphrases cannot. For example, there are a number of questions that can be connected to the sentence *Fay went to the store*. For the questions below, the words following them are typical answers—and also complete phrases:

(33)   Who went to the store? Fay.

(34)   Where did Fay go to? The store.

(35)   Where did Fay go? To the store.

(36)   What did Fay do yesterday? (She) went to the store.

However, there is no question that can elicit an answer like (37).

(37)   *Went to.

The following two exercises give you a chance to practice using the above tests to identify phrases.

EXERCISE 1

Find as many phrases as possible in the following paragraph. Discuss any sequences of words where the phrase boundaries are not clear.

> He pulled the brake. But it did not hold, though he put all his strength into it. The car tipped toward the edge, rolled a little. Without doubt, it was going over the bank.
>
> (from Eudora Welty, "Death of a Traveling Salesman")

EXERCISE 2

Use a paragraph of your own writing and identify as many phrases in it as possible. Discuss any sequences of words where the phrase boundaries are not clear.

Classifying Phrases

Now that we have the means to identify phrases, we need a way to name them, because different phrases have different properties. Here we must rely on our knowledge of parts of speech to give phrases the appropriate labels.

Fortunately, all of the major parts of speech have their own phrases. We find **noun phrases** (NP), **verb phrases** (VP), **adjective phrases** (AdjP) and **ad-**

verb phrases (AdvP). The other phrases that will loom large in our analysis of sentences will be **prepositional phrases** (PP).

Let's consider the phrase *a cat* from the sentence

(38)   Very important people own a cat.

If we sought to reduce this phrase to its most central element, we would say it is the word *cat*. Identifying the part of speech which *cat* belongs to in (38) then identifies the kind of phrase it inhabits. In this case, *cat* is a noun, and so *a cat* must be a noun phrase.

Our phrase identification tests will also identify *very important people* as a phrase. Take a moment and apply these tests to demonstrate to yourself why *very important people* is a phrase.

Again, if we shrink this phrase down to its most important element, we find that it is the word *people*. The word *people* is a noun, and so we see that we have identified another noun phrase.

If you think about the pro-form tests that we can use to identify phrases, you may have noticed that we can apply our pro-adjective test by substituting *such* for *very important,* which gives us the following sentence:

(39)   Such people own a cat.

This tells us that *very important*—a qualifier plus an adjective—is a phrase as well. Let's try to shrink this phrase down to its most important word. If *very* is the core word, then we should be able to realize a sentence like the following:

(40)   *Very people own a cat.

However, we all recognize this sentence as ill formed. Instead, we can shrink the phrase down to the word *important,* as sentence (41) shows:

(41)   Important people own a cat.

The word *important* is an adjective, so the phrase *very important* must be an adjective phrase.

This leaves one last word from the original sentence that is not in a phrase, the verb *own*. Every word must be a part of phrase, so we will need to find the phrase that will include the word *own*. Let's take stock for a moment to consider what we have identified so far. We will draw lines underneath the relevant words with their labels to show the NPs and AdjPs.

<u>Very important</u> people own   <u>a cat</u>.
     AdjP   NP

_____
       NP

We find one AdjP inside a NP, but once a phrase is a part of another phrase, we consider the larger phrase when we are identifying the rest of the sentence structure. We also find that there is one NP before the verb and one NP after the verb. That leaves us with three possibilities for the phrasehood of *own*.

First, *own* could be its own phrase. We can rule this out right away because we find that it doesn't meet any of the tests for phrasehood. For example, we might try to replace it with a pro-verb, but this gives us an ill-formed sentence:

(42)   *Very important people do a cat.

The second possibility is that *own* combines with the NP before it. Again though, the words *very important people own* does not act like a phrase according to our tests. For example, it cannot function as the answer to a question:

(43)   Who owns a cat? *Very important people own.

Neither is there any pro-form that can substitute for those words.

Therefore that leaves the word *own* to combine with the NP that follows it. We find that the pro-verb can substitute for *own a cat*, as in the answer to the following question shows:

(44)   Who owns a cat? Very important people do.

This phrase can also be the answer to a question:

(45)   What would you like to do? Own a cat.

Hence, we have identified the phrases that make up *Very important people own a cat*.

We haven't yet given an example of an adverb phrase. An adverb phrase will take an adverb, words like *slowly* and *quickly*, and any words that modify that adverb, such as qualifiers. Sentence (46) gives an example:

(46)   Greta walked quite slowly.

We see the adverb *slowly*, so we know that we will be building an AdvP containing *slowly*. We only need to ask ourselves whether or not the word before *slowly*, in this case the qualifier *quite*, is a part of the adverb phrase. If you think about the meaning of the sentence, you will have the intuition that the meaning of *quite* is closely linked to the meaning of *slowly*. *Quite* tells us how slowly Greta walked. If you apply a test, such as pro-form substitution, then you can further confirm that indeed *quite slowly* is an AdvP. For example, we can turn this sentence into a kind of question in which *how* takes the place of the AdvP, as the following shows. Likewise, the words *quite slowly* can function as the answer to that question:

(47)   How did Greta walk?   <u>Answer</u>: Quite slowly.

Prepositional phrases work a little bit differently than the other phrases we have looked at. PPs normally consist of a preposition and a NP that follows that preposition. For example, in

(48)   My horse trotted to the trough.

the words *to the trough* are the PP. The preposition is what determines the grammatical properties of the entire PP.

Heads

Every phrase has a **head,** the particular word that determines the phrase type. NPs have a noun as head. VPs have a verb as head, and the same is true for the other kinds of phrases. Some examples are given below showing the heads of various phrases:

the rotten <u>apple</u>	(NP)	<u>head</u> ⮥ apple
very <u>angry</u>	(AdjP)	<u>head</u> ⮥ angry
<u>go</u> home	(VP)	<u>head</u> ⮥ go
quite <u>quickly</u>	(AdvP)	<u>head</u> ⮥ quickly
<u>in</u> the camper	(PP)	<u>head</u> ⮥ in

This gives us a further way of understanding phrases in English: they consist of a word that is typically expanded into a phrase by the addition of other words and phrases. However, sometimes a phrase will consist of a head by itself. We can see two examples of this in the following sentence:

(49)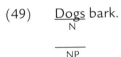

The word *dogs* is a noun in (49), but it also functions as an entire NP in this sentence as well. We know this because we can substitute other NPs in place of *dogs:* for example, we could replace it with the NP *the Great Dane,* as in sentence (50). However, we could not replace it with a noun by itself such as the word *dog* in sentence (51):

(50)   The Great Dane barks.   [*the Great Dane* = NP]

(51)   *Dog barks.   [*dog* = noun]

Now, a writer can elaborate and add further words to the NP in (49). Examples are given in sentences (52)–(56):

(52)   <u>The **dogs**</u> bark.
         NP

(53)   <u>Many black **dogs**</u> bark.
              NP

(54)   <u>Most but not all tall and athletic **dogs**</u> bark.
                        NP

(55)   <u>Fifty frisky **dogs** in the yard</u> bark.
                  NP

(56)   <u>Some sweet **dogs** that Francisco sent to the Animal Shelter</u> bark.
                        NP

The NPs in (49) and (52)–(56) all have something in common: they contain the same head, the word *dogs*.

It turns out that plural nouns without determiners or other modifiers can make up an entire NP by themselves. However, if the determiner is present, then the determiner plus noun combination makes up the NP. Note that in sentence (52), the NP would be the sequence *the dogs,* not just the word *dogs* by itself.

Now apply this approach to the verb *bark* in the next exercise.

EXERCISE 3

The verb *bark* is the VP in sentence (49) and also the head of that VP. Compose four new sentences that add other words and phrases to that VP. Make sure that the word *bark* is the head of the VP in each of your new sentences.

When you need to analyze the structure of a sentence, you can start with the knowledge that the sentence will contain words that will be the heads of their respective phrases. You can then be on the lookout for adjacent words that will elaborate on their heads and so make up a full phrase. It is important that you be able to identify both the entire phrase and the head of that phrase when you are analyzing sentences, so that you don't make the mistake of treating a head in a multiword phrase as if it were a phrase by itself. Remember the contrast between sentences (49) and (52). The word *dogs* is the entire NP in (49), but not in (52).

Clauses

Another kind of phrase is the **clause,** a group of words that form the foundation of a sentence. Clauses convey the meaning of a sentence, and structurally, they are composed of a subject and a verb. In fact, the sentence itself is a clause.

What then is the difference between a sentence and a clause? All sentences are clauses, but not all clauses are sentences. Sentences are clauses that can stand alone, complete by themselves. We call them independent clauses. However, there are also clauses that must be attached to other words to make a complete sentence. We call them dependent clauses or subordinate clauses. In English, dependent clauses are formed by adding subordinate conjunctions to the front of what would otherwise be an independent clause or complete sentence. The words in (57) are an independent clause. There is a subject, *the sky,* and a verb, *is.* The addition of the subordinate conjunction *if* turns the independent clause in (57) into the dependent clause in (58):

(57)   The sky is cloudy.

(58)   If the sky is cloudy . . .

Just as phrases are the basic building blocks of structure in language, clauses are the basic building blocks of discourse, connected language. One reason that language is so powerful is that it allows us to combine clauses in multiple ways. There is no limit to how many clauses can occur inside a single sentence.

Now you may be surprised that we consider clauses to be a kind of phrase. Let's try to justify this way of looking at language. Remember that phrases have two aspects to them. The first is the structural aspect: the parts of the phrase are adjacent to one another. This is certainly true of a clause. For example, a writer couldn't take the parts of a sentence like (53) and scatter them throughout a paragraph, as (59) shows.

(59)   *__Many black__ it is a sunny day in the neighborhood. Kids play in the streets. Moms and dads are on their front steps shooting the breeze **dogs**. Some cats sunbathe on the window sills. **Bark**.

No, the parts of the clause need to stay together.

The second aspect relates to meaning. The meaning of the parts of the phrase are closely connected to each other. We can see this if we reorder the paragraph in (59):

(59a)   It is a sunny day in the neighborhood. Kids play in the streets. Moms and dads are on their front steps shooting the breeze. Some cats sunbathe on the window sills. **Many black dogs bark**.

The phrase *many black dogs* and the phrase *bark* have a closer connection in meaning to each other than they do to the rest of the paragraph.

Likewise, the three tests we gave earlier for diagnosing phrases also apply to clauses. They can be substituted by pro-forms, as sentences (60) and (61) show:

(60)   Wally believes <u>the moon is made of parmesan cheese</u>.

(61)   Wally believes <u>it</u>.

They can move around in a sentence, as (62) shows:

(62)   That the moon is made of parmesan cheese, Wally certainly believes.

They can also stand alone as a well-formed answer to a question, as sentences (63) and (64) demonstrate:

(63)   What does Wally believe?

(64)   That the moon is made of parmesan cheese.

These are all good reasons for treating clauses as phrases themselves.

The following exercise will encourage you to make sure that you can distinguish clauses from nonclauses.

EXERCISE 4

Circle or underline all of the clauses in the following strings of words. Write a zero if there are no clauses in the string.

1. We have been doing grammar all day long.

2. In the bag.

3. The man from Maryland.

4. Arlo's excitement.

5. Since Gigi confessed, not a lot has changed in this town.

6. Since Gigi's confession, life hasn't been the same.

7. Because I love you.

8. Going across town, through the tunnel, past the museum, and over the last bridge.

9. The Texans play the Cowboys on Sunday, and the Steelers play the Eagles on Monday.

10. The area around the park will be cordoned off before the building is detonated, but traffic will be allowed down Crispin Avenue after the dust has settled.

11. The thought that he might not finish his education renewed Edgar's determination.

12. The candidate promised that she would attract new businesses to depressed areas of the state.

Phrases are the heart of sentence structure, and the ability to determine where phrases begin and end will help us make informed decisions about how we order words in our sentences, what kind of punctuation we use, and where we use punctuation in the sentence. The next chapter will discuss the sentence structure of some more-complicated sentences so that you have a fuller understanding of phrases across a variety of sentence types.

COMPREHENSION QUESTIONS

1. What is a phrase?

2. What is the structural aspect of a phrase?

3. What is the meaning aspect of a phrase?

4. What are three tests that can be used to identify phrases? Explain how each works.

5. List the different kinds of phrases this chapter presents.

6. What is the head of a phrase?

7. How big or small can phrases be?

8. What is a clause? What is the relationship between phrases and clauses?

More on Phrases

PREVIEW *This chapter explains how to draw tree diagrams as a visual representation of sentence structure. It also shows how phrases are arranged in some more-complex sentences of English.*

"Aargh! Diagramming sentences." While you surely have never said that yourself, too many people, like a scary visit to the dentist when they were six, have unpleasant memories of drawing diagrams on paper to represent how sentences are put together. I think there are two reasons why people dislike sentence diagrams. First, they found that it was difficult to do, and second, they never saw any point to what they were doing. The world went on just fine, totally oblivious to whether or not they drew an accurate sentence diagram.

We can't do anything about the first reason. It *is* difficult to draw sentence diagrams, because language is a complex system. There are linguists whose entire career is devoted to figuring out how English structure works, and they themselves don't agree on the exact structure for every sentence. However, we can do something about the second reason. Knowledge about structure empowers us to make conscious (and sometimes better!) decisions about our words when writing and editing our texts. Diagrams are not an end in themselves. They are a way of making your knowledge of language more robust and therefore more useful.

Sentence Diagrams

There are a number of ways that phrases can be marked in a sentence. One way is to draw lines above the sentence to form a tree diagram, as in Figure 5.1. The line above each word is connected to its part-of-speech label. Next, lines are

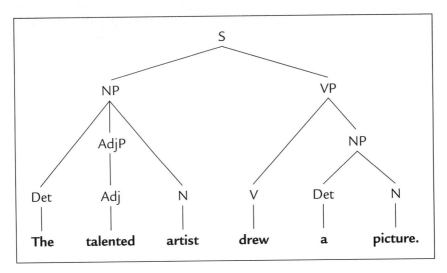

FIGURE 5.1

drawn from each part-of-speech label to the phrase label where they belong. For example, at the end of Figure 5.1, lines connect the symbols *Det* and *N* to meet at the symbol *NP*, because the determiner *a* and the noun *picture* make up the noun phrase *a picture* at the end of the sentence.

Lines can also be drawn underneath each word and phrase, with the appropriate label under those lines, as in

(1)   <u>The</u>   <u>talented</u>   <u>artist</u>   <u>drew</u>   <u>a</u>   <u>picture</u>.
      Det   Adj   N   V   Det   N

I will use both kinds of diagrams in this book. Follow whatever practice your instructor prefers for your own diagrams.

The last phrase indicated is always the sentence itself (S). As Chapter 4 pointed out, sentences are phrases, chunks of words that are tightly connected to each other, just like the smaller phrases that are inside them. Don't forget to indicate that last phrase as well when you analyze the structure of a sentence.

Counting Phrases

The principles of this chapter will also help you to identify phrases in more complicated sentences like the following, in (2)–(6). We will look at each of these sentences in turn:

(2) Cornelia promises to finish her taxes.

(3) The new kid was chewing gum in class.

(4) Our neighbor could eat a hot dog under water.

(5) The clock chimed when the ball hit it.

(6) Ichabod believes that Santa Claus lives in Pasadena.

One thing you can do when you encounter sentences like those above is to figure out the number of phrases each sentence will have, based on its parts of speech. That knowledge will act as a check when you identify all its phrases. Each separate noun will have its own noun phrase. Each pronoun will constitute its own phrase as well. Every verb will have a verb phrase corresponding to it. Likewise, every separate adjective, adverb, and preposition will form its own phrase. Finally, there will be the phrase that constitutes the entire sentence. Based on the parts of speech in a sentence like (2), we can know in advance the number of phrases we should identify:

1 noun (*taxes*), 1 proper noun (*Cornelia*), 1 pronoun (*her*)	3 NPs
2 verbs (*promises, to finish*)	2 VPs
1 sentence	<u>1 S</u>
	6 phrases

Now let's look at some specific kinds of sentences in order to understand their arrangement of phrases.

Diagramming Infinitive-Verb Phrases and Possessive-Noun Phrases

An analysis of the six phrases of sentence (2) is shown in Figure 5.2. Let's consider two phrases in particular. First, the possessive pronoun *her* is a phrase, in this case a possessive-noun phrase, by itself. This follows from our first test for identifying phrases in Chapter 4, where we saw that pronouns can substitute for noun phrases. We can also make a prediction. If the pronoun *her* is a phrase, we should be able to replace it with other similar possessive-noun phrases. This

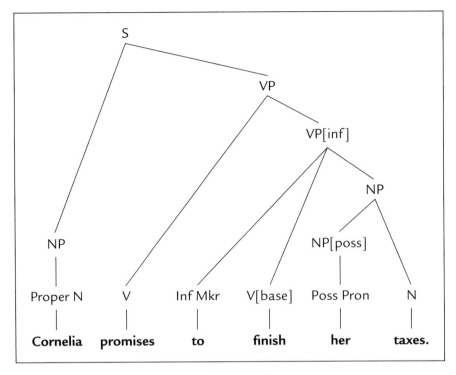

FIGURE 5.2

we can do. The following possessive-noun phrases (a–d) can all appear in place of *her* to form the sentences in (2a–d):

(a)   Pete's

(b)   the neighbor's

(c)   their rich landlord's

(d)   the president of the company's

(2a)   Cornelia promises to finish <u>Pete's</u> taxes.

(2b)   Cornelia promises to finish <u>the neighbor's</u> taxes.

(2c)   Cornelia promises to finish <u>their rich landlord's</u> taxes.

(2d)   Cornelia promises to finish <u>the president of the company's</u> taxes.

Recognizing that possessive pronouns are a kind of phrase can help us to appreciate one of the benefits of understanding phrases. Phrases are places in the sentence that can be expanded.

Sentence (2) also shows us an example of an **infinitive-verb phrase** (VP[inf]). The discussion of heads in Chapter 4 reminds us that every separate head will form its own phrase. In sentence (2), there are two separate verbs, and so there will have to be two verb phrases. The verb *finish* will be the head of an infinitive-verb phrase. Infinitive-verb phrases consist of a verb in its base form (the form we would find in a dictionary entry), the infinitive marker *to*, and whatever phrases modify the verb. In sentence (2), the noun phrase *her taxes* makes up part of the infinitive-verb phrase.

We again make a prediction here. If the sequence *to finish her taxes* is a phrase, then we should be able to replace those words with similar phrases, in this case with other infinitive-verb phrases. This we can do, as the following sentences show. The infinitive-verb phrases in (e–h) can appear in place of *to finish her taxes* to form the sentences (2e–h):

(e)   to sleep

(f)   to answer the call of duty

(g)   to give her fortune to worthy causes across the country

(h)   to deny that the moon is made of white chocolate

(2e)   Cornelia promises <u>to sleep</u>.

(2f)   Cornelia promises <u>to answer the call of duty</u>.

(2g)   Cornelia promises <u>to give her fortune to worthy causes across the country</u>.

(2h)   Cornelia promises <u>to deny that the moon is made of white chocolate</u>.

You should also observe that the infinitive-verb phrase is inside the main-verb phrase of sentence (2). In English, you will find that verb phrases may be contained within other verb phrases as long as the forms of the verb differ.

Diagramming Present-Participle Verb Phrases

Sentence (3) has a structure similar to sentence (2), with a verb phrase inside the sentence's main verb phrase. (See Figure 5.3.) However, in (3) we find a present-participle verb phrase (VP[pres part]), a form that will be discussed further in Chapter 10. The present-participle is the verb plus the suffix *-ing*. Notice again how the present-participle verb phrase in (3) can be replaced with the similar phrases (a–d).

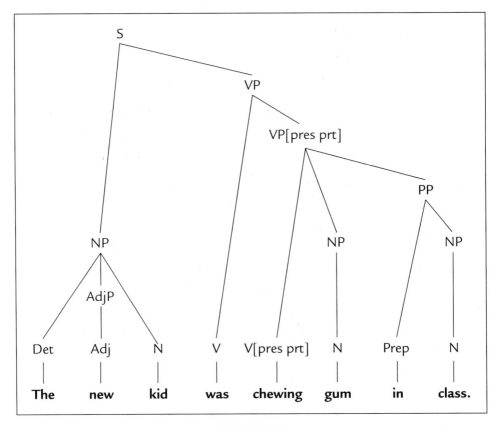

FIGURE 5.3

(a)   running

(b)   breaking a sweat

(c)   promising to finish his chores

(d)   thinking that the moon was made of pasta

(3a)   The new kid was <u>running</u>.

(3b)   The new kid was <u>breaking a sweat</u>.

(3c)   The new kid was <u>promising to finish his chores</u>.

(3d)   The new kid was <u>thinking that the moon was made of pasta</u>.

Notice also in (3) that the prepositional phrase *in class* attaches to the verb phrase. The prepositional phrase provides the location for where the chewing took place. We will further discuss how to diagram prepositional phrases later in this chapter.

Diagramming Modal Phrases

We will treat a sentence like (4) that has a modal as forming a **modal phrase,** which consists of the modal plus a base verb phrase (VP[base]). (See Figure 5.4.) The **base form** of the verb is the form you would find in a dictionary entry. Crucially, modals must be followed by base verbs rather than other forms of the verb, as (7)–(9) show:

(7)   *Our neighbor could <u>to eat</u> hot dogs under water.

(8)   *Our neighbor could <u>eating</u> hot dogs under water.

(9)   *Our neighbor could <u>eaten</u> hot dogs under water.

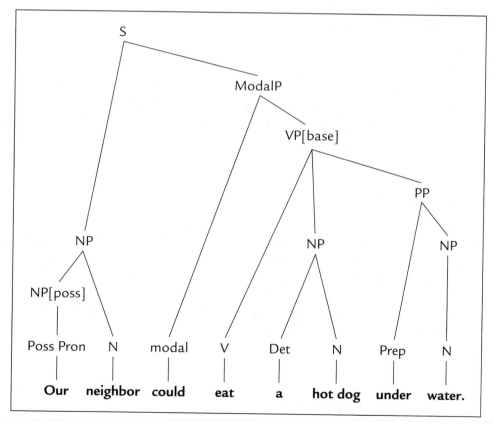

FIGURE 5.4

The base verb will be the head of its own verb phrase. Thus, we could again replace the verb phrase with similar verb phrases (a–d), as shown below:

(a)   sing

(b)   dance a jig

(c)   donate thousands to charity every year

(d)   affirm that the moon was made of pistachios

(4a)   Our neighbor could <u>sing</u>.

(4b)   Our neighbor could <u>dance a jig</u>.

(4c)   Our neighbor could <u>donate thousands to charity every year</u>.

(4d)   Our neighbor could <u>affirm that the moon was made of pistachios</u>.

Diagramming Subordinate Clauses

Sentences (5) and (6) have subordinate clauses, but each occurs in a different position. In sentence (5), the subordinate clause is outside the main clause *The clock chimed*. When diagramming such sentences, you must be careful to build up the phrases in each clause individually before the subordinate clause becomes a part of the entire sentence. Also, the subordinate conjunction combines with its own clause to form a subordinate clause, as Figure 5.5 shows.

The structure of sentence (6) is different from sentence (5), because its subordinate clause is actually inside the verb phrase of the main clause. Notice that if we removed the subordinate clause from sentence (5), the remaining words would still form a complete sentence (5a), but if we do the same for sentence (6), the remaining words form an incomplete sentence (6a):

(5a)   The clock chimed.

(6a)   *Ichabod believes.

In sentence (6) then, the subordinate clause attaches to the verb phrase headed by the verb *believes*. (See Figure 5.6.)

The Challenges of Phrase Boundaries

Sometimes it is a little more difficult to determine the boundaries of phrases. A good case to begin with is when a prepositional phrase follows a noun phrase, as in the two following sentences:

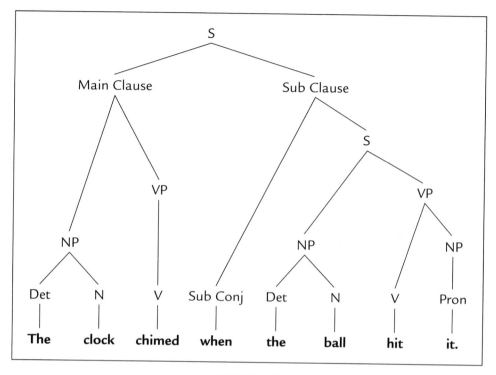

FIGURE 5.5

(10)   Mick gave the package to the store.

(11)   Mick found the keys to the car.

These two sentences have the same parts of speech in the same order—proper noun—verb—determiner—noun—preposition—determiner—noun. However, it turns out that their structure is different. If we apply our phrasal tests, we will identify *to the store* and *to the car* as prepositional phrases, but this is where the fun begins. The prepositional phrases function differently in each sentence. In the first, *to the store* is a separate prepositional phrase and not a part of the noun phrase that precedes it. For example, let's try the pro-form test to see what would replace the phrases after the verb *gave*. If we insert the pronoun *it*, we would come up with the sentence below:

(12)   Mick gave it to the store.

That is, the pronoun *it* replaces the words *the package,* showing that *the package* is a phrase by itself, in this case a noun phrase. However, the pronoun

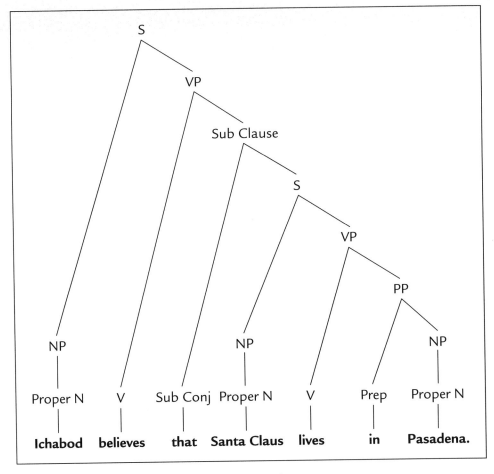

FIGURE 5.6

it cannot take the place of the sequence *the package to the store*. The following sentence,

(13)   Mick gave it.   [*it* replaces *the package to the store*]

is not equivalent to sentence (12).

We also find that we can substitute the pro-form *there* for the prepositional phrase *to the store* and realize the sentence below:

(14)   Mick gave it there.   [*it* replaces *the package; there* replaces *to the store*]

This shows us that the noun phrase *the package* and the prepositional phrase *to the store* are truly separate phrases.

Frank and Ernest

Let's try to make a pro-form substitution for the phrases in sentence (11). In this sentence, a pronoun could take the place of the entire sequence *the keys to the car*. Thus, the sentence below could stand in for the sentence *Mick found the keys to the car*:

(15)   Mick found them.   [*them* replaces *the keys to the car*]

Notice what happens if we try to substitute the pronoun *them* for only the words *the keys* in (11), as a test to see if *the keys* is a separate phrase from the words *to the car*. Then we get the following ill-formed sentence:

(16)   *Mick found them to the car.   [*them* replaces *the keys*]

The other tests give the same results. If *the package to the store* is a phrase in the sentence in (10), we should be able to move it as a unit elsewhere in the sentence, but a couple of experiments show that this sequence does not move as a unit:

(17)   *The package to the store Mick gave.

(18)   *It was the package to the store that Mick gave.

However, the whole phrase *the keys to the car* in (11) can be moved:

(19)   It was the keys to the car that Mick found.

Finally, treating the sequence as a stand-alone answer to a question shows the same result:

(20)   What did Mick give?   Answer: *The package to the store.

(21)   What did Mick find?   Answer: The keys to the car.

All of these tests taken together give us evidence that the sequence *the keys to the car* in (11) is a single phrase, but the sequence *the package* and the sequence *to the store* are separate phrases in (10). In other words, if a prepositional phrase (like *to the store* and *to the car*) follows a noun, sometimes it belongs to that noun phrase, and sometimes it is completely separate from that noun phrase.

The following exercises will give you practice in determining the structure of a variety of English sentences and then using your knowledge of structure to compose sentences.

EXERCISE 1

Draw diagrams that identify all of the phrases by name in the following sentences.

 1. I like coffee.

 2. The silly antelope chased the surprised tiger.

 3. Joan sent the bank a bad check.

 4. Unfortunately, my semester is terribly busy.

 5. Aunt Evie procured a used howitzer from the antique collector last night.

 6. Under intense pressure from stockholders, the board of Diligent Can Company restated its earnings for the past two years.

 7. An ordinary buyer would fail to notice the many extras in this house.

 8. Rick ripped Reg's red rag.

 9. To be Toby is my life's goal.

10. After the expedition climbed Mount Everest, I was too tired to climb Bunker Hill.

11. Dr. Zipporah Deaver wanted to cross the Atlantic in a plastic flotation device.

12. Your brother tried washing the floors with apple vinegar.

13. The very daring gambler bet ten dollars that the United States would win the World Cup.

14. Billy Joe McAllister jumped off the Tallahatchee Bridge.

15. New York City gets water through the Delaware Aqueduct.

16. I would like to feed the pigeons in the Piazza San Marco.

17. Richard J. Gatling invented the machine gun in 1862.

18. The Grinch intended to steal Christmas.

EXERCISE 2

Write your own sentences that consist of the following phrases and parts of speech in the order given. (V[pres prt] is a verb with an -ing suffix. VP[inf] is a verb phrase that begins with the infinitive marker to and a base form of the verb.)

1. NP–V–NP

2. Sub. Clause–NP–modal–V–NP–PP

3. PP–NP–V–Inf. Mkr.–V[base]

4. Poss. Pron–Noun compound–V–V[pres prt]–AdjP

5. Det–N–PP–V–NP–Sub Clause

6. V–NP–NP

7. VP[inf]–V–NP

8. NP–V–NP–NP–PP

9. NP–modal–V[base]–PP

10. Pron–V–AdvP

 # Application to Writing

Phrases are the building blocks of our sentences. Knowing where phrases begin and end gives us an advantage when it comes to the writing and editing process. There are a couple of principles we can apply immediately to what we have discussed above.

First, phrases are positions in the sentence that can be expanded. This was demonstrated earlier in this chapter, where we saw that possessive-noun phrases can replace possessive pronouns, to name one example. You can jazz up (or tone down) your writing by elaborating (or simplifying) individual phrases in your prose.

Second, phrases present us with the possibilities for different word orders in the sentence. In Chapter 4, we learned that movement, the ability to appear in different positions in the sentence, was one test to determine phrasehood. It follows then that the phrases we identified in the sentences above may appear in other locations in the sentence. Consider again the phrases we found in sentence (4). Many of these phrases could occur elsewhere in that same sentence, as in (4e–i) below:

(4)   Our neighbor could eat a hot dog under water.

(4e)   Our neighbor could eat, <u>under water</u>, a hot dog.

(4f)   <u>Under water</u>, our neighbor could eat a hot dog.

(4g)   <u>A hot dog</u> our neighbor could eat under water.

(4h)   <u>Eat a hot dog under water</u>, our neighbor could.

(4i)   Our neighbor, <u>under water</u>, could eat a hot dog.

If we add some more words to the sentence, there are still more alternative word orders we could produce, as in

(4j)   It was <u>water</u> that our neighbor could eat a hot dog under.

Alternative word orders are the lifeblood of writing, and each of the possible sentences above conveys a slightly different emphasis and sense to the content that the words themselves supply. A knowledge of structure can heighten your awareness of the possibilities a single sentence contains.

The following exercise will ask you to practice these skills of expanding and reordering phrases.

EXERCISE 3

Part A

Rewrite sentences 1, 2, 3, 8, 9, 14, 16, 17, and 18 by expanding one of the phrases in each example. Make sure your new phrase contains at least eight words. Do not make any other changes to the sentence.

Part B

For sentences 4, 5, 6, 7, 10, 11, 12, 13, 15, and 16, rewrite each example with as many other possible word orders as you can discover. Do not add any new words to the sentence.

Now that you have some familiarity with the phrases that make up sentences in English, you can use this knowledge to talk more specifically about error correction when revising and editing a text. For example, suppose you needed to proofread sentences like the following:

> The hot, dusty plains looked <u>uninvited</u> compared to the <u>luscious</u> rain forest I had just left. The hitchhiker in the seat next to me was <u>very asleep</u> and never noticed the change in climate.

You could put a name to the area where this writer struggles. All of the underlined problems are in the adjective phrases in the sentence. In the first two instances, the word choice is not accurate. The writer probably means to write *un-inviting* rather than *uninvited* and *lush* rather than *luscious*. In the third case, the word *asleep* is one of those adjectives that is not modifiable by the qualifier *very*. The writer might want to try *deeply asleep* instead. Knowing parts of speech and phrases will enable you to be that much clearer when you talk about what is going on in a text.

EXERCISE 4

Identify the phrases or parts of speech where problems arise in the following paragraph.

EXAMPLE: The dancers <u>was</u> fired after the last show.

PROBLEM: verb

<u>A police</u> came to arrest my neighbor last night because of <u>an altercation</u> between two gang members. <u>Much beers</u> had flowed at his party, and <u>temper</u> had begun to <u>flay</u> about midnight. The two antagonists <u>fired at 11:00 shots</u>, but no one was injured in <u>the fracture</u>. Why my neighbor served beer to <u>drinkers underage</u> is a mystery to me.

The ability to consciously determine how words chunk together in a sentence is central to applying rules of punctuation and style and to making conscious decisions about how to write and refine the sentences of your written discourse. Making this process explicit in your mind will enable you to diagnose and analyze your own writing. The rest of this book will require you to pick out phrases in a variety of sentences. Once you are confident and adept at consciously identifying the chunks of words that make up sentences, you will be in a position to craft and sculpt your language to your purposes.

COMPREHENSION QUESTIONS

1. How can we determine in advance how many phrases a sentence has?

2. If there is more than one verb in a clause and the verbs appear in different verb forms, what will be the structural relationship between the verbs?

3. Prepositional phrases can attach to many different categories in the sentence. How can we tell whether a prepositional phrase attaches to a noun phrase or a verb phrase?

4. How do phrase boundaries relate to expanding and reordering a sentence?

6

Grammatical Roles: Distinguishing Identical Elements

PREVIEW *Grammatical roles* *is a cover term that encompasses subjects, direct objects, indirect objects, subject complements, and object complements. This chapter will explain what grammatical roles are, with special focus given to how we can distinguish them.*

In reading through these chapters, you may have been noticing that there is a connection between structure and meaning. We saw this in Chapter 5 when we compared the sentences

(5.10)   Mick gave the package to the store.

(5.11)   Mick found the keys to the car.

In (1), the prepositional phrase *to the store* attaches to the verb phrase headed by the verb *gave*, and this matches the meaning of the sentence because *to the store* tells us who was the recipient of Mick's giving. In (2), the prepositional phrase *to the car* attaches to the noun phrase headed by the noun *keys*, because *to the car* describes which keys Mick found.

In this chapter, we will observe another way in which structure contributes meaning, by examining the roles that noun phrases can play in an English sentence. We'll see that the various meanings of noun phrases follow patterns that are determined by the verbs of the sentence.

Verb-Phrase Patterns

Declarative sentences, sentences that make a statement, can normally be broken down into two main parts: the subject and the predicate. The subject is the part of the sentence that the whole thing is about. The predicate is the part of the sentence that comments on the subject. The following sentences have been divided into their subjects and predicates (a vertical line will mark the boundary between the two parts of the sentence):

(1)   Cheesy pizzas | give me gas.

(2)   A horse with no name | ran down the road.

(3)   I | prefer to rely on the kindness of strangers, wanderers, and dreamers.

(4)   The counselor who worked nights and weekends to aid his students | wept.

We can't identify subjects and predicates by size because the size of the subject and predicate can vary greatly. In the third sentence above, the subject has only one word. In the fourth sentence, the predicate has only one word. However, we can see a pattern emerging. The subjects in the above sentences are all noun phrases, and in English, subjects are usually noun phrases, though they don't have to be. The predicates in the above sentences are all verb phrases, and we will see that that is typical for English as well. The boundary line between the subject and the predicate goes right before the verb (though we'll also see there are exceptions to this generalization when other words are added to the sentence).

In Chapters 4 and 5, you gained practice in identifying phrases by name. As you think back to the various phrases you identified—NPs, VPs, AdjPs, PPs, AdvPs, and so forth—which phrases did you notice the most variation in?

Most likely you said verb phrases. The verb phrases in Chapters 4 and 5 exhibited a number of different patterns, more patterns than you saw in noun phrases or any of the other phrases. One of the things this chapter will do is to give you a way to understand the various patterns you observed in verb phrases.

Frank and Ernest

©1986 Thaves. Reprinted with permission. Newspaper dist. by NEA, Inc.

This knowledge can be organized under the heading **grammatical roles.** Grammatical roles are names we give to phrases that have a unique relationship to the verbs in their sentences. In doing so, we will also be naming a number of different verb-phrase patterns based on the kinds of phrases and grammatical roles that distinguish them.

There are five particular verb-phrase patterns that we will pay attention to. Other verb-phrase patterns exist, in fact many of them, but the ability to identify these five will enable you to understand the basic workings of most sentences in English.

INTRANSITIVE-VERB PHRASES The first verb-phrase pattern is the intransitive pattern. The necessary part of this verb phrase consists of only one thing—a verb that is intransitive. We use *intransitive* to classify verbs that make a complete verb phrase by themselves. Here are some examples of **intransitive verbs:**

(5)   The sleepy student | snored.

(6)   Mary | jogs.

(7)   This concert | rocks.

Snored, jogs, and *rocks* in these sentences are intransitive verbs. In each case they constitute the entire verb phrase and the entire predicate by themselves. Only intransitive verbs can function as a complete verb phrase alone.

TRANSITIVE-VERB PHRASES The second verb-phrase pattern is the transitive pattern. The necessary parts of this verb phrase consist of two elements—a verb that is transitive and a noun phrase. We use the label *transitive* to classify verbs that require a noun phrase to make a complete verb phrase. We call this noun phrase a *direct object,* its grammatical role. Here are some examples of **transitive verbs:**

(8)   Agnes | tamed <u>a tiger</u>.
                        NP
                        Dir. Obj.

(9)   The aggressive cat | clawed <u>my brand-new sofa</u>.
                                        NP
                                        Dir. Obj.

(10)   They | opened <u>a Persian teashop</u>.
                            NP
                            Dir. Obj.

Tamed, clawed, and *opened* in these sentences are transitive verbs. They combine with a noun phrase to make up the verb phrase and predicate. So, for example, *tamed* combines with the noun phrase *a tiger* to make the verb phrase *tamed a tiger.*

SUBJECT-COMPLEMENT VERB PHRASES The third verb-phrase pattern is the subject-complement pattern. The necessary parts of this verb phrase consist of two elements—a verb that falls into the subject-complement class and a noun phrase. We call this noun phrase a **subject complement.** Here are some examples of subject-complement verbs:

(11)　　Oscar ｜ is <u>a tightrope walker</u>.
　　　　　　　　　　　　NP
　　　　　　　　　　Subj. Comp.

(12)　　Rhonda ｜ became <u>a judge</u>.
　　　　　　　　　　　　　NP
　　　　　　　　　　　Subj. Comp.

(13)　　Dr. Baines ｜ remained <u>the dean</u>.
　　　　　　　　　　　　　　NP
　　　　　　　　　　　　Subj. Comp.

Is, became, and *remained* in these sentences are subject-complement verbs. They combine with a noun phrase to make up the verb phrase and the predicate. So, for example, the verb *is* combines with the noun phrase *a tightrope walker* to make the verb phrase *is a tightrope walker.*

DITRANSITIVE VERB PHRASES A fourth verb-phrase pattern is the ditransitive pattern. The necessary parts of this verb phrase consist of three elements—a verb that is ditransitive and two noun phrases. We call the first noun phrase an **indirect object** and the second noun phrase a **direct object.** Here are some examples of ditransitive sentences:

(14)　　Glenda ｜ gave <u>the server</u> <u>a large tip</u>.
　　　　　　　　　　　　NP　　　　NP
　　　　　　　　　　Ind. Obj.　　Dir. Obj.

(15)　　Huey ｜ baked <u>his mother</u> <u>a chocolate cake</u>.
　　　　　　　　　　　　NP　　　　NP
　　　　　　　　　　Ind. Obj.　　Dir. Obj.

(16)　　The pitcher ｜ threw <u>the catcher</u> <u>a curve ball</u>.
　　　　　　　　　　　　　NP　　　　NP
　　　　　　　　　　　Ind. Obj.　　Dir. Obj.

Gave, baked, and *threw* in these sentences are ditransitive verbs. They are the kind of verb that combines with two noun phrases to make up their verb phrase. So, for example, *gave* combines with the noun phrase *the server* and the noun phrase *a tip* to make the verb phrase *gave the server a tip.*

OBJECT-COMPLEMENT VERB PHRASES A fifth verb-phrase pattern is the object-complement pattern. The necessary parts of this verb phrase consist of three elements — an object-complement verb and two noun phrases. We call the first noun phrase a *direct object* and the second noun phrase an **object comple-ment.** Here are some examples of object-complement sentences:

(17) The administration | proclaimed <u>February fourteenth</u> <u>a university</u>
      holiday.   NP   NP
                                           Dir. Obj.   Obj. Comp.

(18) The student in row ten | called <u>him</u> <u>a nasty name</u>.
                                       NP   NP
                                    Dir. Obj.   Obj. Comp.

(19) Ling | considered <u>the party</u> <u>a complete success</u>.
                          NP   NP
                       Dir. Obj.   Obj. Comp.

Proclaimed, called, and *considered* in these sentences are object-complement verbs. They combine with two noun phrases to make up the verb phrase. So, for example, the verb *proclaimed* combines with the noun phrase *February fourteenth* and the noun phrase *a university holiday* to form the verb phrase *proclaimed February fourteenth a university holiday.*

Table 6.1 lists the five verb-phrase patterns discussed above.

Identification Rules for Grammatical Roles

I hope you are wondering about something at this point. The first pattern seems simple enough: the verb is the only unit required to be in the verb phrase. However, all the rest consist of one or two noun phrases, and the noun phrases assume different grammatical roles — direct object, subject complement, indirect object, or object complement. If we need to identify a grammatical role, it is easy to become confused. When a single noun phrase follows the verb, it can be either a direct object or a subject complement. When two noun phrases follow the verb, they can be either an indirect object plus a direct object or a direct object plus an object complement.

We need a way to distinguish these patterns and these grammatical roles, so here are some rules for identifying grammatical roles, similar to those I gave you for identifying phrases and parts of speech.

DISTINGUISHING DIRECT OBJECTS FROM SUBJECT COMPLEMENTS
Here is the first set of rules for verb phrases with one noun phrase following the

TABLE 6.1 Verb-Phrase Patterns

PATTERN	NAME	NECESSARY UNITS IN THE VP	SAMPLE SENTENCE
Pattern 1	intransitive verb phrase	verb	Mary jogs.
Pattern 2	transitive verb phrase	verb + direct object (NP)	Agnes tamed a tiger.
Pattern 3	subject-complement verb phrase	verb + subject complement (NP)	Oscar is a tightrope walker.
Pattern 4	ditransitive verb phrase	verb + indirect object (NP) + direct object (NP)	Glenda gave the server a large tip.
Pattern 5	object-complement verb phrase	verb + direct object (NP) + object complement (NP)	Ling considered the party a complete success.

subject and verb. We know that we have either a direct object or a subject complement. There are three ways to tell the difference between these patterns.

Identification Rule 1

Take the two noun phrases of the original sentence and make a new sentence with them by supplying the appropriate form of the verb be. If the original sentence implies the meaning of your newly constructed sentence, the noun phrase following the verb is a subject complement. If the original sentence does not imply the meaning of your newly constructed sentence, the noun phrase following the verb is a direct object. Right away, you can see that if a sentence has only a be-verb, then the noun phrase following the verb must be a subject complement.

Let's apply this principle to some sentences. If I am trying to figure out the grammatical role of the noun phrase *the dean* in sentence (13), *Dr. Baines re-*

mained the dean, I can take the two noun phrases of the original sentence and insert a *be*-verb between them. That would give me the following:

Dr. Baines remained the dean.

↻

Dr. Baines was the dean.

Then I ask whether the sentence *Dr. Baines remained the dean* implies the meaning of the sentence *Dr. Baines was a dean,* and the answer is yes. Therefore, the noun phrase *the dean* must be a subject complement.

The test works the same way for the sentence in (12), *Rhonda became a judge.* I take the two noun phrases and make a new sentence with them: *Rhonda was a judge.* The first sentence implies the meaning of the second sentence; therefore, the noun phrase *a judge* must be a subject complement:

Rhonda became a judge.

↻

Rhonda was a judge.

Now let's apply this test to a couple of sentences that don't have subject complements. Suppose I am trying to figure out the grammatical role of the noun phrase *a tiger* in sentence (8), *Agnes tamed a tiger.* I can apply this first test and make a new sentence with the two noun phrases, *Agnes* and *a tiger.* That would give me

Agnes tamed a tiger.

↻

Agnes was a tiger.

Now Agnes might be really fierce, and her friends may call her a tiger, but the sentence *Agnes tamed a tiger* does not imply the meaning of *Agnes was a tiger.* Therefore, the noun phrase *a tiger* must not be a subject complement in the sentence *Agnes tamed a tiger.* By process of elimination, it must then be a direct object.

The same process works for sentence (9), *The aggressive cat clawed my brand-new sofa.* I take the two noun phrases and add a *be*-verb to obtain the following:

The aggressive cat clawed my brand-new sofa.

↻

The aggressive cat is my brand-new sofa.

The cat is in no way my brand-new sofa, and certainly the first sentence does not imply the second sentence. Therefore, the noun phrase *my brand-new sofa* is not a subject complement; it must be a direct object.

To make sure we understand the identification rule, let's review it closely. As we have seen, it verifies the meaning relationship between noun phrases. Sometimes the noun phrases have a very close relationship, so close that they refer to the same individual. In the sentence *Dr. Baines remained the dean,* the noun phrase *Dr. Baines* describes the same person in reality as does the noun phrase *the dean.* This identity is the essence of a subject complement. The subject complement "complements" the subject: it gives us some information about the subject.

This is not true for direct objects. Direct objects describe a different entity from the subject. In the sentence *The aggressive cat clawed my brand-new sofa,* the aggressive cat and the brand-new sofa are not the same entity in the world outside the sentence. Instead, my brand-new sofa is the recipient of the clawing that is inflicted by the aggressive cat. This nonidentity is the essence of a direct object. It is distinct from the subject and has a certain relationship to the verb: it refers to something out in the world that experiences the action conveyed by the verb.

Identification Rule 2

Replace the noun phrase following the verb with an adjective phrase. If the sentence still is grammatical, the original noun phrase is a subject complement. If the sentence is ungrammatical, the original noun phrase is a direct object.

We saw in the first test that subject-complement noun phrases are like descriptions of the subjects they are connected to. In English, when we describe a noun we often use adjectives, and adjective phrases can often take the place of noun phrases that are subject complements. However, they can never take the place of noun phrases that are direct objects, because direct objects refer to distinct individuals, whereas adjective phrases do not.

Let's try this out on some of our sentences. For sentence (13), we replace the noun phrase *the dean* with an adjective phrase like *very calm.* The result is a perfectly fine sentence:

Dr. Baines remained the dean.

◖◗

Dr. Baines remained very calm.

This result indicates that the noun phrase *the dean* is a subject complement. If we try the same test with the sentence in (8), we get an ungrammatical sentence:

> Agnes tamed a tiger.
>
> ◑
>
> *Agnes tamed very calm.

This result indicates that the noun phrase *a tiger* was not a subject complement. Therefore, it must be a direct object.

The test works the same way for our other sentences. The following change to sentence (12) shows that the noun phrase *a judge* is a subject complement:

> Rhonda became a judge.
>
> ◑
>
> Rhonda became very calm.

Likewise, that sentence (9) cannot be turned into a grammatical sentence by replacing its final noun phrase with an adjective phrase shows that the noun phrase *my brand-new sofa* is a direct object and not a subject complement:

> The aggressive cat clawed my brand-new sofa.
>
> ◑
>
> *The aggressive cat clawed very calm.

Identification Rule 3

Replace the noun phrase following the verb with an object pronoun (*him, her, it,* or *them*) and see if the meaning stays the same. If it does, the noun phrase is a direct object. It if does not, the noun phrase is a subject complement.

Let's apply this third test to some sentences. Replacing the last noun phrase in (8) with a pronoun gives us

> Agnes tamed a tiger.
>
> ◑
>
> Agnes tamed it.

The sentence *Agnes tamed it* means the same thing as the sentence *Agnes tamed a tiger*. Therefore, the noun phrase *a tiger* must be a direct object.

Notice, though, how this test works for subject-complement sentences. Inserting a pronoun into the sentence in (13) results in the following:

Dr. Baines remained the dean.

⟃

*Dr. Baines remained him.

The resulting sentence sounds distinctly odd, and it does not have the same meaning as the original sentence. Therefore, the noun phrase *the dean* must not be a direct object but rather a subject complement.

This test also makes sense if we think about the kinds of meaning associated with direct objects and subject complements. As the chapter pointed out earlier, direct objects are distinct entities, clearly differentiated from the subjects of the sentences. We use pronouns to refer to distinct entities, and so it is no surprise that pronouns can be used as direct objects. However, subject complements do not pick out distinct entities in the world outside the sentence but rather describe the subject in some way. Therefore, it is not surprising that pronouns do not substitute for subject complements.

The three identification rules give us multiple ways of distinguishing sentences with direct objects from sentences with subject complements. You may need to apply more than one test to a sentence to determine its grammatical structure. As mentioned earlier, the system of language is so complex that all the rules we give to describe language have exceptions.

Let's look at one example to show how a test may not give conclusive results, so multiple tests must be used. Consider the following sentence:

(20)   Jacinth had a cold.

If we try to replace the noun phrase *a cold* with an adjective phrase like *very calm,* we get an ungrammatical sentence:

(21)   *Jacinth had very calm.

If we take the two noun phrases out of this sentence and add a *be*-verb, we get the sentence

(22)   *Jacinth was a cold.

The meaning of (22) is not implied by the meaning of the original sentence. These two tests together tell us that the noun phrase *a cold* is not a subject complement. By process of elimination then, we would want to call that noun phrase a direct object. However, if we try to replace the noun phrase *a cold* with an object pronoun, we get the sentence

(23)   Jacinth had it.

This sentence is not easily understood to mean the same thing as the original sentence. Now we might start questioning ourselves. Is the noun phrase *a cold* a direct object or not?

This is where language becomes so much fun, so much richer than we realize when we use it effortlessly. We previously described a direct object as an entity out in the world that is distinct from the subject. Using this idea, can we say that the noun phrase *a cold* describes a distinct entity? Here we might find some debate. Some may say that the noun phrase *a cold* is not a distinct entity. It seems rather to be a condition or state that the subject of the sentence is in, rather than a separate object from the subject. However, others may counter by saying that we could conceive of the noun phrase *a cold* as pointing to something distinct from the subject, especially if we think of that cold in terms of the germs or viral component that invades the subject's body.

Can we solve this dilemma? Not here. What we can say is this: noun phrases like *a cold* are clearly not subject complements. They do have some characteristics of direct objects: they follow transitive verbs. They also lack some characteristics of direct objects: they can't be replaced with pronouns. That gives us two ways of classifying them. It may be that we need to make another category for such noun phrases. Or we could classify them as direct objects but note that they may be a different kind of direct object. These are the kinds of questions that linguists wrestle with as they study language.

DISTINGUISHING DITRANSITIVE VERBS FROM OBJECT-COMPLEMENT VERBS Now we need a way to distinguish the last two sentence patterns. The indirect-object-plus-direct-object pattern on the surface looks the same as the direct-object-plus-object-complement pattern. Both consist of a verb phrase with a verb followed by two noun phrases. Here are three ways to separate the two patterns:

Identification Rule 4

Take the two noun phrases out of the verb phrase and make them into a new sentence with an appropriate *be*-verb. If the original sentence implies the meaning of your newly constructed sentence, then the pattern is direct object plus object complement. If it does not, then you have the indirect-object-plus-direct-object pattern.

Let's try this with the following sentence:

(19)   Ling considered the party a complete success.

I take the noun phrase *the party* and the noun phrase *a complete success* and make a new sentence out of them with a *be*-verb. This gives me

> Ling considered the party a complete success.

> ☝

> The party was a complete success.

Then I check the relationship between the two sentences. Does the sentence *Ling considered the party a complete success* imply the meaning of *The party was a complete success*? Yes, it does. Therefore, the noun phrase *the party* must be a direct object and the noun phrase *a complete success* must be an object complement.

You can really see how this test works by applying it to a different pattern. Consider sentence (15) again:

> (15)   Huey baked his mother a chocolate cake.

If I take the two noun phrases out of the verb phrase to make a new sentence with a *be*-verb, I get

> Huey baked his mother a chocolate cake.

> ☝

> *His mother was a chocolate cake.

Clearly, the first sentence implies nothing like the meaning of the second sentence. Therefore, the noun phrases *his mother* and *a chocolate cake* must not be the direct-object-plus-object-complement pattern. By process of elimination, they must be the indirect-object-plus-direct-object pattern.

This particular test is doing much the same thing as the first test we used to distinguish between direct objects and subject complements. When we have the direct-object-plus-object-complement pattern, the two noun phrases both refer to the same individual, with the object complement being a description of the direct object. Hence, the noun phrase *a complete success* is pointing to the same thing in the world outside the sentence as the noun phrase *the party*. However, in the indirect-object-plus-direct-object pattern, the two noun phrases are pointing to different entities outside the sentence. The noun phrases *his mother* and *a chocolate cake* are two different objects in the world. That is why the last sentence fails the test.

Identification Rule 5

Replace the second of two noun phrases in the verb phrase with an adjective phrase. If this allows you to make a grammatical sentence, the pattern in the verb phrase is direct object plus object complement. If this leads to an ungrammatical sentence, the pattern in the verb phrase is indirect object plus direct object.

Let's try this test:

(19)   Ling considered the party a complete success.

I replace the noun phrase *a complete success* with an adjective phrase like *very boring*. This gives us the sentence

Ling considered the party a complete success.

◑

Ling considered the party very boring.

This is a grammatical sentence, and it tells us that the original sentence must have a direct-object-plus-object-complement pattern.

Now let's try this test on sentence (15). That sentence becomes

Huey baked his mother a chocolate cake.

◑

*Huey baked his mother very boring.

This is not a grammatical sentence. Therefore, the original sentence must have an indirect-object-plus-direct-object pattern.

We can understand how this tests works. If the second noun phrase is an object complement, it acts like a description of the noun phrase before it. Adjective phrases function as descriptions. Therefore, we should be able to insert them in object-complement positions. However, if the two noun phrases refer to separate individuals, it should not be possible to insert an adjective phrase into a direct-object position, because a direct-object position needs a phrase that can refer to an individual, that is, a noun phrase.

Identification Rule 6

Take a sentence that has two noun phrases following the verb; switch the order of the two noun phrases and add a preposition, normally the preposition *to,* in front of the second noun phrase. If this leads to a grammatical sentence that has the same meaning as the original, then the pattern of the original is indirect object plus direct object. If this leads to a sentence whose meaning is different, then the pattern of the original is direct object plus object complement.

Let's try this test:

(14)   Glenda gave the server a large tip.

I make a new sentence that is exactly the same as the one above except that I switch the order of the noun phrase *the server* and the noun phrase *a large tip*. Then I add the preposition *to* before the last noun phrase:

Glenda gave the server a large tip.

◖◗

Glenda gave a large tip to the server.

This sentence has the same meaning as the original. Therefore, the original sentence must have an indirect-object-plus-direct-object pattern.

Now let's try this test for a different pattern. Applying it to sentence (19) results in an ungrammatical sentence:

Ling considered the party a complete success.

◖◗

*Ling considered a complete success to the party.

That sentence is ill formed; therefore, the pattern in our original sentence must be direct object plus object complement.

As identification rule 6 is stated above, it tells you to add the preposition *to*. Sometimes, however, a different preposition is required. Often the preposition *for* works for this test. We would want to use the preposition *for* instead of the preposition *to* for a sentence like (15). Rearranging the noun phrases and adding a preposition works when we add *for*, as the sentences below demonstrate:

Huey baked his mother a chocolate cake.

◖◗

Huey baked a chocolate cake for his mother.

Adding the preposition *to* would result in the ill-formed sentence

(24)   *Huey baked a chocolate cake to his mother.

Therefore, you might need to try more than one preposition when applying test 6 to verb phrases that have two noun phrases in them.

This last test works because it turns out that English has two different sentence structures to express the roles that indirect objects and direct objects together contribute to the sentence. Often the role contributed by an indirect object can be expressed with a prepositional phrase. The noun phrase that has the role of the direct object can then be positioned immediately after the verb.

Now, just as we saw for the tests that distinguished transitive verbs and subject-complement verbs, there will be exceptions to our tests that distinguish ditransitive verbs from object-complement verbs. For example, consider the sentence

(25)   We named our daughter Moon Unit.

Analyzing the structure of the verb phrase shows us that the verb *named* is followed by two noun phrases, the noun phrase *our daughter* and the noun phrase *Moon Unit*. Hence, we know right away that we need to determine whether this is a ditransitive verb phrase or an object-complement verb phrase. We then apply test 4 and make a new sentence with the two noun phrases and a *be*-verb. That gives us the sentence

(26)   Our daughter is Moon Unit.

The meaning of this sentence implies the meaning of the original sentence. That tells us that the original sentence must have the direct-object-plus-object-complement pattern.

Now let's apply test 6 where we reorder the two noun phrases and add a preposition to the last one. No matter which preposition we use, *to* or *for*, we get an ungrammatical sentence:

(27)   *We named Moon Unit to our daughter.

(28)   *We named Moon Unit for our daughter.

This confirms our earlier test. The sentence does not have a ditransitive pattern. Therefore, it must have a direct-object-plus-object-complement pattern.

A difficulty arises when we try test 5 and replace the second noun phrase with an adjective phrase. If the last noun phrase is an object complement, we should be able to do this. However, we get a sentence like the following:

(29)   *We named our daughter silly.

This sentence would make sense if *silly* were a proper name, but it doesn't work with *silly* as an adjective. What's the moral here? If we had started with this test, we might have erroneously thought that the sentence didn't have a direct-object-plus-object-complement pattern. However, the other two tests confirm that we do have a direct-object-plus-object-complement pattern. The lesson is that not all examples of a pattern are alike. The verb *name* does fit the direct-object-plus-object-complement pattern but does not allow the object complement to be an adjective phrase. Table 6.2 summarizes the identification rules for grammatical roles.

TABLE 6.2   Identification Rules for Grammatical Roles

For verb phrases containing one noun phrase

RULE NUMBER	RULE	EXAMPLE	RESULTS OK?
Rule 1	Insert form of *be*	Dr. Baines remained the dean ⟳ Dr. Baines was the dean.	Yes ◑ Subject Complement No ◑ Direct Object
Rule 2	Replace with adjective phrase	Dr. Baines remained the dean. ⟳ Dr. Baines remained very calm.	Yes ◑ Subject Complement No ◑ Direct Object
Rule 3	Replace with object pronoun	Agnes tamed a tiger. ⟳ Agnes tamed it.	Yes ◑ Direct Object No ◑ Subject Complement

For verb phrases containing two noun phrases

RULE NUMBER	RULE	EXAMPLE	RESULTS OK?
Rule 4	Insert form of *be*	Ling considered the party a complete success. ⟳ The party was a complete success.	Yes ◑ Dir Obj + Obj Comp No ◑ Ind Obj + Dir Obj
Rule 5	Replace with adjective phrase	Ling considered the party a complete success. ⟳ Ling considered the party very boring.	Yes ◑ Dir Obj + Obj Comp No ◑ Ind Obj + Dir Obj
Rule 6	Reorder noun phrases	Glenda gave the server a large tip. ⟳ Glenda gave a large tip to the server.	Yes ◑ Ind Obj + Dir Obj No ◑ Dir Obj + Obj Comp

The following two exercises will give you some practice at distinguishing grammatical roles.

EXERCISE 1

Identify all of the grammatical roles in the following sentences, giving the entire phrase that fills each role.

1. Mervin is pursuing trivial pursuits.

2. The stable hired Vargas.

3. Brandy felt sick.

4. The president called the conference a success.

5. After the flood, the local philanthropist gave the town $50,000.

6. During the conference, the delegate from the red team snored.

7. This babysitter read Susie a book about reptiles.

8. Last year's runner-up became this year's front-runner due to Carl's ineligibility.

9. Betsy painted the room a deep shade of purple.

10. We drove through the pouring rain.

11. The tongue is the strongest muscle in the body.

12. Gina played baseball for the Antelopes.

13. The quartet sang a Bach cantata at the opening of the new music store in the mall.

14. The committee made Frank treasurer because he could count backwards and forwards.

15. The new carpenter in town built the Ridleys a fantastic back porch.

16. With over $810,000 in annual sales, Pop's Grocery is listed as the largest company in the neighborhood.

EXERCISE 2

Choose a paragraph from a favorite text and identify all of the grammatical roles in each sentence. Make sure that you give the entire phrase that fills each role.

Application to Writing

Grammatical roles can make us more aware of the rich world of verbs. Verbs are juicy words, not only because of their individual meanings but also because of the multifold patterns they form. Furthermore, some verbs can appear with more than one pattern. The verb *eat* can occur as an intransitive (30) or a transitive verb (31):

(30)   Yes, we ate.

(31)   No, we ate the crabs.

You can begin to think about the verbs you use in your writing in terms of the phrases that accompany them. The following exercise will encourage you to think about verbs in terms of the patterns they form.

EXERCISE 3

Write a paragraph or poem that uses all five of the verb-phrase patterns listed in this chapter. Discuss what difficulties you encountered when including particular patterns in your text.

COMPREHENSION QUESTIONS

1. What are the two main parts of a declarative sentence?

2. What kind of phrases display the most variation in English?

3. What are the five basic verb-phrase patterns of English?

4. What are the three tests that distinguish transitive verbs from subject-complement verbs?

5. What are the three tests that distinguish ditransitive verbs from object-complement verbs?

Adverbials and Other Elements in the Clause

PREVIEW *This chapter will introduce the idea of grammatical necessity: what elements a clause must have to form a complete sentence. Adverbials, those elements that are not necessary for the structure, take many different forms and carry out many different functions. This distinction is crucial to understanding the rules of English punctuation.*

The Other Elements: Examples of Grammatical Necessity

Grammatical roles are another way of referring to what we might call the "necessary stuff" of the sentence. By "necessary," I am not talking about how important the content or information of a phrase is to what you may be writing. I refer to grammatical necessity. What does a particular sentence need to even qualify as a complete sentence? We could begin to make a list of grammatical necessities in a sentence. That list would include

> main verb(s)
>
> all phrases that have a grammatical role (subject, direct object, indirect object, subject complement, object complement)

English is a language that requires sentences to have a verb. We can see that if we take away a verb from a sentence like (1), we get an ungrammatical sequence like (2):

> (1)   Granville saw a gopher west of his computer desk.
>
> (2)   *Granville a gopher west of his computer desk.   [missing verb]

Likewise, phrases that carry grammatical roles are necessary, too. For example, subjects are just as necessary as verbs for declarative sentences in English. Take away the subject from (1), and you get the ungrammatical sequence

(3)   *Saw a gopher west of his computer desk.   [missing subject]

However, it may be a little harder to recognize the grammatical necessity of other grammatical roles. Sometimes, removing a phrase like a direct object will result in a sentence that sounds ill formed. Thus, if we remove the direct object from (1), the resulting sentence clearly sounds awkward:

(4)   *Granville saw.   [missing direct object]

Nonetheless, in some cases the sentence with a missing direct object may still be grammatical. However, the meaning of that sentence, in particular the meaning of the verb, will be changed. Sentences (5)–(8) demonstrate this:

(5)   Devon bathed her daughter.

(6)   Devon bathed.

(7)   Devon ate spaghetti.

(8)   Devon ate.

The direct object *her daughter* in (5) is removed in (6). However, (6) is still grammatical. This makes it look like the direct object is not grammatically necessary in (5). We must compare, though, the meaning of the verbs in both sentences, and when we do we see that they are different in meaning. The verb *bathed* in (6) conveys to us that Devon bathed herself, whereas in (5) the bathing is done to someone else. What we can say then is that the verb *bathe* requires a direct object when the person doing the bathing is bathing someone else.

The difference between the sentences in (7) and (8) is more subtle but nonetheless still present. The verb *ate* in (8) conveys the idea that Devon ate a meal. The sentence could describe a setting in which Devon ate any kind of food. However, the verb *ate* in (7) does not convey the idea of eating a meal but rather a food. Therefore, the direct object is necessary for the verb *eat* when it pertains to a specific food. Sentences (5)–(8) show that some verbs can be transitive or intransitive. However, the meanings of the transitive and intransitive verbs are subtly different, as demonstrated above, and the direct object is necessary in the sentence when we want to convey the transitive meaning of the verb.

There are two other elements we can add to our list of necessary stuff. If a modal appears in the sentence, it is a necessary element or core part of the sentence. When we remove a modal from a sentence like (9), we get an ungrammatical sequence, as in (10):

(9)   Yancy will attend Northern Springfield Technical School of Multi-media Engineering next year.

(10)   *Yancy attend Northern Springfield Technical School of Multi-media Engineering next year.

Likewise, certain prepositional phrases are necessary stuff. This is shown in a sentence like

(11)   I rely on the kindness of strangers and children.

If we remove the prepositional phrase *on the kindness of strangers and children* from the sentence, we get the ungrammatical sequence

(12)   *I rely.

Clearly, the prepositional phrase in (12) is a necessary or core element in some sentences, just like phrases with grammatical roles. Sometimes a verb may require both a phrase with a grammatical role and a prepositional phrase:

(13)   Joyce gave ten pairs of pants to the Save the Whippoorwill auction.

The prepositional phrase *to the Save the Whippoorwill auction* is a necessary prepositional phrase like the one in (11). One of our tests for distinguishing ditransitive sentences from object-complement sentences depended on the relationship between a sentence like (13) and its corresponding ditransitive form:

(14)   Joyce gave <u>the Save the Whippoorwill auction</u> <u>ten pairs of pants</u>.
              Indirect object   Direct object

As a matter of fact, you may have been taught in school that the prepositional phrase *to the Save the Whippoorwill auction* in (13) is an indirect object. In this book, however, we will not apply grammatical role labels to prepositional phrases but only to bare noun phrases, noun phrases with no preposition before them. We will do this for the sake of consistency. Bare noun phrases all look alike, and so we will always need to determine what contribution a bare noun phrase makes to the sentence. However, when we have a prepositional phrase, the preposition tells us how the entire phrase will relate to the rest of the sentence.

Thus, to sum up, the necessary stuff of the sentence includes the following:

main verb(s)

phrases that carry grammatical roles

modals

certain PPs

Adverbials

If there is necessary stuff, then there must also be extra stuff. Again, by "extra stuff" I refer to those elements in the sentence that are not grammatically required to make a complete sentence. I am not referring to the importance of their content or meaning to the discourse you may be writing. Often the key information in a sentence is conveyed by the grammatically optional elements of a sentence. Also, in this chapter we are only considering those phrases that are not inside other noun phrases. (These are called adjectivals and will be discussed in Chapter 10.)

Many people refer to the extra stuff as **adverbials,** a term I will use in this book. It is important that you distinguish between the terms *adverbial* and *adverb*. **Adverbs** are a part of speech, a formal category of the language: they can be identified on the basis of their form and on the basis of the structure of the sentence. Adverbials are a functional category that consists of many different kinds of word classes. That is, adverbials all function in a similar way: they play a similar role across a wide variety of sentences. For example, the adverbial *yesterday* plays the same role, or contributes the same information, in all of the following sentences. That is, it conveys when the event of the sentence took place.

> <u>Yesterday</u>, a water pipe broke in our kitchen and caused $14,000 in damages.

> The Grower's Association <u>yesterday</u> appealed to the state for relief funds because of the drought.

> I saw you <u>yesterday</u> at the courthouse.

> The class was completely filled <u>yesterday</u>.

These can be contrasted with the different functions expressed by phrases carrying grammatical roles. For example, the noun phrase *Lucinda* may convey to us a person by that name, but in sentence (15) Lucinda is the doer of the action, while in (16) she is the recipient of the action.

PEANUTS reprinted by permission of the United Feature Syndicate, Inc.

(15)   <u>Lucinda</u> ran the Biloxi Marathon.

(16)   Celeste defeated <u>Lucinda</u>.

Adverbials can contribute the following kinds of information to a sentence:

temporality: Pierre went to Lourdes <u>two years ago</u>.

frequency: Denny brushes his teeth <u>five times a day</u>.

location: The two cars collided <u>at the corner of Elm and Wisteria</u>.

purpose: Sandy bought a doberman <u>to protect her house</u>.

manner: Ronald laughed <u>hysterically</u> at the biology teacher's joke.

cause: I sent you gumbo <u>because I like you</u>.

Many people remember adverbials as those phrases that answer the questions *when, how often, where, why,* and *how* in a sentence. The following exercise will give you practice in recognizing the meaning different adverbials contribute.

EXERCISE 1

Identify the kinds of adverbials in the following sentences by function. Be careful to identify the entire phrase that functions as an adverbial. There may be more than one adverbial in a sentence, and some sentences may have no adverbials in them.

1. I fell off my bike.

2. On September 3rd, school started with a bang.

3. Duke was running late because his car had broken down.

4. Six times a day, the trash gets taken out at that diner.

5. Hedda studies hard in order to go to medical school.

6. Lewis E. Waterman invented the fountain pen.

7. Paul is walking barefoot on the cover of *Abbey Road.*

8. The Olympic Games were canceled once during World War II.

9. On account of the rain, the picnic was postponed till next Saturday.

10. Dover Donny ran skillfully at Palmetto Downs.

11. Hilary knows that truffles are edible.

12. Irene may be at the corner of Devon and Spenser.

Adverbials also take different phrasal forms, as shown below.

   noun phrases: The Jets and the Falcons played <u>last night</u>.

   adverb phrases: Tickets for the home opener were sold out <u>very quickly</u>.

   prepositional phrases: Baby Johnny eats his mush <u>with gusto</u>.

   subordinate clauses (discussed further in Chapter 9): "<u>Until you get all A's and B's on your report card</u>, you're not staying out late, young lady!"

   infinitive verb phrases: I'd walk a mile <u>to buy a can of Jolt</u>.

The next exercise asks you to recognize the form of adverbials.

EXERCISE 2

Identify all of the adverbials in the following sentences by kind of phrase.

1. The Indianapolis 500 is run on Memorial Day.

2. Adolf Hitler irrationally believed that the number seven possessed supernatural power.

3. Curly sings to keep the blues away.

4. We will drive next week to the Hamptons.

5. After he played football at Florida State, Burt had quite an acting career.

6. That patron is walking rather erratically down the alley.

7. The offense has run that play forty-eight times.

8. To remain competitive, Sonya will have to increase her daily workouts.

9. It got quite cold last night, though the orange crop probably survived.

10. Theodore Roosevelt was the first U.S. president to travel in a car, plane, and submarine.

11. My aerobics class, while they were warming up, heard a loud bang from the pool area.

12. Quickly and efficiently, the thief found an unlocked window.

13. Inside the tunnel, the engineer whistled with great fervor.

14. Today, the sun will not shine for me.

Now try an exercise that puts together function and form for adverbials.

EXERCISE 3

Identify by function and kind of phrase all of the adverbials in the following sentences.

> EXAMPLE: We skied <u>in Vail</u>.
> PP, location

1. Gasohol is made at this plant during the fall.

2. To win this game, you need nerves of steel and patience.

3. After you leave work, can you go to the store and buy me some drain cleaner?

4. That drawing by Moreau mysteriously disappeared once the war ended.

5. Joe stayed around the corner at Kelly's house three weeks.

6. Last month Tanya stomped her feet angrily in Doc's office because he reprimanded her.

7. Little White Dove was undoubtedly the maiden in that song.

8. Stuart bought that old house to be closer to work.

9. Once Camille unscrewed the lid, the aroma began to seep out into the hall.

10. Dee and Pete bought an island with their retirement account.

Now we need to bring some of these concepts together. For example, since some noun phrases can be adverbials, you need to make sure you identify all adverbials in a sentence before you look for grammatical roles. The sentence below, for example, has two noun phrases in the verb phrase.

> Neville soaked <u>his head</u> <u>this morning</u>.
>   NP   NP

We wouldn't mistakenly want to treat this verb phrase as either a ditransitive with an indirect object plus direct object or as a verb taking a direct object plus object complement, because the second noun phrase in the verb phrase, *this morning,* is an adverbial. The adverbials are eliminated from consideration for any grammatical role, so that the sentence would have either the direct object or the subject-complement pattern. In this case, our tests would identify the noun phrase *his head* as a direct object.

The following exercises will give you some practice in distinguishing necessary stuff and adverbials from each other.

EXERCISE 4

Identify all adverbials and phrases that take grammatical roles in the following sentences.

1. Napoleon's army first used canned foods.

2. Our lot borders the Thompsons' lot on the north.

3. Crass rudeness will get you nowhere with that division head.

4. Although her house is small, Lana's parties make her friends jealous.

5. In two weeks, that cheese is going to smell rancid unless you put it in an air-tight container.

6. Probably Ulysses gave the maintenance man the key before he left for vacation.

7. Anne told the children at the orphanage a story about knights in shining armor.

8. Despite our loud singing and vigorous thumping, Colson slept through the night.

9. Carelessly, Ralph dropped a bowling ball on his big toe outside the alley.

10. The curator's idea sounded intriguing to the museum director.

EXERCISE 5

Write two sentences of your own for each of the verb patterns listed below. Try to include verbs not used in the example sentences found in Chapters 6 and 7.

1. Intransitive verb

2. Transitive verb

3. Subject-complement verb

4. Ditransitive verb

5. Object-complement verb

6. Verb that requires a PP

7. Transitive verb that also requires a PP

EXERCISE—APPLY YOUR KNOWLEDGE

The following sentences display some verb patterns not discussed in Chapters 6 and 7. Identify verb patterns below by listing the main phrases found in each verb phrase.

1. Phaedrus wants to buy a trailer.

2. The class of 2006 persuaded the president to build a new recreation center.

3. Arnie acknowledged that his last movie didn't live up to his expectations.

4. Sarah told the clerk that the pants were too big.

5. The Porter sisters bet the Franklin brothers ten dollars that the homecoming game would be canceled because of the hurricane.

 # Application to Writing

The content of the last two chapters gives us a number of ways to think about our writing or the writing of our students. In Chapter 8, we will use the concept of grammatical roles to talk about voice and the distinction between active and passive sentences and sentences that are neither active nor passive.

The necessary stuff is what the reader must identify to pull together the structure of a sentence in her mind. Because our minds operate on the basis of grammar, the necessary stuff is crucial for deciphering meaning. When the grammatical patterns of a sentence are not well formed, meaning breaks down.

The most basic rule for punctuation follows this distinction between necessary stuff and extra stuff. A single piece of punctuation, with one important exception, does not separate necessary units from one another in the sentence. For example, we would not put a single comma between a verb and its direct object:

> *Old Bessie <u>chews</u>, <u>her cud</u>.
>   V   Dir Obj

or between a modal and a verb:

> *You <u>could</u>, <u>compete</u> in the quarterfinals.
>   Modal   V

or between an indirect object and a direct object:

> *Inez gave <u>Fido</u>, <u>her love</u>.
>   Ind Obj Dir Obj

The necessary stuff of the sentence is based on patterns in which each element plays a crucial role. None can be missing and all must occur in the positions determined by the language. A single piece of punctuation interferes with the reader grouping all of the necessary stuff together. Research has shown that punctuation slows down the reader. We will see later in this book that there are times when it is appropriate to slow the reader down, but not when the reader is trying to recognize the overall pattern of the sentence and so needs to combine each element in that pattern. As this discussion implies, most sentence-internal punctuation appears when there is extra stuff in the sentence, and we will see examples of this in later chapters.

There is one exception to this generalization about punctuation. We insert a comma after a verb of speaking and before the clause that is the content of direct speech, as the following sentence demonstrates:

(17)   Kip said, "The hosts are all out of cheese crackers."

The clause *the hosts are all out of cheese crackers* is a necessary unit. We can see this if we eliminate it from the sentence:

*Kip said.

Nonetheless, it is quite important to mark clause boundaries when more than one clause is in a sentence. Even though direct speech is set off by quotation marks before and after, we still insert a comma after the verb to reinforce in the reader's mind that a clause and not just a noun phrase is the object of the verb. Your readers encounter words in a linear order and will try to assemble them into a coherent sentence as in (18).

(18)   Kip said "The Hosts. . . .

Notice that this could be enough content to make a complete sentence by itself, as in (19).

(19)   Kip said "The Hosts."

Instead, the comma signals to the reader that an entire clause is following the verb, so he will also realize that there are more words following the noun phrase *the hosts*. This is an example of redundancy in written language, some aspect of the language being marked in more than one way. The need to clearly identify clause boundaries will be discussed more fully in Chapter 9.

While the necessary stuff is grammatically crucial, the extra stuff is often where writers put the content that is most important for their rhetorical purposes. We can see this by observing what is necessary and what is extra in a piece of real-world writing. The two paragraphs below are from Lewis Carroll's *Through the Looking Glass.*

> And then (as Alice afterwards described it) all sorts of things happened in a moment. The candles all grew up to the ceiling, looking something like a bed of rushes with fireworks at the top. As to the bottles, they each took a pair of plates, which they hastily fitted on as wings, and so, with forks for legs, went fluttering about: "and very like birds they look," Alice thought to herself, as well as she could in the dreadful confusion that was beginning.

> At this moment she heard a hoarse laugh at her side, and turned to see what was the matter with the White Queen; but instead of the Queen, there was the leg of mutton sitting in the chair. "Here I am!" cried a voice from the soup-tureen, and Alice turned again, just in time to see the Queen's broad good-natured face grinning at her for a moment over the edge of the tureen, before she disappeared into the soup.

Most of the important content of the story is conveyed through extra stuff. We can see this if we eliminate all of the adverbials from the above paragraphs so that we have left only the phrases that make up the necessary stuff.

> All sorts of things happened. The candles grew. They took a pair of plates and went fluttering: "like birds they look," Alice thought.
>
> She heard a hoarse laugh and turned; there was the leg of mutton. "Here I am!" cried a voice, and Alice turned.

Our paragraphs have shrunk enormously without the extra stuff. The story has become virtually impossible to understand without the adverbials. In your writing as well, adverbials may carry the most-important information that you want to convey. The necessary stuff provides the structure that helps your reader organize meaning, but the extra stuff will probably get most of your points across. These ideas will be discussed in later chapters as we talk in more detail about the order and sequencing of our words from a grammatical and rhetorical point of view.

The following exercises ask you to manipulate writing by eliminating the adverbials in order to see how they affect written communication and to reinforce in your mind the distinctions between adverbials and other elements of the structure.

EXERCISE 6

Find a paragraph from a favorite text and eliminate all of the adverbials in it. Then discuss what effect this has on the paragraph.

EXERCISE 7

Write a normal paragraph about a subject you know well, but use no adverbials in your sentences. Then rewrite the paragraph using adverbials as appropriate. Compare the two paragraphs and discuss how they differ in their effect on the reader.

COMPREHENSION QUESTIONS

1. Grammatically speaking, what is the "necessary stuff" of a sentence?

2. What forms are grammatically necessary in a sentence?

3. Grammatically speaking, what is the "extra stuff" of a sentence?

4. What functions do adverbials carry out in a sentence?

5. What forms can adverbials take?

Passive? Tense? What's on that Verb?

PREVIEW *This chapter brings together two separate issues, tense and passives. Because both are marked on the verb, it is easy to confuse both of them. We will learn how to distinguish these two and how to change active sentences to passive and passive sentences to active.*

Tense

Verbs in English are a fun lot. We normally think about them primarily in terms of tense, the information that signals the time conveyed by a sentence. Tense is a linguistic category that shows itself on the different forms that verbs take. For example, we know the following sentence

(1)   Sheila mowed the grass.

is in the past tense because of the *-ed* form that shows up on the end of the verb *mow*. If the sentence had been the following:

(2)   Sheila mows the grass.

then the *-s* form would have told us that the sentence was in the present tense.

If we think about tense this way, as something that manifests itself on the form of verbs, how many tenses would you say that English has?

Did you say two or three tenses? If you said three, then you were probably thinking of the traditional list of past, present, and future tense. We know that past and present tense are signaled by changes to the verb. What about future tense? In English, future tense is conveyed a number of different ways. The one we think of first is by adding the modal *will* to the sentence:

(3)   Sheila will mow the grass.

Frank and Ernest

ENVIRONMENTAL GRAMMAR

PASTURE   PRESENTURE   FUTURE

©1994 Thaves. Reprinted with permission. Newspaper dist. by NEA, Inc.

When we add *will*, we always use the base form of the verb. If we examine the forms of verbs themselves, it looks like English does not have a future tense, and that is exactly what linguists who study the language would say. In terms of form, English has only two tenses: past and present.

Let's ask another question about tense. Does tense always refer to time? Does the past-tense form always convey past time information in the sentence? Does the present-tense form always convey present time information?

If you said no, you were correct. Let's consider the present tense first. The present tense by itself often does not locate the sentence in present time. For example, the sentence below,

(4)   Jud eats anchovy pizzas.

does not tell us what Jud is eating right now. That would require a sentence like

(5)   Jud is eating an anchovy pizza.

Rather, the previous sentence tells us about Jud's habits or preferences. That is, it conveys both past, present, and future time information.

Here's another example of how the present-tense form does not necessarily mean present time. If someone asked when your flight to Hawaii took off, you could say, for instance:

(6)   My flight leaves at 1:00 p.m.

Even though the event is in the future, this sentence uses a present-tense verb. Sentences like (6) make it clear that present-tense forms do not simply correspond to present time.

Past-tense verb forms more often refer to past time than present-tense verb forms refer to present time. However, even here there are a few exceptions. Consider the sentence

(7)   If you baked the cake tomorrow, you would still have time for the party at 6:00.

The first clause in the sentence, *if you baked the cake tomorrow,* is talking about a future event. Nonetheless, the verb *baked* has a past-tense form. As a matter of fact, if we tried to use the word *will* in that clause, we would get an awkward sentence:

(8)   *If you will bake the cake tomorrow, you would still have time for the party at 6:00.

Sentence (8) shows how the past tense may convey a sense of tentativeness or uncertainty rather than information about time.

The moral of the story is that tense forms do not always refer to time.

More than Temporal Information

There's another difficulty for us here. Traditionally, the terminology makes it sound as if the forms of the verbal system of English conveyed a single kind of information—time. However, the tense system communicates another type of information as well. We can see this by comparing the following two sentences

(9)   Gretchen sat on the desk.

(10)   Gretchen was sitting on the desk.

Each sentence has past tense, but they differ as well. In particular, we see a *be* verb and an *-ing* on the end of *sit* in (10). Both sentences tell us that Gretchen's sitting on the desk took place in the past, yet both view that action of sitting differently. In the second, the sitting is viewed as a process or as incomplete. Because this view of the action is not really related to past, present, or future time, we will give it a different name. Linguists call this phenomenon **aspect.** All sentences have an aspect besides their tense. In English, tense and aspect are displayed together in the various forms that verbs take and the auxiliary verbs they combine with.

Tense-Aspect Forms

Now that we have added this part of the discussion, let's look at the **tense-aspect** system in terms of its forms, because you will need to keep those distinct from passives when we get to them.

There are six primary tense-aspect forms in English. They are

simple present

simple past

present perfect

past perfect

present progressive

past progressive

The **simple present** consists of the main verb either in a form with no suffix or with an -s ending. No other verb or modal is in the clause (except in the case of passive sentences). The sentences below give examples:

(11)   Fleas <u>sit</u> on my dog's back.

(12)   A flea <u>sits</u> on my dog's back.

The **simple past** consists of the main verb in its past form, usually the -ed ending or one of the irregular forms. No other verb or modal is in the sentence (except in the case of passive sentences). The next sentences give examples:

(13)   Fleas <u>chased</u> my dog.

(14)   Fleas <u>sat</u> on my dog.

Both **present perfect** and **past perfect** consist of a *have*-verb and the **past participle** or -en form of the content verb. Regular verbs form their past participle by adding the suffix -ed. Irregular verbs form their past participle most often by adding the suffix -en but sometimes in other ways. Below is a representative list of verbs with their past-participle forms.

Verb	Past participle
take	taken
be	been
have	had
jump	jumped
give	given
make	made
sing	sung
think	thought
cut	cut

The term *past participle* is the traditional term for this form, but some teachers refer to the form as the **-en verb form,** because it is the only place where verbs ending in the -en suffix occur.

For the present perfect, the *have*-verb is in the present tense:

(15)   Fleas <u>have</u> <u>chased</u> my dog. [*chased* is the past participle]

(16)   A flea <u>has</u> <u>sat</u> on my dog.   [*sat* is the past participle]

For the past perfect, the *have*-verb is in the past tense:

(17)   Fleas <u>had</u> <u>chased</u> my dog.

(18)   Fleas <u>had</u> <u>sat</u> on my dog.

Both **present progressive** and **past progressive** consist of a *be*-verb and the present participle or *-ing* form of the content verb. Again, the term **present participle** is the traditional name for the form. Unlike past participles, which take many different forms, present participles are always formed by adding the suffix *-ing.* For the present progressive, the *be*-verb is in the present tense:

(19)   Fleas <u>are</u> <u>chasing</u> my dog.

(20)   Fleas <u>are</u> <u>sitting</u> on my dog.

 For the past progressive, the *be*-verb is in the past tense:

(21)   Fleas <u>were</u> <u>chasing</u> my dog.

(22)   A flea <u>was</u> <u>sitting</u> on my dog.

How to Tell Them Apart

Here comes the fun part. Can you tell these tense-aspect combinations apart as they occur in real sentences in authentic text? Just as I did for phrases, I will give you a series of tests that you can run through so that you can identify the tense-aspect of any English sentence. If you apply these tests in order when you need to determine the tense-aspect of an English sentence, you too will be able to do what even many educated people cannot do—figure out the tense-aspect of every sentence that you meet.

Basically, what we want to do is look for easily recognizable characteristics in a specific order. One of the problems students have in figuring out the tense of sentences is that they look at everything at one time and so get lost in the process. The sheer amount of words in the sentence can be overwhelming. However, if you look for specific indicators of tenses, then you can't go wrong.

STEPS FOR TENSE IDENTIFICATION

Step 1

For our purposes, we will only worry about identifying the tense of sentences that don't have modals. So the first thing we want to do is look for a modal (See Chapter 3.). If there is a modal, we will call that sentence a modal sentence. If there is no modal, then we will go ahead and look for the tense of the sentence.

After we have examined a sentence for modals and found none, we will start by looking for the more specialized tenses. This will work through a process of elimination. Each test will either identify a tense or eliminate a tense. We can do this because we have a short list to work with, only six primary tenses. The first tense we will test for are the perfects.

Step 2

First, look for a *have*-verb in the sentence. If there is no *have*-verb, then we know that the sentence is not a perfect and we can go on to step 3. That's great. By looking for one little word, we might eliminate two possible tenses from further consideration. If there is a *have*-verb, then we need to ask another question. Is there an *-en* verb form after the *have*-verb? If there is not, then we also don't have a perfect and we can go on to step 3.

If there is an *-en* verb form, then we know that it is a perfect. However, that leaves us with two choices, present perfect or past perfect. Now we must go back to the *have*-verb, and check its tense. If it is the form *have* or *has,* then the sentence is a present perfect. If it is the form *had,* then the sentence is a past perfect.

Step 3

Once we eliminate the possibility of perfects, we can check for the progressive. The first thing we look for is a *be*-verb. If there is no *be*-verb, then the sentence is not a progressive and we can go on to step 4. If there is a *be*-verb, then we next look for an *-ing* verb form after the *be*-verb. If there is no *-ing* form, then the sentence is not a progressive and we can go on to step 4.

If there is an *-ing* form, then the sentence is a progressive. All that remains is to look at the tense of the *be*-verb to determine whether the sentence is present progressive or past progressive. If the *be*-verb is present tense, (*am, is, are*), then the sentence is present progressive. If the *be*-verb is past tense (*was, were*), then the sentence is past progressive.

Step 4

Once we eliminate the possibility of either perfects or progressives, we can check for the simple present and simple past tense. Now we only need to check the form of the verb itself. If the verb has no suffix or ends in -s, we have a simple present. (Note that the simple present forms of *be* are *am, is,* and *are.*) If the verb ends in -*ed* or some other irregular form, we have a simple past. All of these tests are laid out in Figure 8.1 to help you with your decision making.

Let's try these rules out on some sentences. Consider the sentence below.

(23)   Grandy has eaten the cake.

Starting at step 1, we look for a modal and find none. Then we move to step 2 and look for a *have*-verb and find one, the second word *has.* Next we look for an -*en* verb form following the *have*-verb, and we find one, the third word *eaten.* Hence, we know that the sentence is a perfect. Finally, we identify the tense of the *have*-verb. We see that it is present tense, the verb *has.* Therefore, we identify the tense as a present perfect.

Now let's try the same thing for the next sentence.

(24)   Grandy has the cake.

Starting at step 1, we look for a modal and find none. Then we move to step 2 and look for a *have*-verb and again find one, the second word *has.* Next we look for an -*en* verb form after the *have*-verb, but this time we don't find one, so we know that sentence is not a perfect.

We then go to step 3 and look for a *be*-verb and see that there is no *be*-verb. Hence, we know that the sentence is not in the progressive tense. That leaves two possibilities, either simple present or simple past. We identify the tense of the one verb in the sentence and observe that *has* is present tense. Therefore, we know that the sentence is simple present. These two examples demonstrate how similar sentences can have different tenses. The verb *has* in (23) marks the present-perfect tense. In (24), the verb *has* is the main verb of the sentence and appears in the simple present.

The following two sentences also illustrate a potential confusion:

(25)   The firefighter was sleeping at the fire station.

(26)   The firefighter was at the fire station.

We start at step 1 and look for a modal in (25) and find none. Then we move to step 2 and look for a *have*-verb. There is none, so we know the sentence is not

Tense Identification

1. Look for modal.
    Yes ➔ This is a modal sentence.
    No ➔ This is not a modal sentence. Go to step 2.

2. Look for a *have*-verb.
    Yes ➔ Go to step 2a.
    No ➔ This is not a perfect. Go to step 3.

    2a. Look for an -*en* verb form after the *have*-verb.
        Yes ➔ This is a perfect. Go to step 2b.
        No ➔ This is not a perfect. Go to step 3.

    2b. Check the tense of the *have*-verb. (*have*, *has*) ➔ This is a present perfect.
        (*had*) ➔ This is a past perfect.

3. Look for a *be*-verb.
    Yes ➔ Go to step 3a.
    No ➔ This is not a progressive. Go to step 4.

    3a. Look for an -*ing* verb form after the *be*-verb.
        Yes ➔ This is a progressive. Go to step 3b.
        No ➔ This is not a progressive. Go to step 4.

    3b. Check the tense of the *be*-verb.
        (*am*, *is*, *are*) ➔ This is a present progressive.
        (*was*, *were*) ➔ This is past progressive.

4. Check the tense of the first verb form.
    (no ending or -*s* verb form or irregular form) ➔ This is a simple present.
    (-*ed* verb form or other irregular past) ➔ This is a simple past.

FIGURE 8.1

a perfect. We move to step 3 and look for a *be*-verb. We find the verb *was*, so now we must check for an *-ing* verb form following the *be*-verb. We find one, the verb *sleeping*, so we know that sentence (25) is in the progressive. Now we identify the tense of the *be*-verb. The verb *was* is past tense, so the sentence is in past-progressive tense.

For the sentence in (26), we find no modal, and we find no *have*-verb, so it is not a perfect. However, we do find a *be*-verb, so we must look for an *-ing* verb form following the *be*-verb. There is none, so we know that the sentence is also not a progressive. Therefore, we have narrowed down our choices to simple present or simple past. We look at the tense of the verb and see that *was* is past tense. Therefore, the sentence is in simple past.

Going through the steps in order will allow you to distinguish these two uses of *have*-verbs and these two uses of *be*-verbs. The verb *have* may signal a perfect construction, or it may be the sole verb of the sentence. The verb *be* may signal a progressive construction, or it may be the sole verb of the sentence.

The following exercise will give you some practice in identifying tense forms.

EXERCISE 1

Identify the tense of the following sentences. If the sentence has a modal, simply write modal *for its tense.*

1. An ostrich can roar like a lion.
2. Donatello was the foremost sculptor of the Renaissance.
3. The authorities had the fire under control.
4. Mercy was hitching a ride to New Mexico.
5. C-Span has been Dirk's favorite channel for years.
6. "You are being a complete jerk!"
7. The physical plant locks the doors to the music building at 10:00 every night.
8. The CFO had resigned before the scandal broke.
9. Next week Tiffany should present her research on pulmonary functions in rodents.
10. "They sit out there night after night."
11. The detective is watching the house at the end of the street.
12. Radar operators at Station Omega have detected incursions into our airspace.
13. Attila the Hun was called the "Scourge of God."

14. "I cried all the way to the bank."

15. There are approximately 20,000,000 camels in the world.

16. The Pinsky twins were writing their autobiography at the park.

There are some more complicated tense-aspects that occur in English that are not discussed above. Using the tests for tense identification, give a name to the tense-aspects that appear in the following sentences.

1. Many families in town have been eating at Figaro's Restaurant for over thirty years.

2. Six patients had been waiting for four hours to see a doctor before the electricity went out.

3. Chantelle will be sunbathing in Nice next month.

4. That driver might have been drunk when he drove his Hummer into the river.

5. "You should have been studying last night."

 # Tense in Writing

Tense is one of the factors writers can control to make their writing communicate many nuances. Because tense conveys more than just time information, it is almost always possible to convey the same content with respect to tense in more than one way. For example, in English, speakers can tell a story that occurred in the past by using either past or present tense. The following paragraphs demonstrate this possibility:

> A rhinoceros walks into a busy video store. He browses the aisles and passes up *Tarzan* and *The African Queen*. Finally he goes up to a clerk and asks, "Do you have *The Jungle Book*?" The clerk turns to the shelf behind her and picks up a DVD. She smiles and says, "That will be $25 for a three-day rental." The rhinoceros digs into his pocket and places the money on the counter. The clerk looks at the rhinoceros and says, "We don't get many rhinoceroses in here." "That's no surprise," the rhinoceros says, "at these prices."

> A rhinoceros walked into a busy video store. He browsed the aisles and passed up *Tarzan* and *The African Queen*. Finally he went up to a clerk and asked, "Do you have *The Jungle Book*?" The clerk turned to the shelf

behind her and picked up a DVD. She smiled and said, "That will be $25 for a three-day rental." The rhinoceros dug into his pocket and placed the money on the counter. The clerk looked at the rhinoceros and said, "We don't get many rhinoceroses in here." "That's no surprise," the rhinoceros said, "at these prices."

The paragraph in present tense gives a sense of immediacy to the writing. The reader is more likely to feel as if he is living the experience described by the story. The paragraph in past tense puts more distance between the experience of the story and the reader. That is why jokes are often told in the present tense; the immediacy contributes to the humor.

The following exercise asks you to manipulate tense so that you can experience how it affects writing.

EXERCISE 2

1. Find a paragraph from a text that is written in past tense. Then rewrite the paragraph in present tense. Discuss the difference in effect each version has.
2. Find a paragraph from a text that is written in present tense. Then rewrite the paragraph in past tense. Discuss the difference in effect each version has.

Passives

Now that you can identify the tense of a sentence, we can turn our attention to passives. You might be wondering why several pages of this book should be devoted to this topic. This is what I am wondering: can you reliably pick out passive sentences from an authentic text? When your writing teacher tells you to use fewer passive sentences, do you know which ones she is referring to? Writing guides offer a lot of advice today about active and passive sentences, how to use them and when to use them, but this advice assumes that a writer can pick out active and passive sentences reliably and can easily move from one form to another. However, many writers are not comfortable doing this.

That is why half a chapter is being devoted to this topic. It illustrates one of the main ideas of this book—that you are better off knowing some grammar if you want to write or edit well and if you want to teach others how to write and read well. There's no point telling someone to change an active sentence to passive if that person can't distinguish active and passive sentences. To write active and passive sentences, you have to know how phrases and grammatical roles work in English.

Active and passive constructions belong to an area of grammar that linguists call **voice.** Voice refers to the relationship between a transitive verb and its two noun phrases, the subject and the direct object. In English, we generally only concern ourselves with two voices, **active voice** and **passive voice.** Active voice is the name we give to sentences where the verb is in its ordinary form. Typically, the subject acts on the direct object in some way. Sentences (27)–(29) are examples of active voice:

(27) Grover bit a hot pepper to his surprise.

(28) Genevieve squeezed the lemon over the pasta.

(29) Gus-Gus carried the kernel of corn into a remote corner.

Passive voice is a rearranging of the relationships in (27)–(29), a sort of flip so that the direct object of the active sentence becomes the subject of the passive sentence, and the subject of the active sentence gets demoted. The passive equivalents of (27)–(29) are the following:

(30) A hot pepper was bitten by Grover to his surprise.

(31) The lemon was squeezed over the pasta by Genevieve.

(32) The kernel of corn was carried by Gus-Gus into a remote corner.

The first thing we need to do is find a way to distinguish between active and passive sentences. Fortunately, there are some reliable tests that accurately pick out passive and active sentences, as well as those that are neither active nor passive.

Passive-Voice Identification Tests

1. A passive sentence must have a *be*-verb.

2. A passive sentence must have an *-en* verb form or past participle.

3. In a passive sentence, the action of the verb is done to the subject.

All three of these criteria will be true of every passive sentence. Let's apply the criteria to sentence (30). First, we see a *be*-verb, *were*. Then we find an *-en* verb form, *teased.* Then we examine the relationship between the subject, *the freshmen,* and the content verb *teased.* Are the freshmen doing the teasing, or is the teasing being done to the freshmen? The meaning of (30) is that the teasing is being done to the freshmen, satisfying test 3. Therefore, sentence (30) is a passive sentence.

Active-Voice Identification Test

To identify active sentences, we need to find a direct object or an indirect object in the verb phrase. If we examine sentence (27), we see that the noun phrase *the freshmen* is a direct object, thus establishing that sentence as active.

Sentences That Are Neither Active Nor Passive

Now there is one other possibility. Many sentences will be neither active nor passive. Why? Because the active/passive labels apply only to sentences with transitive verbs, those that take a direct object. Here is where you will need to apply what you learned in Chapter 6 about grammatical roles. If you encounter sentences with nontransitive verbs, you must be careful not to put those into the active or passive category. Let's take an example:

(33)   Walker became a doctor.

This sentence does not have a *be*-verb. It also does not have an *-en* verb form. When I apply the third test and ask if Walker doing the becoming or if the becoming being done to Walker, I end up with a nonsensical question. Clearly, sentence (33) is not a passive sentence.

Furthermore, if I examine the sentence for grammatical roles, I find out that the noun phrase *a doctor* is a subject complement, not a direct object. Sentences that contain a subject complement are neither active nor passive.

The following exercise asks you to identify voice in a variety of sentences.

EXERCISE 3

Identify whether the following sentences are active, passive, or neither.

1. It rained and rained for forty days.

2. Queen Elizabeth I feared roses.

3. The new parents named their baby Spunky.

4. Our aspirations were furthered by the unexpected windfall.

5. Sigmund Freud was afraid of train travel.

6. Sophistication crowns Juliet's head.

7. Achilles was fatally wounded by Paris.

8. "Faithful computer, you are christened Excalibur."

9. Presidents Gerald Ford and Bill Clinton were adopted.

10. The Franklins had seventeen children.

11. The city collects property taxes on homesteads and automobiles.

12. Hu fired the shot heard round the Chinese restaurant on the corner.

13. Camp Red Oak hosted 1,500 campers last week.

14. That struggling politician has burnt all her bridges behind her.

15. "We were robbed by that officiating team."

16. Snoopy Loop drove his Corvette through a brick wall at the train station.

Changing Voice

Once we can reliably identify active and passive sentences, we need to be able to change one form into the other, active into passive and passive into active. If we can do this for all English sentences, it demonstrates that we truly understand their structure. Fortunately, there is a systematic way of altering voice. We will start by changing active into passive, taking sentence (34) as our example:

(34)   Dagmar baked a cake yesterday.

We need to get a new subject for the passive sentence, and that will be the entire noun phrase that was the direct object in the active sentence. In (34), this would be the phrase *a cake*. Our new sentence begins with

(34a)   A cake . . .

Then we need a verb. When we go from active to passive, we always add a *be*-verb to the sentence. The form of the *be*-verb will depend on the tense of the original active sentence. Using the rules for tense identification will reveal that the tense of (34) is simple past. Therefore, we need a past-tense form of *be* that will agree with our subject. Hence we add the form *was* to (34a) to get

(34b)   A cake was . . .

Next we need to add the content verb in its *-en* form. The *-en* form of *bake* is *baked,* and we add that after the verb *was:*

(34c)   A cake was baked . . .

The former subject in the active sentence can be placed in the passive sentence in a prepositional phrase that begins with *by:*

(34d)   A cake was baked by Dagmar . . .

Then anything else left in the original active sentence can be added to the passive sentence. In this case, we include the adverbial phrase *yesterday:*

(34e)   A cake was baked by Dagmar yesterday.

Here are the steps needed to turn an active sentence into a passive sentence:

Active ➲ Passive

1. Turn the entire direct object into the new subject.

2. Add a *be*-verb to the new sentence, making sure you keep the tense the same.

3. Turn the content verb into its *-en* verb form.

4. Turn the subject into a *by*-prepositional phrase.

5. Add everything else left over from the original active sentence.

To go from passive to active, we reverse the steps. Starting from

(35)   A party was hosted by Dante last night.

we need to get a subject for the active sentence, and we find that in the prepositional phrase with *by,* in this case *Dante:*

(35a)   Dante . . .

Next, whenever we go from passive to active, we must always get rid of one *be*-verb. However, we must also note the tense of the passive sentence so that we can keep that same tense in the active sentence. Applying our tense identification rules to (35), we can determine that the tense of the sentence is simple past.

Then we take the content verb of the passive sentence and put it into our new active sentence with the appropriate tense. In this case, we take the verb *hosted* from (35) and put it into sentence (35b) in its simple past form, which turns out to be the form *hosted:*

(35b)   Dante hosted . . .

We need to be careful at this step, because we don't simply copy the form of the content verb from the passive into the active sentence. The form *hosted* in (35) looks the same as the form *hosted* in (14b), but that is just an accident of the English language. The form *hosted* in (35) is actually a past participle, and the form *hosted* in (35b) is in simple-past form.

Next we take the subject of the passive sentence and make it our new direct object, in this case the NP *a party:*

(35c)   Dante hosted a party . . .

Finally we add everything else that is left in the sentence, in this case the phrase *last night:*

(35d)   Dante hosted a party last night.

One thing to consider when we go from passive to active voice is that the prepositional phrase with *by*, which conveys the doer of an action in a passive sentence, may be missing. In fact, the agent of the action is often left unexpressed in real-world writing. For example, in the sentence below,

(36)   The road repairs were completed on time.

it isn't specified who did road repairs. Normally, in a text somewhere, the context would tell us who did the road repairs. If you were to turn this sentence into its active counterpart, you would supply the missing agent. You might write something like the following:

(36a)   The contractor completed the road repairs on time.

Here are the steps needed to turn a passive sentence into an active sentence:

Passive ➲ Active

1. Get a new subject by either taking the NP from the *by*-PP or supplying an appropriate subject.

2. Eliminate one *be*-verb from the passive sentence.

3. Put the content verb of the passive sentence into the active sentence, keeping the tense the same.

4. Turn the subject of the passive sentence into the direct object of the active sentence.

5. Add everything else left over from the original passive sentence.

The Interaction of Tense with Voice

This chapter has talked about two topics, tense and voice in the system we call the English language. There has been a specific reason why I have brought these two together. Both are expressed through the verb system of English, and so life gets interesting when the two interact.

We have seen how tense is expressed in English. Apart from more complicated tenses, we have our simple tenses, which normally consist of a content verb alone. We have our perfects, which consist of a form of *have* plus an *-en* verb form. And we have our progressives, which consist of a form of *be* plus an *-ing* verb form.

We have also seen how voice is expressed in English. Active sentences typically consist of a content verb alone. Passive sentences, though, are more complicated and consist of a form of *be* plus an *-en* verb form. When we combine tense and voice, potential areas of confusion arise.

First, there is some similarity between an active sentence in the perfect tense and a passive sentence. They are similar because both have *-en* verb forms. They differ because the perfect has a *have*-verb and the passive has a *be*-verb. Compare sentences (37) and (38):

(37)   Agnes has raked the yard.

(38)   The yard was raked by Agnes.

It is easy to get confused here because both sentences have the *-en* verb form *raked*. However, this is where our rules discussed earlier in the chapter help us out. If I am evaluating sentences (37) and (38) for passive voice, I see right away that sentence (37) cannot be passive because there is no *be*-verb. That rule by itself keeps me from confusing perfect sentences in active voice with those in passive voice.

A similar confusion may arise between an active sentence in the progressive tense and a passive sentence. They are similar because they both have *be*-verbs. However, they are different because the progressive has an *-ing* verb form and the passive has an *-en* verb form. Compare sentences (39) and (40):

(39)   Anthony was painting the colonel's boat.

(40)   The colonel's boat was painted by Anthony.

Here is another place where we can get confused. Both sentences have the verb *was*. However, our rules will come to our rescue. If I am evaluating sentences (39) and (40) for passive voice, although both have a *be*-verb, I must next look for an *-en* verb form. In sentence (39), the verb *painting* is not an *-en* form. Therefore, sentence (39) cannot be a passive.

The next exercise asks you to determine tense and voice both.

EXERCISE 4

Identify the tense and voice of each sentence.

1. Luis was being unfair when he didn't pick Samuel for the team.

2. The airport has been strafed by bombers.

3. Sierra is reaching for the cookie tin on the top shelf.

4. Dolan could be demoted by tomorrow.

5. Klingon mating rituals fascinate Jerry.

6. The cream has risen to the top of the pail.

7. Cassandra is having a baby next month.

8. A dog can depend on its owner.

9. The unhappy man had unfortunately stolen a car from the police yard.

10. Mungo was stripped of his title because of steroid use.

11. The king of diamonds resembles Julius Caesar.

12. Mount Olympus had been conquered by the gods long before you came along.

13. Julia's house was being raided for illegal aliens.

14. Before the war broke out, *Life* had already hit the newsstands.

15. Eustace can snore like a lumber mill when he has a cold.

Now let's take a look at active and passive voice when they combine with the more complicated tenses in English, perfects and progressives.

The rules work the same as explained previously. In changing from active to passive or passive to active, we simply must keep track of more things. Let's start with an active sentence in perfect tense, such as:

(41)   A Canadian air mass has dumped rain over the Great Lakes.

First, we find a *have*-verb (*has*) and an *-en* verb form, *dumped*, confirming that the tense is perfect. Then we apply the five steps to turn an active sentence into a passive one. We look for the direct-object noun phrase and find it in the word *rain*. This becomes our new subject:

(41a)   Rain . . .

Then, as we always do when moving from active to passive, we add a *be*-verb, but we must do this in a way that keeps the perfect tense of the original. That means the *be*-verb must be added after the *have*-verb. In this case, the *be*-verb must be put in its *-en* verb form, *been*. That gives us

(41b)   Rain has been . . .

Then we add the content verb in its *-en* verb form.

(41c)   Rain has been dumped . . .

Notice that a passive sentence in perfect tense has two *-en* verb forms, one to mark the perfect tense (which is always *been*) and one to mark the passive voice (the content verb). Finally, we add the agent in a *by*-prepositional phrase and the leftovers of the sentence:

(41d)   Rain has been dumped by a Canadian air mass over the Great Lakes.

Now let's go from passive to active in a sentence with perfect tense, starting with

(42)   Our basketball team has been demoralized by many losses.

We find a new subject in the *by*-prepositional phrase:

(42a)   Many losses . . .

Then we find our verb but keep the tense the same. This step will entail getting rid of one *be*-verb, as always happens when we move from passive to active. The content verb is *demoralize,* and it must be in the present-perfect tense. That means we use a form of *have* that matches our subject and the content verb in its *-en* form, *demoralized:*

(42b)   Many losses have demoralized . . .

Finally, we turn the old subject into our new direct object:

(42c)   Many losses have demoralized our basketball team.

Notice what happens with progressive tense sentences. An active sentence with progressive tense always has a *be*-verb. We add a *be*-verb when we make it passive so that a passive sentence in the progressive tense will have two *be*-verbs:

(43)   Charlton is running the show.   (active: one *be*-verb)

(43a)   The show is being run by Charlton.   (passive: two *be*-verbs)

Likewise, when we change a passive sentence in the progressive tense into an active one, we move from two *be*-verbs to one *be*-verb.

When there is a modal in the sentence, we must add a *be*-verb in changing an active sentence into a passive, and the *be*-verb will always appear in its base form, *be*. The content verb, which was formerly in its base form following the modal, will now appear in its *-en* form, following *be*. In the active sentence (44), the content verb *cancel* appears in its base form after the modal. In the passive sentence (44a), the base form *be* follows the modal, and the content verb *canceled* appears as an *-en* verb form:

(44)   The league may cancel the game because of poor field conditions.

(44a)   The game may be canceled (by the league) because of poor field conditions.

The following exercises ask you to bring all your knowledge together in identifying the tense and voice of a sentence and then changing the voice.

EXERCISE 5

Identify the tense of each sentence. Then make all of these active sentences passive. Be careful to keep the tense the same.

1. You crush half a pineapple for this recipe.

2. Without a doubt, Ursula could co-chair the committee on program review.

3. Shea is making a mistake about Mr. Davenport.

4. A guy in the mailroom has discovered the greatest technology for this company.

5. "They may entertain me for free."

6. Big Jake has lost three pounds since he started the pumpkin diet!

7. The Potter family climbed the highest mountain in Florida—"The Matterhorn" at Disney World.

8. The Volkswagen Beetle had already broken the sales record held by the Model T.

9. Cleo, Pinocchio's pet goldfish, was swallowing a fly.

10. Birdwatchers rarely see the common loon in some states.

11. Sinead had landed that fish before her brother inadvertently knocked it back into the water.

12. Around the dam, the water is eroding the bank.

13. Camels store fat in their humps, not water.

14. Galileo invented the astronomical telescope.

15. Our school might cancel the tournament if there are not enough entries.

16. Carrie and Cary were selling floral arrangements to raise money for a children's petting zoo.

EXERCISE 6

Identify the tense of each sentence. Then make all of these passive sentences active. Be careful to keep the tense the same. Add subjects where necessary.

1. The White House is depicted on the back of a U.S. twenty-dollar bill.

2. President Merkin Muffley was played by Peter Sellers in *Dr. Strangelove*.

3. Shirley has been healed of her cancer.

4. Bernard had been sacked by his boss for insubordination.

5. A comic rendition of *Macbeth* is being staged by the Hillman Players.

6. The road to Centerville can be reached from Route 39.

7. We are amazed by the amount of time you spend with Sheila.

8. Malta was bombed more than any other strategic site during World War II.

9. The Mattoon-Decatur route was being driven in the seventies by people with low seniority.

10. The new employee had been hired to maintain the company's web content.

11. I am puzzled by your symptoms.

12. A telegram is being sent to the president at this very moment.

13. The first U.S. presidential trip to China was made by Richard Nixon in 1972.

14. Our pizza has been delivered via bicycle.

15. The monkey wrench was named after the English blacksmith Charles Moncke.

16. Pet rocks were being sold in 1976.

Follow-up Questions: Do any of the above passive sentences sound more natural than their active counterparts? Why?

EXERCISE 7

Identify the tense of each sentence, and identify whether the sentence is active, passive, or neither. Then change active sentences to passive and passive sentences to active. Be careful to keep the tense the same. If a sentence is neither active or passive, write neither *next to it.*

1. Freddie skips rocks across Lake Bartholomew.

2. Hank Ketchum created the cartoon "Dennis the Menace."

3. St. Appolonia is the patron saint of toothaches.

4. Yul Brynner and Burt Lancaster had worked in the circus before they became actors.

5. Zoe is meeting York's art teacher tomorrow.

6. Donovan could be chased by a bear in those woods.

7. "Yours truly has sold bric-a-brac for forty years at this flea market."

8. This department is equipped with the latest night-vision binoculars.

9. Moira has observed National Squid Day for almost thirty years.

10. The victim was unlocking his car when the roof fell in.

11. Next week our fencing team will beat ZSU.

12. A weary messenger is bringing tidings from afar to the Duke of Gloucester.

13. The kitchen has been scoured and the drains have been unclogged.

14. Castle Dinan is falling apart from neglect.

15. Karnov the Magnificent had requested that book on pottery through inter-library loan.

16. "Doby, you were fooled on that pass play."

 # Application to Writing

Mastering the information in this chapter will enable you to determine whether any sentence you encounter is active, passive, or neither active nor passive. It will also enable you to accurately convert active sentences into their passive counterparts and passive sentences into their active counterparts. This knowledge empowers you to change only the voice of a sentence while keeping the tense and all other information the same.

This kind of understanding will allow you to take full advantage of the advice teachers and textbooks give you concerning the use of passive sentences in writing. For the most part, instructors are concerned with the overuse and the misuse of passive sentences. I have never seen a teacher critique a student for using too many active sentences! There are good reasons why passive sentences are faulted in students' writing. First, they are longer than their active counterparts, and they have a more complicated structure than active sentences, as the above discussion has shown. That means passive sentences will be harder to understand than their active counterparts, and they could potentially obscure the message you are trying to convey in your text.

Second, passive sentences are less direct than active sentences. Much of our writing is most effective when we are direct and clear about our points.

Third, many passive sentences are awkward and downright ugly. Take a look again at the passive version you constructed for sentence 3 in Exercise 5 on page 127. I wouldn't want a sentence like that defacing my writing.

This is not to say that passive sentences aren't useful in the proper context. Sometimes we may wish to de-emphasize or hide the doer of an action. Sometimes we may not know who was responsible for it. Furthermore, some verbs only occur in the passive voice, for example, the verb *rumor:*

(45)   It was rumored that the flu epidemic would close down the university. (passive)

(46)   *Students rumored that the flu epidemic would close down the university. (active)

and often passive-voice constructions sound natural and are appropriate to use.

The next two exercises prompt you to evaluate the effectiveness of active and passive sentences in context.

EXERCISE 8

Examine the sentences in Exercises 4–6.

Which of your passive sentences sound more natural than their active counterparts? Which sound awkward? What distinguishes the natural-sounding passives from the awkward-sounding passives? Give reasons for your choices.

EXERCISE 9

1. In a separate list, change each of the active clauses in the following paragraph into passive voice. Would the paragraph benefit from replacing any of its active clauses with the corresponding passive? Explain your rationale for choosing the active or passive clause in each case.

The blackcurrant may make a comeback in the state of New York. The state banned the tart little berry in 1911 because people believed it carried a disease that harmed white pine trees. Later research showed how people could grow blackcurrants in ways that would avoid spreading the dreaded white pine blister rust.

2. In a separate list, change each of the passive clauses in the following paragraph into active voice. Would the paragraph benefit from replacing any of its passive clauses with the corresponding active? Explain your rationale for choosing the active or passive clause in each case.

Bert's hair was smoothed by the hair stylist with great deliberation. The greasiness and the grit were rubbed away, and now that his head had been transformed by the stylist's deft handiwork, her patience could be dispensed with. She had seen greasy hair a thousand times before, yet her stomach was rarely upset by such dirtiness, and her mind was already distracted by the next customer. His unruly mop had been noticed by a small crowd gathering outside the window, and they stopped to see what might happen to that magnificent disarray.

Postscript

This chapter illustrates how the many different aspects of grammar are all connected. Consider for a moment all the bits of knowledge you relied on in Chapter 8. You identified parts of speech. You figured out where phrases begin and end. You recognized the grammatical roles in a sentence. You determined the tense and voice of different sentences. Finally, you were able to change sentences into their active and passive counterparts. All of this understanding went into a single concept, the passive sentence.

I have a question for you. Is it worth it? It seems like we had to go through a lot of intellectual trudging for something as "trivial" as passive sentences. For many writers, writing or editing passive sentences is rarely a problem. The grammatical knowledge might seem superfluous.

Ultimately, you will have to decide whether all of this knowledge is worth it to you. We can say this: if you have a flair for writing and find yourself able to unconsciously put the words on the page in an effective manner, this chapter may not have improved your ability to create with words. What it might have done is give you the ability to communicate with others and yourself about what your exact structures are when you pen active and passive sentences. That is, it has made your unconscious knowledge conscious and accessible to reflection. If you ever need to talk to someone about active and passive sentences, then you do need all of the information brought together in this chapter. If you ever get into a difficult sentence, one where you consciously need to manipulate structure, you will need to understand what we have talked about so far in this book.

And you can't scrimp on the grammatical knowledge, because it is all tied together. You can't simply know parts of speech and phrases and tense and voice and not know grammatical roles. It may be exactly this aspect of grammar that applies to a specific sentence in your or someone else's writing, a sentence that you suddenly find yourself needing to spend some time on because you just can't find the best way to put the words together.

That is why my wish for you is that you develop a working knowledge of these aspects of grammar, so that if you need to consciously work with English structure, you will be able to do so.

COMPREHENSION QUESTIONS

1. What is tense, and what kind of information does it convey?

2. Based on the forms of the verbs themselves, how many tenses does English have?

3. What are the six primary tenses of English?

4. What steps in what order can we follow to identify the tense of every sentence?

5. What is voice in language?

6. What tests can we use to identify passive sentences?

7. How do we identify active sentences?

8. How do we identify sentences that are neither active nor passive?

9. What specific changes do we make when we change an active sentence into its passive counterpart and a passive sentence into its active counterpart?

10. How does tense interact with passive? What tense forms may be confused with a passive construction?

Putting Words Together: Coordination, Subordination, and Parallelism

PREVIEW *So far we have primarily examined the structure of sentences that contain a single clause—a single subject with its predicate. In real-world writing, though, we typically encounter sentences that have numerous clauses, and that phenomenon will be the focus of this chapter. We will examine the ways in which we use multiple clauses to make larger and more complex sentences, paying attention to their structure and then using that knowledge of structure to understand the rules for their punctuation and style.*

Coordination

The primary way we combine smaller bits of language into larger units is through **coordination.** One way of doing this is by using a word class called a coordinate conjunction and combining it with two or more pieces of language that are the same grammatical unit. We can demonstrate this with the most common coordinate conjunction, *and.* The conjunction *and* can be used to join individual categories themselves, such as

> N and N
>
> V and V
>
> Adj and Adj
>
> Adv and Adv
>
> P and P

and so on.

It also can join together all phrasal categories:

NP and NP

VP and VP

PP and PP

AdjP and AdjP

AdvP and AdvP

S and S

and so forth.

Before you read any further, try your hand at Exercise 1 and then compare your results with the following discussion.

EXERCISE 1

1. Write two sentences that use the conjunction *and* to combine two noun phrases.

2. Write two sentences that use the conjunction *and* to combine two nouns.

A little practice with coordination will demonstrate what these various units look like. Two noun phrases joined by the conjunction *and* will look different from two nouns joined by the conjunction *and*. The sentence in (1) illustrates the conjunction of two noun phrases:

(1) <u>My laptop</u> and <u>my mom's spaghetti</u> would be necessary for me
         NP   NP

  on a deserted island.

Here the noun phrase *my laptop* and the noun phrase *my mom's spaghetti* are the two noun phrases put together with the conjunction *and*.

A sentence that coordinates only nouns rather than noun phrases will look different. In particular, the nouns have to share some element in common, as in

(2) <u>Cats</u> and <u>dogs</u> don't always get along.
         NP   NP

In this sentence, however, the conjunction *and* is still combining whole noun phrases rather than nouns alone. This becomes apparent when we simplify the sentence so that it contains only one of the conjuncts, or combined units:

(3)   Cats don't always get along.

We know from our previous chapters that while the word *cats* in this sentence is a noun, it is also a noun phrase by itself. Plural nouns without any determiner can function as an entire noun phrase in English. The word *cats* is a noun phrase, and that clues us in that it is also a noun phrase in sentence (2). Therefore, the conjunction *and* in that sentence is joining together two noun phrases rather than two simple nouns.

If, however, the conjunction *and* combines two single nouns that also share some element in common, then we are likely to have noun coordination. The easiest way to do that is to have both nouns share the same determiner. That gives us a sentence like

(4)   My sister and brother are here for the weekend.

Here is an unambiguous example of noun coordination. The possessive pronoun *my* applies to both the noun *sister* and the noun *brother*. That is, the subject phrase is equivalent to saying,

my sister and my brother

If we draw lines underneath our units, then we see that the proper combination is the following:

(4)   My <u>sister</u> and <u>brother</u> are here for the weekend.
            N   N

_____
            N

_____
            NP

That is, the nouns *sister* and *brother* are combined first to make a dual-noun combination, and then that unit combines with the possessive pronoun *my* to make the noun phrase.

Notice why the following combination won't work:

*<u>My sister</u> and <u>brother</u> are here for the weekend.
  NP   N

_____
            NP

In this diagram, the words *my sister* constitutes a noun phrase. The word *brother* alone would be a noun. However, the conjunction *and* must combine identical grammatical units. It can't put together a noun phrase with a noun. So *my sister and brother* must be either two noun phrases or two nouns. Therefore, the former phrasal analysis describes correctly the structure of the sentence.

The following exercise asks you to apply your understanding of coordination to a variety of structures.

EXERCISE 2

Write a sentence for each of the coordination possibilities listed on pages 133–134. Consider in particular how a conjunction like *and* would coordinate two verbs alone as compared to two verb phrases.

When identical grammatical units are conjoined with a coordinate conjunction, the resulting phrase always has the same label as the individual conjuncts. Thus, two noun phrases combined with *and* result in a larger phrase that is itself a noun phrase. Two prepositional phrases combined with *and* result in a prepositional phrase.

There are seven coordinate conjunctions in English: *and, but, or, for, yet, nor,* and *so.* The coordinate conjunctions *and, or,* and *nor* are used freely to coordinate any grammatical unit in English. The other four conjunctions, *but, for, yet,* and *so,* are more typically used to coordinate complete sentences.

Punctuation for Coordination

Let's consider the punctuation rules for coordinating two units at a time, such as two noun phrases, two verb phrases, and so forth. The rule is very simple: When two sentences are conjoined with a coordinate conjunction, a comma is inserted after the first sentence and before the conjunction. Otherwise, no punctuation should be added. If we draw this schematically, we have

> NP and NP   [no comma]
> VP and VP   [no comma]
> PP and PP   [no comma]

but

> S, and S.   [comma after first S]

Hence, the sentence in (5) has a punctuation mistake:

(5)   *The senators, and the representatives adjourned for the year.
        NP   NP

A comma has incorrectly been inserted between the two noun-phrase conjuncts.

There is a good reason for this punctuation rule. As I hinted at earlier in the book, punctuation is not a torture device thought up by teachers to make life miserable for writers. Rather, punctuation is added to make a text more readable. In particular, it helps readers to chunk together the words in a sentence. You might have expected that the purpose of a comma is to increase the readability of the text, and if you thought this you were right. Consider again the previous sentence, now written correctly:

(5a)   The senators and the representatives adjourned for the year.

Is there any possibility that a reader would be unsure how to chunk together the words in this sentence? Would he wonder what words the conjunction *and* was joining together? Almost certainly not, but let's imagine for a moment that he might try to join only a single word on either side of the *and,* as notated below:

(5a)   The <u>senators</u> and <u>the</u> representatives adjourned for the year.
                N   Det

               _____
                     ?

That would give us the anomalous situation whereby the conjunction *and* would be joining together a noun with a determiner, an impossible combination because coordinate conjunctions must put together identical grammatical units.

No, it is clear that the conjunction *and* combines the noun phrase *the senators* and the noun phrase *the representatives.* There is no real possibility of misreading the sentence, and so no punctuation is used.

Now let's see what happens with sentence coordination. It turns out that in this case there is the possibility of misreading the coordination. Suppose I want to combine the following sentences:

(6)   I like macaroni.

(7)   Cheese is my favorite food.

Without using punctuation, my sentence would look like

(8)   *I like macaroni and cheese is my favorite food.

As a reader begins to read such a sentence, he will try to combine words into a single clause as long as he can. He would read

    I   like   macaroni   and   cheese

and combine these words together before reading further and finding out that, whoops, the word *macaroni* is the direct object of the first clause, and the word *cheese* is the subject of the second clause. Sentence (8) is not written in a user-friendly way, and so the reader is forced to reread, something we should avoid making the reader do if we want to write successful prose. Sentence (8a) displays the comma in the correct position:

(8a)   I like macaroni, and cheese is my favorite food.

The comma slows the reader down and signals to him that a new clause follows the word *macaroni.*

What this example illustrates is that there is the potential for misreading the boundaries when complete sentences are conjoined. A lot of sentences end in a noun phrase and begin with a noun phrase, but we don't want our readers to conjoin only those two noun phrases when we intend both sentences to be conjoined. Especially as sentences grow longer, we need to help the reader find the end of the first one, and the means we have for doing that is putting that comma before the coordinate conjunction.

Now you might be wondering about short sentences. If I conjoin two short sentences, do I have to use a comma? Well, you raise a good question, and the answer is no. If the sentences are short and there is no real danger that the reader will misread the sentence, the comma is often left out, as in

(9)   I'm tired and I'm hungry.

Now let's consider the opposite problem. Some writers put in commas when they are not necessary. In particular, a common mistake is to put a comma in when two verb phrases are conjoined, as the sentence in (10) demonstrates:

(10)   *The team <u>gave its best performance of the season</u>, and
                      VP

<u>almost beat the reigning champions</u>.
         VP

The conjunction *and* combines the verb phrase *gave its best performance of the season* and the verb phrase *almost beat the reigning champions*. People sometimes erroneously add this comma because there is a tendency to pause after the first verb phrase. Some students have even been taught to put in commas where they pause, but this unfortunately is a bad rule for punctuation. The standard rules of punctuation are not based on where we pause in a sentence but on the structure of the sentence. The comma after the word *season* leads the knowledgeable reader to expect to find an entire sentence following, even though only a verb phrase shows up. Therefore, this sentence should be punctuated as follows:

(10a)   The team gave its best performance of the season and almost beat the reigning champions.

There are two other problems that arise when two complete sentences are combined into one sentence. Sometimes the writer forgets to put any punctuation or a conjunction between the clauses and produces a *run-on sentence:*

(11)   *Envying their neighbors destroyed John

Philip was devastated too.
              S

Sometimes the writer puts only a comma between the clauses and produces a *comma splice:*

(11a)   *Envying their neighbors destroyed John,
                                        S

Philip was devastated too.
              S

These errors cause the same difficulties that arose for the previous sentence — they make it difficult for the reader to chunk together words. In the former case, the reader runs into the ambiguous sequence

Envying   their   neighbors   destroyed   John   Philip

Uh-oh. Are the words *John Philip* one person or two? The run-on makes the reading of the sentence ambiguous.

In the latter case, the reader runs into another ambiguous sequence:

Envying   their   neighbors   destroyed   John,   Philip

Another problem. Is the reader encountering a list like *John, Philip, and Egbert?* The reader can't tell by the time he has read this sequence. You the writer must make those clause boundaries unambiguous. You could make the clauses into separate sentences. You could separate the clauses with a comma and the conjunction *and* (11b), or you could use a semicolon (11c):

(11b)   Envying their neighbors destroyed John, and Philip was devastated too.

(11c)   Envying their neighbors destroyed John; Philip was devastated too.

For further details on the use of semicolons, see the note on punctuation at the end of this chapter.

Subordination

Another way we combine bits of language is through **subordination**: we can put two units together in a grammatically unequal way. This allows a writer to emphasize certain pieces of information in a sentence and also specify the logical relationship between two clauses.

The easiest way to combine information is to use the coordinate conjunction *and*. As mentioned in Chapter 1, spoken language is dominated by coordination with *and*. Coordination has a simple structure, as seen in the previous section, and the meaning of *and* is simple as well. In the following sentence,

(12)   Doris bought the cake, and Douglas ate the cake.

we have added two clauses together, but the relationship between them is not precise. With subordination, we can be more precise, as the following alternatives show:

(12a)   When Doris bought the cake, Douglas ate the cake.

(12b)   Because Doris bought the cake, Douglas ate the cake.

(12c)   Though Doris bought the cake, Douglas ate the cake.

(12d)   If Doris bought the cake, Douglas ate the cake.

(12e)   After Doris bought the cake, Douglas ate the cake.

For example, if I want to specify a cause-and-effect relationship between two clauses, I can use the subordinate conjunction *because* with the clause that gives the cause.

English has a wide range of subordinate conjunctions: *that, if, though, although, because, when, while, after, before,* and so forth. (See the list on page 45.) They are placed before a complete sentence or independent clause to make that clause dependent. This dependent clause now needs to attach to another clause that is independent. Otherwise, a sentence fragment results:

(12f)   *When Doris bought the cake.

Punctuation for Subordinate Clauses

Subordinate clauses can occur in the three different locations within the sentence: at the beginning of the sentence, at the end of the sentence, and in the middle of the independent clause to which they are attached. Where they occur determines the punctuation needed. When they occur at the beginning of a sentence, the rule is easy and consistent: always place a comma at the end of the subordinate clause. The following sentences illustrate this rule:

(13)   If you never take chances, you will never make anything in the stock market.

(14)   After the music died down, the crowd began to grow restless.

(15)   Until the rain stops, we can't search the creek for Fifi.

When subordinate clauses appear in the middle of the independent clause to which they are attached, the punctuation rule is also consistent and easy. Put commas before and after the dependent clause so that it is set off from the rest of the clause:

(16)   I, while my mother never knew it, drove a car when I was fourteen.

(17)   The governor proposed a tax cut, though the legislature didn't like it, for the coming year.

(18)   Last night my friends believed, before they heard the news on the radio, that the game had gone into overtime.

These commas serve the important purpose of helping the reader determine where the clause boundaries are in a sentence. Without punctuation, the reader may mistake where one clause ends and the other begins. The sentence below illustrates this potential problem:

(19)   *After the eager salesperson sailed through the morning appointments started coming in left and right.

The problem is similar to what we saw earlier for sentences conjoined with *and*. A reader will try to include words in the clause he is constructing for as long as it makes sense. Thus, he will read the sentence as follows:

(19a)   After the eager salesperson sailed through the morning appointments

It makes sense to include the noun *appointments* with the noun *morning*. Only too late will the reader discover that the word *appointments* was supposed to be the subject of a new clause rather than a part of the direct object of the beginning subordinate clause. The comma at the end of an initial subordinate clause keeps the reader from making that mistake:

(19b)   After the eager salesperson sailed through the morning, appointments started coming in left and right.

When the subordinate clause is in the middle of another clause, commas mark the beginning and the end of that clause so that there is no difficulty for the reader in determining where things begin and end. We are asking a reader to do something difficult in this case. He must begin to construct one clause and then stop and construct a second before the first clause has been completed. Notice how this works for sentence (18).

The reader apprehends the main clause:

Last   night   my   friends   believed

Then he holds part of the clause in memory as he puts together the subordinate clause:

before   they   heard   the   news   on   the   radio

Once he has finished that, he returns to finish building the first clause. In this process note that both commas play a very important role. The comma at the beginning of the subordinate clause signals the reader to interrupt the main clause, and the comma at the end of the subordinate clause signals the end of that clause. We must take special care to write in a way that aids our readers in chunking together words because of the unique challenges that occur in reading as compared to listening.

When subordinate clauses appear at the end of the independent clause, the rule is less clear-cut. Commas are used when the subordinate clause begins with the conjunctions *though* and *although* and sometimes when they begin with the conjunction *because*.

Let's first consider why commas are not used for the majority of sentence-concluding subordinate clauses. Earlier we saw that subordinate clauses at the beginning and in the middle of sentences are set off by commas, and these commas serve the very useful purpose of communicating where the clause boundaries are. This problem does not occur for sentence-concluding subordinate clauses because the subordinate conjunction at the beginning of the subordinate clause clearly signals where the clause boundary is, as in

(20)   <u>I want to be there in that number</u> <u>when the saints go marching in</u>.
                 clause   clause

There is no possibility of mistaking the boundary between *I want to be there in that number* and *the saints go marching in* because the subordinate conjunction *when* occurs between them.

This gives us a clue that the commas that occur before the conjunctions *though, although,* and *because* must be there for a different reason than simply marking clause boundaries. When a person reads a text, punctuation marks slow the reader down. This slight slowdown is beneficial to the reader in key places. We can see this benefit when a contrast is introduced into a sentence with a subordinate clause headed by the conjunction *though* or *although*. Notice what the reader must do when reading sentence (21):

(21)   The food was great, though the service was slow.

The first clause, *The food was great,* sets up a positive evaluation in the reader's mind. The second clause, *the service was slow,* detracts from the positive evaluation of the first clause. It changes the reader's first positive impression to an evaluation that is both positive and negative. Whenever a sentence gives content that goes against what was stated earlier in that sentence, it is harder for a reader to process, because he must alter the representation stored in his mind. If a writer slows the reader down at this point, it aids the reader's comprehension, and the comma before subordinate clauses that end with *though* or *although* does just that.

The situation with sentence-concluding subordinate clauses headed by *because* is trickier: sometimes a comma is used (22), and sometimes it is not (23):

(22)   Pepe is home, because his car is in the driveway.

(23)   Pepe is home because his mother brought him home.

Each of the subordinate clauses in sentences (22) and (23) has a different relationship to its independent clause. In (23), the final clause, *his mother brought him home,* is the reason why Pepe is at home. The subordinate clause here is directly connected to its independent clause. In (22), the final clause, *his car is in the driveway,* is the reason the speaker believes Pepe is at home. This subordinate clause is not directly connected to its dependent clause. The reader of a sentence like (22) must go through a longer chain of reasoning to understand the sentence, something like the following:

1.   The writer says Pepe is at home.

2.   The writer says Pepe's car is in the driveway.

3.   Pepe drives his car when he goes out.

4.   Hence, if Pepe's car is in the driveway, it should be inferred that Pepe didn't go out.

The reader has to do a fair amount of reasoning over the stretch of one sentence. The comma here is useful to slow the reader down ever so slightly as an aid to comprehension.

The following exercise asks you to recognize when commas are used correctly.

EXERCISE 3

Add commas to or remove commas from the following sentences that contain subordinate clauses. Some sentences may be correct as written.

1. Before the hurricane made landfall, the police were out in force to oversee the evacuation.

2. Ollie while his teacher wasn't looking threw an eraser out the window.

3. Her coworkers gave Annette a big sendoff after she accepted a fantastic offer from a rival firm.

4. When the saints go marching in I want to be there in that number.

5. Jeanette snored, although the noise in the hall was horrendous, through the fire alarm.

6. Farmer Scott sold off his herds, although the price of beef was at a ten-year low.

7. "Kline was the culprit because I saw him leave the building at 2:30."

8. "If all my wishes were dishes they'd be realized."

9. The computer once Smythe replaced the motherboard worked like a dream.

10. The rock wall fell, because the heavy rains had eroded the hillside.

11. The puzzle was easy once I figured out the formula.

12. The guarantee is in force, wherever you go.

13. The roof, whenever it rains leaks like a sieve.

I am asking you to make deliberate errors in the next exercise, because that forces you to know the material.

EXERCISE 4

Write sentences that contain the deliberate errors indicated.

1. Write two sentences that begin with a subordinate clause and that lack proper punctuation after that clause.

2. Write two sentences that have a subordinate clause in the middle and that lack proper punctuation before and after that clause.

3. Write two sentences that end with a subordinate clause: one that has a comma that shouldn't be there and one that lacks a comma that it should have.

Parallelism

As I think back to writing papers for English classes, I remember my teachers red-inking my essays because I used nonparallel structures. **Parallelism** in writing means that two or more items in a list have common characteristics. One characteristic that coordinated phrases must share is grammatical similarity. The coordinate conjunctions *and* and *or* can be used to join together two or more conjuncts, but the conjuncts need to be the same grammatical unit. For example, three noun phrases could be joined by the word *and* but not two noun phrases and a verb phrase. Unfortunately, we are more likely to make a mistake and join grammatical units that are not similar when we add together three or more conjuncts. Sentence (24) demonstrates this error:

(24)   *<u>Dog shows</u>, <u>zydeco concerts</u>, and <u>to go to the beach</u> keep me
          NP   NP   VP[inf]
        busy during the summer.

This sentence sounds odd, and its awkwardness comes from the lack of parallelism. If we look carefully to see what the conjunction *and* joins together, we can identify these three conjuncts:

          dog shows   zydeco concerts   to go to the beach

The first two phrases are noun phrases, but the third phrase is an infinitive verb phrase. The last phrase is not the same grammatical unit as the previous two phrases; therefore, the sentence has a parallelism error.

The solution is to make all three phrases grammatically equal. There are a number of ways this could be done. We could make all three units infinitive verb phrases, but probably the easiest thing would be to turn the infinitive verb phrase into a noun phrase. That would result in a sentence like the following:

(24a)   Dog shows, zydeco concerts, and beach activities keep me busy
          during the summer.

You the writer must make sure that your conjuncts are parallel. To ensure that your conjuncts are parallel, you will need to be able to identify where they begin and where they end. It can be tricky to determine a boundary. The list may begin a sentence (25) or end a sentence (26), or it may be in the middle of a sentence (27):

(25)   **Laney, Lori, and Lulu**   went to town.

Item 1, Item 2, and Item 3 | rest of the sentence

(26)   Lars saw   **Laney, Lori, and Lulu.**

rest of the sentence | Item 1, Item 2, and Item 3

(27)   At the bank, the teller gave **Laney, Lori, and Lulu**

part of the sentence | Item 1, Item 2, and Item 3 |

a large sum of money.

part of the sentence

You will need to determine the boundary between the "edge" of the list that is next to the rest of the sentence. In (25), this is where Item 3 ends and the rest of the sentence begins. In (26), this is where the rest of the sentence ends and Item 1 begins. In (27), you will need to find both where Item 1 begins and Item 3 ends. Let's look at the sentence in (28) to practice finding the boundary of a list:

(28)   Jorge will buy the groceries, cut the vegetables, and make the salad.

The last two conjuncts are easy to pick out:

cut the vegetables   make the salad

Grammatically, they are both base-verb phrases. We can sense that this sentence is parallel, so the first conjunct must be a base-verb phrase also. Someone may ask if the first conjunct is the sequence *Jorge will buy the groceries* or the string *will buy the groceries.* However, neither of these choices will work. The first choice is a complete sentence, but a complete sentence cannot be parallel with a verb phrase. The second choice, *will buy the groceries,* is a modal phrase, and it too cannot be parallel with a base-verb phrase. Therefore, we must pick out only those words that constitute the verb-phrase portion of that initial sequence, and those are the words *buy the groceries.* The first two words of the sentence, *Jorge will,* combine with the three conjoined verb phrases. In fact, we could consider this sentence to be an abbreviated way of saying the following:

Jorge will buy the groceries.

Jorge will cut the vegetables.

Jorge will make the salad.

Then we identify the conjuncts by stripping away what each of those three sentences has in common, in this case the subject and the modal *Jorge will*. If we draw our lines to mark the phrases that are conjoined, it would look like this:

Jorge will <u>buy the groceries</u>, <u>cut the vegetables</u>, and <u>make the salad</u>.
VP[base]   VP[base]   VP[base]

VP[base]

As the above example shows, in a conjoined phrase you should identify the grammatical units of the phrases that are easy to pick out and then look for that same kind of phrase at the edge of the list that is adjacent to the rest of the sentence.

Exercises 5–7 will give you practice in applying your knowledge of structure to parallel constructions.

EXERCISE 5

Identify the grammatical units and their boundaries for all of the conjuncts in the following sentences with parallel structures.

EXAMPLE   I met <u>Octavio</u>, <u>Kenyatta</u>, and <u>Pierre</u> at the party.
NP   NP   NP

1. A bricklayer, a carpenter, and an electrician applied for a job today at the construction site.

2. The Girl Scout troop went running, skipping, and hopping along the beach.

3. We looked in, on, and under the stereo for the missing earring.

4. Carter saw the mysterious figure at the store, in the street, and by the bridge.

5. "I want you to pick up the phone, to dial the number, and to call your boss immediately."

6. "I don't need to pick up the phone, dial the number, and call my boss immediately."

7. The manager has met all her staff, evaluated their performance, and made her salary recommendations.

8. Jan ran the race quickly, steadily, and quite elegantly.

9. The food is cooked, the apartment is decorated, and the guests are here.

10. Last year Mickey believed that Santa Claus was real, that the moon was made of green cheese, and that the Chicago Cubs would soon win the World Series.

11. Veronica tallied her receipts, swept the floors, and closed her shop early.

12. The king, bishop, and pawn are all blocking the queen from moving out to attack.

EXERCISE 6

Some of the following sentences are correct as written, and some have parallelism errors. Identify the kinds of grammatical units that are combined by the coordinate conjunctions in each sentence, and correct those sentences that have errors.

1. Magnificent, splendid, and breathtaking—your performance was the best I've seen this year.

2. Money, fame, and to die with the most toys are that socialite's goals.

3. Working for the IRS, being a volunteer dad, and cricket may not be the typical description of a suburban Denverite.

4. The bear licked his lips, steadied his balance, and starting to climb after the treed camper.

5. Dahlia could wrestle steers, catch rattlesnakes, and climb mountains, all with her bare hands.

6. Beatrice knows how to maintain, pamper, and cajoles computers.

7. You are kind to animals, generous with strangers, and magnanimous to all.

8. The stock price has plummeted, the board has resigned, and a complete fiasco brewing.

9. The members of the band strum guitars, bang drums, and keyboards.

10. Winston becomes sick, feigns a headache, and could get out of work.

11. Lady Macbeth gave me the creeps, the willies, and thoroughly frightened me during the University Players' performance of *Macbeth*.

12. That collision with a tractor-trailer broke my windshield, my ribs, and my bank account last year.

EXERCISE 7

Write sentences that contain the parallelism errors indicated.

1. A sentence that conjoins two infinitive-verb phrases and a noun phrase.

2. A sentence that conjoins two clauses and a verb phrase.

3. A sentence that conjoins two verb-participle phrases and an infinitive-verb phrase.

4. A sentence that conjoins two noun phrases and a clause.

5. A sentence that conjoins two prepositional phrases and an adverb phrase.

Conceptual Parallelism

Another kind of parallelism error should be mentioned at this point. Parallelism errors tend to crop up in our writing when we are composing essays about topics that we are not familiar with. Good style in writing also requires that the ideas or content in a coordinate construction be parallel. This can sometimes be a harder problem to detect, but it is one you can become sensitive to as you read closely. The sentence below shows a parallelism error due to nonparallel content:

(29)   *The three main consequences of the government policy were unemployment, tax evasion, and a ten-percent fall in the stock market on March 5.

The three conjuncts are all noun phrases:

unemployment   tax evasion   a ten-percent fall in the stock market on March 5

However, even though they are grammatically parallel, the first two conjuncts are general terms and the last conjunct is specific. That is, the ideas are not parallel because they are not presented at the same level of generality. This sentence could be improved by making the last conjunct more general, as in (30), or by making the first two conjuncts more specific, as in (31):

(30)   The three main consequences of the government policy were unemployment, tax evasion, and falling stock prices.

(31)   The three main consequences of the government policy were a five-percent increase in unemployment, a twelve-percent decrease in income tax compliance, and a ten-percent fall in the stock market on March 5.

Understanding English grammar is what enables you to distinguish between the first kind of faulty parallelism, based on grammatical form, and the second kind, based on concepts. Each requires a different kind of solution.

What's the Problem with Parallelism Errors?

As a convention of writing, why is parallelism important, and why are parallelism errors a problem? Why do they matter? These questions become even more interesting in light of spontaneous speech. If you listen carefully, you might find that people use nonparallel structures quite frequently when they speak in informal situations. It would not be at all unusual to hear the following in a conversation:

(32)   "We had a great time at the beach: perfect weather, super food, and the water was fabulous."

Following the colon, we see a list conjoined by *and*. The list contains two noun phrases, *perfect weather* and *super food*, and also a complete sentence, *the water was fabulous*. What is even more notable is that this sentence is not hard to understand. If we can understand nonparallel structures when we speak, we might wonder why we should worry about them in writing.

This question brings us back to one of the themes of this book: the differences between speaking and writing. Speaking, as was noted in Chapter 1, has the advantage of having extra resources available to aid the listener in understanding the message. The physical context, the nonverbal cues of the speakers, and the tone of voice all give additional help to the listener. An even stronger resource is the speaker's intonation, the rise and fall in the melody of one's voice, which gives specific clues to the listener on how to chunk together the words he hears from the speaker. Finally, we often convey more familiar and less complex ideas when we speak. This latter consideration is a factor why a listener easily could understand the nonparallel coordination above. Most of us are familiar with beaches and beach activities, so the words and ideas of this sentence don't tax our minds. The content in (32) is so familiar that most people would have no problem understanding the sentence in speech or writing.

Alas, most of the valuable resources of speech are absent in writing; therefore, the reader must rely more on the mere words themselves in the order they come to him. Furthermore, parallelism becomes a more serious concern in formal and academic prose, where the reader is likely to encounter novel content and less-familiar ideas. When we are reading difficult material, nonparallel coordination interferes with our attempt to understand the material, because it makes it more likely that our memory will be overloaded as we process a sentence.

A crucial consideration that arises for both a listener and a reader is memory capacity. When we hear or read a sentence, we process it in our short-term memory, a crucial part of our minds that is involved in the hard work of processing language. Short-term memory is remarkably similar for all of us. Research shows that all of us can store seven to twelve bits of information in short-term memory. We differ, though, in what we can include in a single bit of information. Proficient readers can store more content in a single bit in their short-term memory than can those who struggle with a text. There are a number of factors that influence the reader's ability to chunk more stuff into a memory bit. The more familiar a reader is with the content of a text, the more he will be able to chunk into his short-term memory bits. The better written a text is, the more a reader can store in his short-term memory. Effective use of parallelism is one way of enabling the latter. The first instance of a grammatical unit in a list prepares the reader's mind to process similar units later in the list and so facilitates chunking more information in the reader's short-term memory. For example, if the reader processes a noun phrase at the beginning of a list, his mind will be primed to process noun phrases later in the list.

Sentences with lists are often longer and thus put a greater demand on our reader's memory. There is always the danger that our reader's short-term memory will be overloaded before he gets to the end of any long sentence. Disrupting the parallelism forces the reader to devote more short-term memory to fewer linguistic units. Therefore, writers need to be even more careful to make long sentences reader-friendly by using stylistic devices such as parallelism.

A Note on Punctuation in Parallel Structures

When three or more items are combined in a parallel structure with a coordinate conjunction such as *and* or *or,* commas are used to separate the conjuncts. However, the comma before the coordinate conjunction is optional. We could write either of the following:

> hot dogs, buns, and potato chips

> hot dogs, buns and potato chips

This is an area in which the writer's discretion is called for. Most handbooks recommend that you use the optional comma, though journalistic practice often omits it. The value of leaving out unnecessary punctuation from your text is that punctuation always slows down the reader a little bit. A text with lots of punctuation is usually cumbersome to read.

On the other hand, the added comma may improve readability. An example of a difficulty that might arise is when one of the conjuncts itself has a coordinate conjunction inside it. Suppose we wanted to combine the following foods into a list:

> spaghetti   macaroni and cheese   meatloaf

If we leave out the comma before the conjunction *and,* we get a sentence like the following:

(33)   *My favorite foods are spaghetti, macaroni and cheese and meatloaf.

Now the reader faces the difficulty of sorting out which food *cheese* goes with— *macaroni* or *meatloaf.* Even though the reader's knowledge of American culture would probably help her link *cheese* with *macaroni,* there is still the potential for confusion. However, you can eliminate that confusion by including a comma before the conjunction *and:*

(33a)   My favorite foods are spaghetti, macaroni and cheese, and meatloaf.

 # Application to Writing

In seeking to convey nuances and shades of meaning, one of the grammatical choices writers make involves the use of coordination and subordination. The very same information given by two clauses will be understood differently based on the way we link clauses to one another. Consider sentence (21) again:

(21)   The food was great, though the service was slow.

Notice how the meaning subtly changes if the same two clauses are united with the coordinate conjunction *and:*

(21a)   The food was great, and the service was slow.

It is useful to consider the kinds of contexts in which either (21) or (21a) would be more suitable. For example, the coordinate conjunction in (21a) might be used to lessen the potential negative impression given by the clause *the service was slow* or even change it. The sentence in (21) highlights the negativity of the second clause more than the sentence in (21a) does. The wording in (21a) could be used when the writer wanted to say the following:

(34)   The food was great, and the service was slow, just the way I like it so I have a chance to talk to my clients.

Notice how the last part of (34) sounds less natural if added to (21):

(34a)   *The food was great, though the service was slow, just the way I like it so I have a chance to talk to my clients.

Now, you might be wondering what difference there is between coordination and subordination when the conjunctions are similar in meaning. Does it matter whether you use *but* or *though*? If we insert the conjunction *but* in place of the conjunction *though* in sentence (21) above, there seems to be very little difference in meaning:

(21)   The food was great, though the service was slow.

(21b)   The food was great, but the service was slow.

However, there are subtle differences between using *but* with coordination and using *though* with subordination, as (35) and (36) show:

(35)   We went to the park, but it was almost closing time.

(36)   We went to the park, though it was almost closing time.

Sentence (35) implies that we did not know that it was almost closing time when we went to the park. Sentence (36), however, implies that we did know it was almost closing time, yet we went to the park anyway. These two sentences illustrate that subordination makes for a tighter connection between clauses than coordination does. In (36), our going to the park and the nearness of the closing time are portrayed as related in some way because of the subordination, a connection that is missing in (35) because of its coordination.

Keep in mind these choices as you write and compose. In Chapter 11, we will discuss what factors can help you decide the placement of subordinate clauses in your sentences.

The next exercise lets you experiment with coordination and subordination in order to see their effects on a text.

EXERCISE 8

1. Find a paragraph or section from a college textbook that uses coordination to join clauses. Rewrite the paragraph or section so that there is subordination in place of the coordination. Discuss what effects this has on the meaning of the paragraph.

2. Find a paragraph or section from a college textbook that uses subordination to join clauses. Rewrite the paragraph or section so that there is coordination in place of the subordination. Discuss what effects this has on the meaning of the paragraph.

This chapter has shown how an understanding of the basic structures of English sheds light on coordination, subordination, and parallelism, especially as they pertain to the conventions of writing. Knowledge of grammar will help you to be clear in your assessment of problems and to be goal oriented when you refine your writing, because now you can keep in mind this important question: have I made my prose reader-friendly for my audience?

PEANUTS reprinted by permission of the United Feature Syndicate, Inc.

A Note on Some Marks of Punctuation

Earlier in the chapter, we saw that semicolons can be used to separate independent clauses inside a single sentence. The following section describes the semicolon, the colon, the dash, and parentheses so that you can clearly distinguish their use in your writing.

THE SEMICOLON I remember when I was in school that I got the semicolon and the colon confused all the time, partly because their names are similar and partly because they look similar on the printed page (the semicolon is ; and the colon is :). However, they have very different functions.

What helps me today is to remember the meaning of the semicolon—it means *and* and sometimes *but*. We use it between complete sentences when we are simply combining those sentences together. A sentence with a semicolon like (37)

(37)　The advertising flyers came out in today's newspaper; the shelves are stocked.

means the same thing as the following:

(37a)　The advertising flyers came out in today's newspaper (and) the shelves are stocked.

There are two writing situations in which we use semicolons. They can be used to separate independent clauses when the clauses appear in the same sentence. We also use semicolons to separate conjuncts in a list when those conjuncts contain commas themselves. The latter situation does not arise very often, but you should be familiar with it.

Sometimes, especially in academic and formal writing, a writer might need to combine a lot of information in one sentence. Consider the following situation in which the writer wishes to combine the following three complete sentences into one sentence.

(38)　The New York City landscape, always a thing of great beauty, conveys a sense of loneliness.

(39)   The stock market continues to decline, its fragility apparent to all.

(40)   The national mood goes through the motions of normalcy, but not very convincingly.

Normally, the writer would simply add commas between the conjuncts to keep them separate. If we try that with the above conjuncts, we would get a sentence like the following:

(41)   *The New York City landscape, always a thing of great beauty, conveys a sense of loneliness, the stock market continues to decline, its fragility apparent to all, and the national mood goes through the motions of normalcy, but not very convincingly.

This sentence is difficult to read, primarily because of the competing commas. The underlined commas are used to separate one clause from another. The other commas separate items within a single clause. Unfortunately, it becomes hard to sort out which commas perform which function, because they all look the same. The way to solve this problem is to turn the two commas that separate clauses into semicolons. The comma following the word *loneliness* and the comma following the word *all* are changed, resulting in a cleaner sentence:

(42)   The New York City landscape, always a thing of great beauty, conveys a sense of loneliness; the stock market continues to decline, its fragility apparent to all; and the national mood goes through the motions of normalcy, but not very convincingly.

THE COLON The colon carries a different meaning from the semicolon: it signals either that an explanation or a list follows. Sentence (43) illustrates the use of a colon to signal the advent of an explanation, and sentence (44) illustrates the use of a colon to signal a forthcoming list:

(43)   She knew what was bothering Reginald: his paycheck was late.

(44)   There are three things you need to work on in your performance: your forward flips, your toe pointing, and your facial expressions.

Generally, semicolons and colons are not interchangeable in the same context. For example, if we use a colon in the place of the semicolon from sentence (37), we get the strange sentence

(45)   The advertising flyers came out in today's newspaper: the shelves are stocked.

        = " 'The shelves are stocked' explains why the advertising flyers came out in today's newspaper."

The colon leads the reader to believe that the clause *the shelves are stocked* should be an explanation or clarification of something in the first clause, yet that is not a logical conclusion from the content of this sentence.

Likewise, if we use a semicolon in place of the colon in (43), we get another strange sentence:

(43)   *She knew what was bothering Reginald; his paycheck was late.

The semicolon makes the sentence sound like it means "she knew what was bothering Reginald, and his paycheck was late." Assuming that the late paycheck is the reason for Reginald's bother, we can't use this semicolon because it makes it sound as if the two clauses are unrelated to each other. Colons, though, signal a closer relationship between the clauses.

To use a colon correctly, you the writer must consider two things: what kind of grammatical unit precedes the colon and what kind of grammatical unit follows the colon. Let's consider the latter issue first. Colons can be followed by clauses, noun phrases, and infinitive-verb phrases. The sentences below illustrate these cases:

(46)   The weather was atrocious last week: three feet of snow fell at the gap.

(47)   Her boss e-mailed her the good news: a fabulous promotion!

(48)   The detective has one purpose in entering the abandoned warehouse late at night: to find the killer.

Importantly, colons cannot be followed by a main-verb phrase. (This kind of phrase is also known as a finite-verb phrase.)

(49)   *Judy received low marks for her floor exercise: stepped out of bounds.

The main-verb phrase, by itself, doesn't qualify as an explanation.

The more difficult problem for some writers, however, is getting the wording right that goes before the colon. There is one rule, and it is consistent:

A colon must be preceded by a complete sentence.

This rule is often broken. I have seen numerous memos and other documents written by professors and administrators that make this kind of colon mistake. Many writers are accustomed to using colons to introduce lists, but they end up writing sentences that have mistakes like the following:

(50)   *The Boy Scout troop bought: hot dogs, buns, and potato chips.

The problem is that the sequence of words before the colon is not a complete sentence, as the following shows:

(51)   *The Boy Scout troop bought.

There is a good reason why a colon is not used after an incomplete sentence. As Chapter 7 stated, we don't use punctuation to separate the necessary parts of the sentence. We don't, for example, use punctuation to separate the verb from its direct object. However, inserting a colon so that an incomplete sentence precedes it means that the colon will separate necessary parts of the sentence. We can observe this by identifying the phrases that carry grammatical roles:

The Boy Scout troop bought hot dogs, buns, and potato chips.

From this diagram, we see that the verb phrase has one noun phrase. We use one of our tests to identify its grammatical role and try to make a new sentence with the two noun phrases and a *be*-verb:

(50a)   *The Boy Scout troop are hot dogs, buns, and potato chips.

This sentence does not imply the previous sentence, so we know that the noun phrase *hot dogs, buns, and potato chips* is a direct object. The reader needs to read all of the necessary elements of the sentence together to determine grammatical roles and the basic structure of the sentence. Intervening punctuation interferes with that.

Fortunately, the punctuation mistake is easily corrected. All we need to do is add a noun phrase before the colon to make the preceding words into a complete sentence, as in (52), or remove the colon altogether, as in (53):

(52)   The Boy Scout troop bought these food items: hot dogs, buns, and potato chips.

(53)   The Boy Scout troop bought hot dogs, buns, and potato chips.

You will need to be on the lookout for colons following verbs. It is likely that an incomplete sentence precedes the colon.

THE DASH The dash is the long line, the symbol —, that is used to set off elements from a clause. It is important that you do not confuse the dash (—) with the hyphen (-) , a much shorter line that is used inside words. Today, when almost everyone uses computers to write texts, you should learn the commands your word-processing program uses to make a dash so that your texts will have the correct symbol in the correct place.

Dashes are used to set off explanatory or parenthetical material from the main sentence. At the end of the sentence, they are used for virtually the same purposes as colons. The dash is a bolder and physically larger piece of punctuation than the colon and is considered to be a stronger punctuation mark. A writer might use a dash, then, when she wishes to draw more attention to the parenthetical material she includes.

Dashes do have one major difference from colons. Unlike colons, which only set off material at the end of the sentence, and unlike parentheses, which only set off material in the middle and the end of the sentence, dashes can set off material at the front or back of the sentence or in the middle of the sentence. The following sentences demonstrate the latter two possibilities:

(54)   "Raindrops and roses"—I think I heard that in a song somewhere.

(55)   Jody had the nerve to invite her uncle—the one and only survivor of the U.S.S. Minnow—to my beach party.

Commas could be used in place of the dashes in these sentences. The dashes, though, call more attention to the set-off material:

(54a)   "Raindrops and roses," I think I heard that in a song somewhere.

(55a)   Jody had the nerve to invite her uncle, the one and only survivor of the U.S.S. Minnow, to my beach party.

PARENTHESES Similar to dashes, parentheses are used to set off material from the main sentence. They make less of an impact than dashes and so work well for adding explanatory information, especially in academic and formal writing. If the writer wishes to convey a particular tone or emotion along with her information, however, dashes are more appropriate. Thus, dashes work well in (56) and parentheses work well in (57). However, this is a tendency rather than a hard-and-fast rule. The writer could instead use parentheses in (56) and dashes in (57):

(56)   The candidate from Grampton—though I hate to admit it—ran a clean but aggressive campaign.

(57)   The sun's distance from the earth (93 million miles) is close enough to preserve plant and animal life and far enough to avoid burning the planet up.

There are a few rules to remember with regard to punctuating parenthetical material. First, when a sentence ends with material in parentheses, make sure the final period is outside the last parenthesis. (The examples in (59a) and (60a) are all incorrect.)

(58)   A member of royalty came to my party last night (actually, a de-
        posed duke).

(58a)   *A member of royalty came to my party last night (actually, a de-
        posed duke.)

Second, writers may place an entire sentence inside parentheses as an explanatory comment in the text. In this case, the final period goes inside the last
parenthesis:

(59)   The fence separating the two homesteads was in terrible repair.
        (The bottom of each board had rotted from the many floods.)

(59a)   *The fence separating the two homesteads was in terrible repair.
        (The bottom of each board had rotted from the many floods).

Third, don't put punctuation before a parenthesis in the middle of a
sentence:

(60)   Because Wiggins didn't play in the Homecoming Game (he had an
        ankle sprain), we lost by five points.

(61)   *Because Wiggins didn't play in the Homecoming Game, (he had
        an ankle sprain) we lost by five points.

The following exercise gives you an opportunity to apply your knowledge of
punctuation.

EXERCISE 9

*Some of the following sentences are correct as written. Some have punctuation errors.
Explain what is wrong with the latter and then correct them.*

1. William the Conqueror sailed to England in 1066, and the country has never
   been the same since.

2. It is especially difficult for new people in the neighborhood to observe the
   speed limit on Park Street, and to avoid the traffic jams on Main Street.

3. My money, and your brains are the key to success.

4. Granny went over the meadow, and through the woods.

5. Before the test, you should study your notes, but when in doubt, you should
   try to remember what you studied.

6. Going to the store, and buying a new outfit isn't as much fun as it used to be.

7. Daddy was a plumber and Mommy was a carpenter.

8. Skunks, the most exquisite of animals, rarely bother those who don't bother them, and rarely deserve the scorn we heap upon them.

9. My neighbor filed a complaint with the city; after his yard was flooded during last night's rains.

10. The winners of the pie-eating competition are: Simeon Crowley, Watford Drivens, and Percival DeMunster.

11. My last card was the king of spades, and his card was a four of clubs.

12. The sock fell out the window, and under a bush.

13. Ichabod happily lived out his days in Green Valley. (He really wasn't frightened by the Headless Horseman.)

The following exercise asks you to make deliberate errors in the sentences you write. This kind of exercise forces you to have a deeper understanding of a problem than is required by merely recognizing it in a sentence.

EXERCISE 10

Compose sentences that contain the deliberate errors indicated.

1. Write two sentences that are run-ons.

2. Write two sentences that are comma splices.

3. Write two sentences that use a semicolon incorrectly.

4. Write two sentences that use a colon incorrectly.

5. Write two sentences that use a dash or dashes incorrectly.

6. Write two sentences that use parentheses incorrectly.

7. Write two sentences that use a comma to coordinate two phrases that are not complete sentences.

COMPREHENSION QUESTIONS

1. What is coordination? What part of speech is used in coordination?

2. What is the difference between coordinating phrases and coordinating parts of speech?

3. What punctuation options do we have for coordination?

4. How does appropriate punctuation aid a reader in comprehending a text?

5. What is subordination? What part of speech is used in subordination?

6. What are the punctuation rules for subordinate clauses?

7. What is parallelism?

8. How do we detect and correct parallelism errors?

9. How do parallelism errors hinder the reader's efficient comprehension of the text?

10. How do the colon, the semicolon, the dash, and parentheses differ from one another in usage and effect on a text?

The System of Modifiers

PREVIEW *In Chapter 7, I talked about the difference between the "necessary stuff" and the "extra stuff" in the sentence. This chapter will discuss the extra stuff in more detail. I will organize this discussion around the extra stuff that is found in the verb phrase and the extra stuff that is found in the noun phrase. Extra verbal stuff is often referred to as **adverbials.** Extra nominal stuff is often referred to as **adjectivals.** These terms do not refer to parts of speech but to the functions of words and phrases. The same kind of phrase can carry out different functions in the sentence. Adverbials function as chunks that modify verbs, verb phrases, and clauses. Adjectivals function as chunks that modify nouns and noun phrases. In addition, at the end of the chapter I will introduce another kind of modifier known as **absolute phrases.***

Adverbials

As we saw in Chapter 7, much of the richness of what we convey in our writing is due to the **modifiers** known as adverbials that we add to what would otherwise be bare-bones sentences. You can see this if you look at a simple sentence without any adverbials like (1), and compare it to a sentence that has had modifiers added to it, like (2):

(1)   Dempsey saw his shadow.

(2)   <u>Though you could never tell it by his demeanor,</u> <u>last night at 1:15 a.m.</u>, Dempsey, <u>bless his heart</u>, saw his shadow <u>for the first time in twelve years</u>.

The pizzazz, the sizzle in (2) comes from the adverbials in the sentence. They often convey the most important information in our sentences. Let's take a further look at some adverbials, noting their grammatical properties and restrictions and considering their functions.

PREPOSITIONAL PHRASES We saw earlier that prepositional phrases are sometimes necessary stuff, but they also function as adverbials. In sentences (3)–(5), the **prepositional phrases** are not needed to make each sentence grammatically complete:

(3)   The party arrived <u>at 4:00</u>.

(4)   The Simons took a stroll <u>in the park</u>.

(5)   She plays the piano <u>with great gusto</u>.

Prepositional phrases, though, can carry out more than one function. In sentence (3) the prepositional phrase provides temporal information, in sentence (4) location information, and in sentence (5) manner information.

ADVERB PHRASES Adverb phrases consist of an adverb and any modifiers that combine with that adverb.

(6)   Dara ran the race <u>gracefully</u>.

(7)   <u>Extremely carelessly</u>, the flustered butler poured the wine.

(8)   Constantin completed the obstacle course <u>quickly but deliberately</u>.

(9)   <u>Obviously</u>, the dog handler committed the theft.

Adverb phrases typically provide manner information, describing the way in which the action denoted by the verb was done. However, an adverb phrase can also convey the attitude of the speaker of the sentence. In sentence (9), the adverb phrase does not describe how the theft was committed but rather the opinion of the speaker that it is obvious to him that the dog handler carried out the theft. In this case, the adverb phrase modifies the entire sentence rather than the verb phrase by itself.

Can adverb phrases ever be necessary stuff? It turns out that they can be in some sentences, for example:

(10)   This book reads <u>easily</u>.

If we omitted the adverb phrase *easily*, as in (10a), an ungrammatical sentence results, a sure sign that the adverb phrase is required to make (10) a complete sentence:

(10a)   *This book reads.

TIME PHRASES   Time phrases often consist of nouns and noun phrases:

(11)   <u>Yesterday</u>, the Racers won their division.

(12)   We will go to Galveston <u>tomorrow</u>.

(13)   The Baileys lived in England <u>three years</u>.

The functional label **time phrases** is useful because the formal characteristics of such phrases are unique. *Yesterday, today,* and *tomorrow* are nouns in form, but they do not normally take modifiers:

(14)   *<u>The yesterday</u>, the Racers won their division.

(15)   *We will go to Galveston <u>an exciting tomorrow</u>.

They are capable, though, of acting like ordinary nouns in the right context:

(16)   February 16 is a yesterday I won't forget.

(17)   I hope all your tomorrows are filled with joy.

Though this type of phrase is given many different names in various grammar books, I use the label *time phrases* to capture their common characteristic of contributing temporal information to the sentence.

SUBORDINATE   CLAUSES   AND   DANGLING   PHRASES   Subordinate clauses, which were discussed in Chapter 9, can be classified as adverbials:

(18)   <u>When eagles fear to fly</u>, the Storm Patrol dares to soar.

(19)   Anson, <u>while juggling three printers</u>, rode a unicycle across the dam.

(20)   The case was dismissed <u>after the judge detected the frivolous attitude of the attorney</u>.

However, most subordinate clauses modify the entire clause to which they are attached and not necessarily the verb phrase alone.

   Specific problems arise with subordinate clauses when they are elliptical. **Ellipsis** is the technical term used to describe words being left out of a phrase. Speakers do this all time as they seek to deliver their message with efficiency. Writers do this also when the context makes the message clear. I could write the following sentence and be perfectly understood:

(21)   While I was coming home from work, I saw an accident.

However, I could also reduce the subordinate clause without any loss of meaning:

(22)   While coming home from work, I saw an accident.

The subject and the *be*-verb have been eliminated from the subordinate clause, leading to a leaner and less-clunky sentence. The *be*-verb was there for grammatical reasons but otherwise contributed little information to the sentence. The subject ends up being redundant, because its information can be recovered from the main clause. This kind of elliptical subordinate clause works when the subject of the subordinate clause matches the subject of the main clause.

However, sometimes the missing subject from an elliptical clause doesn't match the subject of the main clause, and the resulting difficulty is called a dangling subordinate clause. The following examples show some **dangling clauses:**

(23)   *Though needing five dollars for cab fare to get home, Joyce's last ten dollars was spent on a ticket to the show.

(24)   *After leaving the class, a campus security officer stopped the student for littering.

(25)   *When cooking liver-and-leek soup, the water should be kept at a constant boil.

We can tell these subordinate clauses are dangling by taking the subject of the main clause and making it the subject of the subordinate clause. This gives us the odd sentences below:

(23a)   Though _____ needing five dollars for cab fare to get home, **Joyce's last ten dollars** was spent on a ticket to the show. ➲

         *Though Joyce's last ten dollars needed five dollars for cab fare to get home, they were spent on a ticket to the show.

(24a)   After _____ leaving the class, **a campus security officer** stopped the student for littering. ➲

         *After a campus security officer left the class, he stopped the student for littering.

(25a)   When _____ cooking liver-and-leek soup, **the water** should be kept at a constant boil. ➲

         *When the water cooks liver-and-leek soup, it should be kept at a constant boil.

A dangling elliptical clause is one of those errors that can be especially hard to detect. If you look at the examples above, the first one might have sounded especially strange. The second sentence is ambiguous. The sentence would be fine if the writer intended to talk about the security officer leaving class. If, however, the writer meant to talk about the student leaving class, the sentence is not effective. The last example perhaps originally sounded fine to your ears, because there is no problem with figuring out what the writer wants to convey. You might ask why we should lose sleep over dangling clauses.

Here is another case where the difference between speech and writing comes to our attention. It is not unusual to speak with dangling modifiers, and our audience rarely notices when we do. Why is this? Again, we must think about the many differences between the two forms of language. Chapter 1 has already established that speech need not be as precise as writing because of all the advantages speech has: the immediate context, the intonation of the speaker, and so forth.

The problem has to do with your readers and what they might notice. In real-world writing, you may be fortunate to have hundreds, thousands, maybe even millions of readers. If you write a sentence that includes a dangling modifier, you run the risk that some of your readers may be tripped up by it. Even if the majority miss the difficulty in the first place and if nine out of ten read the sentence effortlessly, what about that one person who notices the dangling modifier and is distracted or led astray by it? This is why writers should take care to avoid dangling modifiers in most sentences.

There are other phrases where dangling can occur. These include infinitive-verb phrases (26) and participial phrases (27):

(26)   To _____ make a delicious cake, eggs should be brought fresh. ➲

       *For eggs to make a delicious cake, they should be brought fresh.

(27)   _____ Having eaten my dinner, the maitre d' brought me the dessert menu. ➲

       *After the maitre d' ate my dinner, he brought me the dessert menu.

If you are aware of this potential problem, you can become sensitive to the presence of dangling clauses in your own writing or the writing of others.

There are two primary strategies for correcting dangling modifiers. One approach is to change the subject of the main clause so that it matches the implied subject of the subordinate clause or phrase. For sentence (27) you would rewrite the main clause so that its new subject, *I*, matches the implied subject of the participial phrase:

(27a)   Having eaten my dinner, I was brought the dessert menu by the maitre d'.

A second approach is to rewrite the subordinate clause or phrase so that its implied subject matches the subject of the main clause. For a sentence like

(28)   *After repainting the home, the old house looked quite inviting.

you would rewrite the subordinate clause so that its implied subject was *the old house*:

(28a)   After being repainted, the old house looked quite inviting.

Exercises 1 and 2 give you a chance to sharpen your ability to detect dangling modifiers.

EXERCISE 1

Correct the dangling modifiers in the following sentences. Some sentences may be correct as written.

1. While fixing a flat tire, a bicyclist noticed a stranded motorist.

2. Though appraised at $60,000, the owner saw that his rare piece of pottery didn't generate much interest at the auction.

3. Putting aside my objections, I heard the counselor suggest that I take a long vacation.

4. To observe Epsilon 25, the telescope should be pointed toward the eastern portion of the southern hemisphere.

5. Though not yet tested, the scientist was confident that her new drug would cure male-pattern baldness.

6. Once inoculated, the doctor was no longer worried about entering the ward.

7. Whether coming or going, a smile can always be found on Sammy's face.

8. Scolded by his master, the dog slunk under the porch.

9. To catch a bass in these waters, Old Charley would use a spinner with a blue tail.

10. Since quitting her job, money has been hard to come by for Ruth.

11. After coming to an agreement, the meeting was continued at the coffeehouse.

The next exercise is particularly challenging. It asks you to create dangling modifiers and so forces you to understand this problem beyond merely recognizing the error.

EXERCISE 2

Combine the following clauses so that the resulting sentence has a dangling modifier. Then write the sentence without a dangling modifier. You may need to rewrite and/or re-order the clauses to do this.

> EXAMPLE The storm petered out after fifteen minutes. Royal wasn't scared of the storm.
>
> ➲ Petering out after fifteen minutes, Royal wasn't scared of the storm. [dangling]
>
> ➲ Petering out after fifteen minutes, the storm didn't scare Royal. [correct]

1. Arlene finished her dessert. The rest of the pie was left on the counter.

2. The calico cat stalked the mouse. The mouse was unaware of his impending danger.

3. The inhabitants speak Gullah on the outer islands. They were isolated from the mainland for centuries.

4. Murdock went to the store to buy some more paper. Then the printer ran out of paper again.

5. A late spring blizzard moved into the county. The principal was afraid he would have to cancel the annual Senior Banquet.

6. Mr. Rogers was a Presbyterian minister. Mr. Rogers's TV show had a wide appeal to a diverse audience.

7. We recently moved into town. The neighbors invited us over for a crawfish boil.

8. Gladys decided not to buy a computer. Computer prices were still falling rapidly.

9. The airline feared bankruptcy was imminent. Contracts were renegotiated between the unions and management.

10. A new Thai restaurant opened up recently on the north side of town. Their satay is excellent.

CLAUSES OF COMPARISON Clauses of comparison allow us to compare objects and situations. Writers usually leave words out of the comparison clause. In fact, some of these clauses would be ungrammatical without the ellipsis, as in

(29)   Shkendra is five inches taller than
       Carrie [is tall].   (*is tall* must be left out)

(30)   Ezra works much harder than
        Mendel [works hard].   (*works hard* must be left out)

Ellipsis is a very precise phenomenon. What is left out of the second clause is an equal portion of the first clause. We can recover the missing material by comparing the second clause, which is missing information, to the first clause:

Ezra works hard.
NP   V   AdjP

. . . Mendel . . .
      NP

Where can the noun phrase *Mendel* be inserted into the first clause? There is only one possibility: it can take the place of the subject noun phrase *Ezra*. If there is only one place where the noun phrase can occur, the clause of comparison is unambiguous.

However, whenever there is an ellipsis, there is the possibility of ambiguity, and this may occur in comparison clauses. It arises when the two clauses being compared are both transitive. Consider the following clause of comparison:

(31)   *Stern likes Johnson better than Andrews.

We set the clauses side by side to determine what is left out of the second clause:

Stern likes Johnson.
NP   V   NP

. . . Andrews . . .
      NP

Where can the noun phrase *Andrews* substitute in the first clause? Unfortunately, it can substitute in two locations, in place of the subject noun phrase *Stern*, as in (32), or in place of the object noun phrase *Johnson*, as in (33):

(32)   Andrews likes Johnson.

(33)   Stern likes Andrews.

The example in (31) is ambiguous in just this way. It can mean both of the following:

(34)   Stern likes Johnson better than Stern likes Andrews.

(35)   Stern likes Johnson better than Andrews likes Johnson.

These are the kinds of comparison clauses that should be avoided in writing. Even if context favors one reading over the other, you still run the risk of your reader being misled by the reading you did not intend.

The secret to sniffing out these problems in your writing is to reconstruct the comparison clause by turning it into a full clause. This will also help you uncover comparison clauses that turn out to be sloppily written or illogical.

(36)   *My school's job placement record is better than your school. ⟳

My school's <u>job placement</u> is good.
            NP

. . . <u>your school</u> . . . ⟳
      NP

My school's job placement is good. Your school is good.

The reconstruction shows that the writer is comparing the job placement of one school to another school itself (not one job placement to another!).

(37)   *The rainfall in Coopersville is higher than South Windport. ⟳

<u>The rainfall in Coopersville</u> is high.
            NP

. . . <u>South Windport</u> . . . ⟳
       NP

The rainfall in Coopersville is high. South Windport is high.

The reconstruction shows that the writer is comparing the rainfall in one town to another town (not the rainfall of one town to that of the other!).

    A final issue that arises in comparison clauses is with pronouns. This is not a problem that leads to real ambiguity, but rather a response that some readers might have to your formal prose. Should we write (38) or (39)?

(38)   Shaquille is taller than me.

(39)   Shaquille is taller than I.

You should know that some readers will object to (38) on the assumption that any pronoun in the comparison clause should appear in the case that pronoun would have in the full clause. If I wanted to compare my height to Shaquille's height, the two underlying clauses would be these:

      Shaquille is tall.

      I am tall.

The comparison sentence then would be

(40)   Shaquille is taller than I.

If I wrote

(41)   Shaquille is taller than me.

that suggests I am comparing

      Shaquille is tall.

      *Me is tall.

Note that sentences like (38) show up in informal writing and speech and pose no problem for comprehension. However, you should know that some readers will object to such sentences in formal writing. If you wish to make a good impression on a sophisticated audience, you might want to choose the pronoun form that fits the reconstructed sentence.

On the other hand, careful use of pronouns allows the writer to write comparison clauses with precision. Thus, the following two clauses lose their ambiguity when the comparison clause contains a pronoun:

(42)   Tim likes David better than me.

(43)   Tim likes David better than I.

In (42), use of a pronoun in the comparison clause produces

(44)   Tim likes David better than Tim likes me.

In (43), it produces

(45)   Tim likes David better than I like David.

Note that many writers find the sentence in (43) stilted. It can be improved by adding the pro-verb *do* to the elliptical clause:

(45)   Tim likes David better than I do.

Comparison clauses are powerful tools in writing because of their properties. They can even be exploited for humor:

(46)   Q: What animal can jump higher than a building?

        A: All of them. Buildings can't jump.

The following exercise asks you to evaluate clauses of comparison.

EXERCISE 3

Correct the following sentences that contain illogical or poorly written clauses of comparison. Some may be correct as written.

1. The pizza at Smiley's Restaurant tastes spicier than the pizza at The Bounce Shack.

2. Tony's grip is stronger than Seth.

3. The capital of Maine is smaller than Louisiana.

4. The residents of Mooresville buy more potato chips than Lincoln.

5. Steak with potatoes is more typical than peas.

6. Newman cooks pasta more than me.

7. The Polecats of Dogpatch sold more Kickapoo Joy Juice than Sioux City.

8. More American soldiers died in the Civil War than World War II.

9. Dumbo the Elephant has more knees than me.

10. Spain produces more Rioja wines than France.

11. The boss gave Yolanda more perks than Wyatt.

Adjectivals

So far we have discussed the extra stuff that modifies verb phrases and clauses. There is also extra stuff that modifies noun phrases—**adjectivals.** As in the case of adverbials, it is important to remember that this term names a functional category, not a formal category. Many different kinds of phrases make up the category of adjectivals.

ADJECTIVE PHRASES The category of adjectivals that we are most familiar with is **adjective phrases.** In fact, **adjectives** are primarily defined as a modifying category for nouns. We have also seen that adjective phrases can contain more than one word. They themselves can be modified by qualifiers. Thus we can say all of the following:

(47)   the <u>happy</u> camper

(48)   the <u>very happy</u> camper

(49)   the <u>very, very happy</u> camper

There is no limit to how many qualifiers we can put in an adjective phrase, apart from the weariness of the writer or reader.

There are a couple of wrinkles to putting adjective phrases inside noun phrases. The first is a punctuation issue that arises when a noun phrase has more than one adjective. Sometimes there must be a comma separating the two adjectives (50), and sometimes not:

(50)   a tired, frustrated father

(51)   a strong federal system

This presence or absence of a comma points to a structural difference in the phrases. In the first example, both adjectives modify the noun on an equal basis. If we identify the phrases, they would look like the following:

a   <u>tired</u>   <u>frustrated</u>   father
    AdjP   AdjP

_____
          NP

In the second example, the adjective closest to the noun, the word _federal_, forms a unit, and then the adjective modifies that adjective + noun unit:

a <u>strong</u>   <u>federal system</u>
  Adj P   noun unit

_____
          NP

The comma is used when the two adjectives combine with the noun on an equal basis.

There are two tests for determining when this comma is called for. When two adjectives modify a noun equally, they are being coordinated. To test whether they are of equal stature, try adding a coordinate conjunction between them. If you can do this, a comma is required:

(50a)   a tired and frustrated father

(51a)   *a strong and federal system

Sometimes, another coordinate conjunction like _but_ or _or_ may sound better between the adjectives:

(52)   an exhausted but triumphant miler

A second test is to change the order of adjectives. When they modify the noun equally, their order can be changed. We see that the order of adjectives can be changed in (50) but not in (51):

(50b)   a frustrated, tired father

(51b)   *a federal strong system

As with other areas of language, it is good to have more than one test to distinguish structure, because there can be cases in which one test is not sufficient. The following noun phrase is an example:

(53)   a tall, muscular football player

We can put the conjunction _and_ in between the two adjectives.

(53a)   a tall and muscular football player

However, reversing the order of the adjectives does not sound good:

(53b)   *a muscular tall football player

As always, you should learn as many tests as you can to help you navigate through the intricacies of language.

The next two exercises will help you to apply these principles to commas between adjectives.

EXERCISE 4

Put in commas where necessary between the two adjectives. If some cases are not clear, explain why including the comma is uncertain.

1. an angry principal flutist

2. the unclear main purpose

3. a tall dark stranger

4. a slimy green lizard

5. that sad leafless tree

6. a powerful tumultuous time

7. his grimy seedy house

8. the fast ferocious bull

9. a wise strategic decision

10. the unrepentant former thief

EXERCISE 5

Evaluate the following sentences for commas between adjectives. Some commas must be deleted. Some sentences need commas added. Some sentences are correct as written.

1. The vivacious, innovative director had a number of new designs to unveil at the launch.

2. In the second half, the quickest strongest linebacker made six tackles.

3. The Double Cross Gang found an old, abandoned mine at the end of the logging trail.

4. The production assistant claimed that poor split-second judgment was common on the set.

5. We only sell juicy spicy burgers at this greasy spoon.

6. The nature of the new planet was not clear from the fuzzy, dim photographs.

7. The expensive, deluxe upgrade was never a big seller.

8. Vicious inflammatory rumors were spreading all over campus about the change in next year's revised, academic calendar.

9. Somewhere over that bright, optimistic rainbow lies a golden future for those two.

10. The ambassador met the former, military dictator without his country's knowledge.

HYPHENS: PUNCTUATION MIRRORS STRUCTURE Other phrases besides adjective phrases can modify nouns and can occur between a determiner and the noun. When multiword phrases occur in this position, the writer must help the reader chunk together these words. Sometimes the chunking is clear, but sometimes it is not.

Consider the following expression:

(54)   a slowly moving river

Knowing the parts of speech makes it easy to identify the phrases above. The participle *moving* modifies the noun *river*. The adverb *slowly* modifies the participle *moving*; it cannot modify the noun *river* because adverbs do not modify nouns.

Contrast the phrase above with the phrase

(55)   *a large box salesman

This phrase has a chunking problem, because the words can combine in more than one way, and so the phrase is ambiguous. On the one hand, the adjective *large* might modify the noun *box*, as below:

a <u>large box</u>   salesman
noun unit

NP

This corresponds to the meaning "a salesman who sells large boxes."

On the other hand, the nouns *box* and *salesman* may form a compound noun, and the adjective *large* might modify that compound, as the diagram below demonstrates:

a   large   <u>box   salesman</u>
                noun compound

<u>   </u>
AdjP

<u>   </u>
NP

This corresponds to the meaning "a box salesman who is large."

Fortunately, there is a piece of punctuation that clears up this ambiguity—the hyphen. The hyphen is inserted between the two words that should be chunked together. *A large-box salesman* means "a salesman who sells large boxes." *A large box-salesman* means "a box salesman who is large."

Hyphens are inserted wherever the possibility for ambiguity arises. For this reason, no hyphen is inserted between an adverb and an adjective because it is clear that the adverb modifies the adjective.

In general, you should add hyphens to prenoun modifiers whenever they are multiword phrases. This includes prepositional phrases when they act as prenoun modifiers:

(56)   the hole-in-the-wall gang

The hyphens here prevent the reader from misconstruing the phrase and reading it as meaning "the hole that is in the wall gang."

Exercise 6 will give you practice with hyphens.

EXERCISE 6

Correct the following sentences with regard to hyphens. Some sentences may need hyphens added. Some may need hyphens removed. Some sentences are correct as written.

1. This is a French-speaking community.

2. Johnnie spilled his drink watching that extremely-scary movie.

3. The newest dot-com ordered seven limousines for their fleet.

4. How much wood can a Norwegian woodchuck chuck in an hour?

5. Dell works at a crocheted sweater shop part time on the weekends.

6. During a full-time game, referees should maintain their hydration by drinking supplements during television time-outs.

7. Vanna turns vowel letter boxes with less enthusiasm than she turns consonant letter boxes.

8. The quickly drying apricots on the blanket were too much of a temptation to the small company manager.

9. A once in a lifetime opportunity awaits you if you call within the next ten minutes.

10. Computer rhetoric courses will be offered by the new department of Technology and Composition.

RELATIVE CLAUSES AND PARTICIPIAL PHRASES Another important adjectival is the **relative clause.** The following sentences demonstrate this construction:

(57)   Our dog, <u>who chases bats at night,</u> is a lovable mutt.

(58)   Please remove the car <u>that is blocking the driveway.</u>

The structure of relative clauses is different from that of subordinate clauses. Subordinate clauses consist of a subordinate conjunction and a complete sentence:

(59)   We still held the picnic, <u>though the weather forecast predicted rain.</u>

In this sentence we see the subordinate clause has the following parts:

subordinate conjunction ➲ though

complete sentence ➲ the weather forecast predicted rain

Relative clauses, however, consist of a **relative pronoun** and an incomplete sentence, as shown by the following analysis:

(57)   Our dog, *which chases bats at night,* is a lovable mutt.

relative pronoun ➲ which

incomplete sentence ➲ _____ chases bats at night

You might think of this incomplete sentence as a sentence with a gap in it. The gap is the size of a phrase that corresponds to the noun and any prenoun modifiers the relative clause is attached to. I will use *the filler* for this phrase that would complete the sentence or fill the gap:

filler ➲ our dog

sentence with a gap ➲ _____ chases bats at night

The gap in the sentence can occur anywhere. In (57) the gap is the subject; in (60), the direct object; and in (61) the object of a preposition:

(60)   Samantha bought the CD that you recommended.

filler ➲ the CD

sentence with a gap ➲ you recommended _____

(61)   I found the name of the doctor that you relied on.

        filler ➲ the doctor

        sentence with a gap ➲ you relied on _____

The relative pronouns in English are *that, who, which,* and *whose*. Another set of words can also head relative clauses—*where, when,* and *why*. When a relative pronoun is headed by *whose*, its structure is slightly different. The word *whose* is a filler for a missing possessive pronoun. Consider the structure of the sentence

(62)   The neighbor <u>whose house sold today</u> is moving to Phoenix.

The relative clause in (62) is based on the full sentence

(63)   The neighbor's house sold today.

        filler ➲ the neighbor

        sentence with a gap ➲ _____ house sold today

In this case, however, the filler does not exactly match the possessive noun needed to complete the sentence with a gap. The possessive suffix is always absent from that noun, and so sentence (62) has the words *the neighbor* instead of *the neighbor's.*

PUNCTUATION OF RELATIVE CLAUSES   There are two ways to punctuate relative clauses. In some cases, the relative clause is set off by commas. In other cases, there is no punctuation around the relative clause. As with other constructions, the punctuation choices correspond to a difference in meaning and structure.

Grammarians distinguish between restrictive and nonrestrictive relative clauses. Restrictive relative clauses are those in which the content in the relative clause restricts or identifies what the head noun refers to. They are not set off by commas, as in

(64)   Would the member who owns a blue Jaguar please move her car?

In this example, the relative clause *who owns a blue Jaguar* identifies who the question is directed to. One can see this difference if you compare sentence (64) to a version without the relative clause (65):

(65)   Would the member please move her car?

The missing relative clause changes the meaning of the core sentence dramatically. The noun phrase *the member* picks out a large number of individuals possibly referred to in the sentence, and the relative clause narrows down that set (hopefully, for the sake of the questioner, to one individual!).

Nonrestrictive relative clauses are those in which the content in the relative clause does not restrict or identify what the head noun refers to. They require commas to set them apart from the rest of the sentence. Nonrestrictive relative clauses, in essence, add extra information to the description evoked by the noun phrase, but they are not necessary to identifying who or what is being talked about. When the head noun refers to a unique individual, the relative clause is nonrestrictive, as in

(66)   My father, who is an engineer, was a first-generation college student.

In a world where I have only one father, the noun phrase *my father* picks out a unique individual. The relative clause doesn't narrow down the set of fathers any further but simply adds some more information about my father to the sentence. Again, it may be useful to compare the original sentence in (66) to a version with the relative clause missing (67):

(67)   My father was a first-generation college student.

The core meaning of the two sentences is not affected by the relative clause.

Distinguishing between restrictive and nonrestrictive relative clauses can be tricky, but there are some useful rules of thumb for making a judgment.

1. If the relative clause is headed by *that,* it is always restrictive. If you can substitute *that* for the relative pronoun, it must be a restrictive relative clause.

2. If the relative clause is headed by *which,* it is usually nonrestrictive. Some writers consistently use *which* only in nonrestrictive clauses, but other writers are less strict in their usage.

3. If the relative pronoun can be eliminated, it is a restrictive relative clause.

4. If the head noun has only one referent, the relative clause is nonrestrictive.

Rule 1 is useful when you encounter relative clauses that you are unsure about. Notice how the relative pronoun *that* cannot be substituted in the example below, and this demonstrates that the sentence contains a nonrestrictive relative clause:

(66a)   *My father, that is an engineer, was a first-generation college student.

Rule 3 is applicable only when the relative clause does not contain a missing subject. The relative pronoun *who* cannot be eliminated from the example below because the subject is missing. Nonetheless, it still contains a restrictive relative clause:

(64a)   *Would the member owns a blue Jaguar please move her car?

Otherwise, this test will distinguish between restrictive and nonrestrictive relative clauses with missing objects. Sentence (67) contains a restrictive relative clause because the relative pronoun can be deleted, as in (67a):

(67)   Samantha bought the CD <u>that</u> you recommended.

(67a)   Samantha bought the CD you recommended.

However, sentence (68) contains a nonrestrictive relative clause because its relative pronoun cannot be deleted, as in (68a):

(68)   My sister, <u>whom</u> her college named "Alumnus of the Year," collects Urdu manuscripts.

(68a)   *My sister, her college named "Alumnus of the Year," collects Urdu manuscripts.

Rule 4 is easiest to apply when the head noun is a proper noun. Other noun phrases like *the sun* and *the world,* along with expressions like *my oldest sister,* also pick out unique referents. Some noun phrases may pick out unique referents in context. For example, in a given setting, the phrase *the customer who is sitting by the window* refers to a unique person sitting by a window; otherwise its frame of reference is the innumerable customers sitting by innumerable windows across the earth!

You should note, though, that all of these phrases may not pick out unique referents in some uses. Proper nouns normally pick out unique referents, but we can use them as common nouns, as (69) shows:

(69)   I have a paper belonging to a Michelle who has bad handwriting.

This exercise asks you to evaluate relative clauses.

EXERCISE 7

Correct the punctuation of the relative clauses in the following sentences. Some need commas added. Some need commas eliminated. Some are correct as written.

1. The president who is staying at Camp David this weekend must decide whether or not to veto the new bill passed by Congress.

2. The police captured the subject, that attempted to jump bail.

3. Strictly speaking, my only sister, who eats snails once a week, is allergic to uncooked vegetables.

4. Our moon which is a big hunk of rock is no place to buy real estate.

5. The proposition that you uttered could come back to haunt you if this dispute goes to the court.

6. Forces, which cross the border, will be attacked on sight.

7. Carol shifted the schedule, that you agreed on, forward one hour.

8. The National Fruit Salad Company moved its headquarters to southeast Asia which is a great place for tropical fruits.

9. Unless the economy improves soon, I'll have to sell my house, which I have lived in for fifteen years.

10. That man, whom the homeowner's association recently approached, is not available to conduct the water-quality study on the lake.

REDUCED RELATIVE CLAUSES Another kind of adjectival relates to relative clauses that are reduced in form. These reduced relative clauses, or participial phrases, are similar to full relative clauses in meaning and function. We have already seen that the relative pronoun can be deleted for certain restrictive relative clauses:

(70)   The apples that you bought dried out quickly.

(70a)   The apples you bought dried out quickly.

One can also delete the auxiliary verbs in a relative clause that are in the progressive tense or passive voice:

(71)   The candidate <u>who is gaining the most votes</u> is Ben Stilman.

(71a)   The candidate <u>gaining the most votes</u> is Ben Stilman.

(72)   A floor <u>that has been mopped by the Turbomopper</u> will maintain its sheen longer.

(72a)   A floor <u>mopped by the Turbomopper</u> will maintain its sheen longer.

Sentences (71a) and (72a) contain examples of participial phrases. Either a past or present participle and its associated phrases can form a participial phrase that functions as an adjectival.

Participial phrases, or reduced relative clauses, can be restrictive or nonrestrictive, just like full relative clauses. Restrictive reduced relative clauses take no commas, while nonrestrictive relative clauses take commas before and after them:

(71a)   The candidate gaining the most votes is Ben Stilman. [restrictive]

(73)   The mountain lion, gathering all his strength, made a mighty leap. [nonrestrictive]

As you did in Exercise 7, evaluate the reduced relative clauses in Exercise 8.

EXERCISE 8

Correct the punctuation for the reduced relative clauses in the following sentences. Some sentences need commas. Some sentences need commas deleted. Some are correct as written.

1. Clouds, gathering on the horizon, threatened the community cleanup.

2. My old laptop, forgotten by my family, gathered dust in the attic.

3. The lawn sprinkled with dew sparkled like a diamond.

4. Sadie could not see the one dog, lying at her feet.

5. The Scillibus sunk in 1504 is likely to be the wreckage you see off the coast.

6. The polar bear using his left paw swatted at the jumping fish.

7. In this picture are teeth, suffering from years of neglect.

8. Thirty-five percent of all the people, using personal ads for dating, are already married.

9. Dr. Angus, filled with creative ideas, started a Chihuahua farm.

10. The player hitting the best right now is the shortstop.

OTHER POSTNOMINAL ADJECTIVALS Other adjectivals that follow the noun include prepositional phrases (74), adjective phrases (75) and (76), and noun phrases (77). We looked at prepositional phrases inside of noun phrases in Chapter 5. These modify the noun just as adjectives do. We can also use adjectives that are coordinated or modified by prepositional phrases. Another postnominal modifier is a full noun phrase, often called an appositive (77).

(74)   The title <u>of the book</u> was *The Clothed Gun.*

(75)   The bull, <u>weary and wounded</u>, nervously eyed the matador.

(76)   The casino manager smiled at the young gambler, <u>flush with money</u>.

(77)   The winning raffle ticket belongs to Betty Burnett, <u>a salesperson in Region 5</u>.

What's interesting is that, apart from the prepositional phrases, these other adjectivals can also appear before the noun phrase they modify:

(75a)   <u>Weary and wounded</u>, the bull nervously eyed the matador.

(76a)   <u>Flush with money</u>, the young gambler caught the casino manager's eye.

(77a)   <u>A salesperson in Region 5</u>, Betty Burnett held the winning raffle ticket.

These phrases can be seen as a kind of reduced relative clauses. All of them could be converted into full relative clauses:

(75b)   The bull, who was weary and wounded, nervously eyed the matador.

(76b)   The casino manager smiled at the young gambler, who was flush with money.

(77b)   The winning raffle ticket belongs to Betty Burnett, who is a salesperson in Region 5.

Absolute Phrases

In addition to adverbials and adjectivals, one last modifier we will look at is the **absolute phrase.** This marvelous phrase can be tricky to recognize because it consists of a subject and a partial verb phrase. Examine the following sentences that contain absolute phrases:

(78)   The wide receiver caught the last-second pass in the end zone, <u>a smile on his face</u>.

(79)   The police officer, <u>her eyes scanning the abandoned car</u>, walked slowly across the country road.

(80)   The real estate agent frowned at the house, <u>its lawn burned by the August sun</u>.

The key to identifying these phrases is understanding how they differ from a complete sentence. Absolute phrases are similar to independent clauses that are missing their *be*-verb. This could be the main verb, as in the absolute clause of sentence (78):

(78a)   a smile on his face ➲ A smile <u>was</u> on his face.

It could be the *be*-verb from a sentence in the present or past progressive tense, as in the absolute clause of (79):

(79a)   her eyes scanning the abandoned car ➲ Her eyes <u>were</u> scanning the abandoned car.

It could also be the *be*-verb from a passive sentence, as in the absolute phrase of (80):

(80a)   its lawn burned by the August sun ➲ Its lawn <u>was</u> burned by the August sun.

You can combine sentences by turning one of them into an absolute phrase if it either has a *be*-verb or can be changed into a sentence with a *be*-verb. For example, suppose you want to combine the following two sentences:

(81)   The fisherman motored his bass boat down the channel.

(82)   His cat stared intently at the surface of the water.

Neither sentence has the required *be*-verb. However, you could rewrite the second sentence so that it has a *be*-verb by changing its tense from simple past to past progressive:

His cat stared intently at the surface of the water. ➲

His cat was staring intently at the surface of the water.

This new sentence can then become the basis for an absolute phrase joining the two sentences together:

(83)   The fisherman motored his bass boat down the channel, his cat staring intently at the surface of the water.

Can all sentences be turned into absolute phrases? Not very easily. Consider sentences (84) and (85). What happens if we wish to combine them by turning one into an absolute phrase?

(84)   Edna had finished painting the house.

(85)   Edison wanted to put in a deck.

Possible sentences include (86) and (87):

(86)   *Edna having finished painting the house, Edison wanted to put in a deck.

(87)   *Edna had finished painting the house, Edison wanting to put in a deck.

Unfortunately, neither one of these sentences makes a good absolute phrase. Notice that neither (84) or (85) easily takes a *be*-verb without dramatically changing the meaning:

(84a)   Edna was finishing painting the house. ⮌ Edna had finished painting the house.

(85a)   Edison was wanting to put in a deck. ➜ Edison wanted to put in a deck.

The following exercise will give you practice in crafting absolute phrases.

Rewrite the following pairs of sentences as a single sentence containing an absolute phrase.

1. Lizzie had too much to do before the end of the semester.

Her term papers had piled up.

2. Buzz Groenen relaxed for the first time in his life.

His drive-in funeral parlor was a great success.

3. Aunt Betty sent for the doctor.

Her brother's condition was worsening.

4. A lone horse trotted out of the canyon.

Its saddle was askew on its back.

5. All three candidates stayed awake during the night.

The election was too close to call.

6. Schraeder laughed hysterically.

His roommate had rolled off the bunk bed without waking.

7. The alien piloted his star cruiser towards our solar system.

The earth looked inviting.

8. Dr. Glenn sent out an S.O.S.

The boat sank under his feet.

9. Sykes ran his first mile under four minutes last June.

His pace was superb.

10. Honeymooners watch the sun set from these cliffs.

Their dreams float over the trees.

The Structure of Sentences with Modifiers

At this point, it might be useful to think about adverbials and adjectivals with respect to the overall structure of the sentence. These modifiers constitute phrases themselves and so will form their own chunk with the sentence. In addition, adverbials after the verb wil be part of the verb phrase. Adjectivals, whether before or after the noun, will be part of the noun phrase. An example of both is given in sentence (88) with its analysis in Figure 10.1.

(88)   The polo field at the club was muddy yesterday.

Here, the adjectival prepositional phrase *at the club* is part of the noun phrase *the polo field at the club*. The adverbial time phrase *yesterday* is part of the verb phrase *was muddy yesterday.*

If an adverbial appears at the front of the sentence, as in sentence (89) with its analysis in Figure 10.2, we can diagram it as a stand-alone phrase that combines with the subject and the verb phrase to make a sentence.

(89)   Without a doubt, Morris the Cat died at the age of seventeen.

In the case of subordinate clauses, we can diagram these adverbials as separate phrases that combine with an independent clause to make a complete sentence, as in sentence (90) with its analysis in Figure 10.3.

(90)   Ellie was enjoying the craps game until she rolled a twelve.

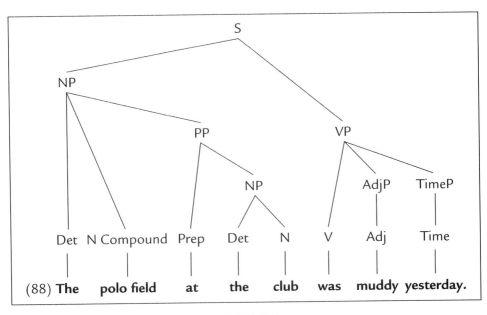

FIGURE 10.1

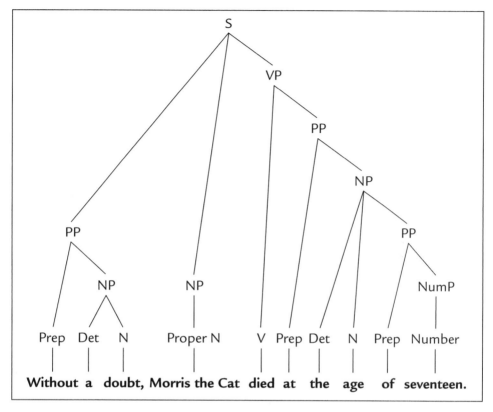

FIGURE 10.2

Modifiers in general, then, follow principles already developed in this book with regard to phrases.

The following exercise gives you practice in recognizing where modifiers go in English sentence structure.

Frank and Ernest

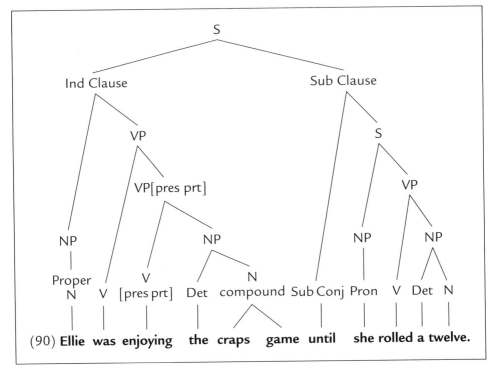

FIGURE 10.3

EXERCISE 10

Identify and diagram all phrases with modifiers in the following sentences.

1. After George invited Rachel for a date, he served her chicken and red wine.

2. Dewey tried to eat fifty eggs in an hour because he saw *Cool Hand Luke*.

3. No bees could be found in the apiary, sitting empty and sad.

4. Before its destruction, the World Trade Center had 43,600 windows.

5. The Luxembourg Garden, located in Paris, is not in Luxembourg.

6. The detective held the shred of flag that was blue and ripped.

7. The bus driver and the sewer worker came upon a stranded motorist, attractive but quiet.

8. Busby could play drafts, the British name for checkers, in Manchester.

9. Whenever you meet a boy born between cannons on a British warship, you have met a son of a gun.

10. At the corners of the infield, the Catamounts had freshmen.

The Placement of Modifiers

Besides knowing what adverbials and adjectivals look like so that you can discern the structure of a sentence, you the writer need to develop your ability to use these modifiers. Much of the power of our writing comes from altering the word order of sentences. In particular, the word order of adverbials and adjectivals allows us to convey nuances and connotations of meaning that give written language its beauty and its power.

As you will see in Chapter 11, one major effect of the placement of modifiers is on **intonation**: the pitch of our voice rises and falls throughout an utterance. When we place a modifier in a less-common place in the sentence, there is a corresponding change in the intonational pattern that potentially changes the attention drawn to individual elements and even the overall meaning of the sentence.

Say the following sentences aloud and notice where the pitch of your voice rises:

(91a)   The weary and wounded bull nervously eyed the matador.

(91b)   The bull, weary and wounded, nervously eyed the matador.

(91c)   Weary and wounded, the bull nervously eyed the matador.

The first example draws attention to the adjectives because they are in their usual prenominal position. A typical utterance of (91a) would have a slight rise in pitch on *weary* and *wounded* but no rise on the noun *bull*:

The WEAry and WOUNded bull NERVOUSly eyed the MATador.

In example (91c), more attention is drawn to the adjectives because they occur before the noun phrase *the bull*, which they modify. Again, there is no rise on the noun *bull* in the subject position:

WEAry and WOUNded, the bull NERVOUSly eyed the MATador.

Example (91b) has a word order that not only draws more attention to the adjectives but also to the noun *bull*:

The BULL, WEARY and WOUNDED, NERvously eyed the MATador.

As you will see in Chapter 11, a comma not only slows the reader down but also leads to a slight rise in pitch on the word before the comma, in this case the noun *bull* in subject position. Subjects in English don't normally receive a peak in pitch, but one way to raise the pitch on the subject is to insert material after it and set off this material by commas.

Exercise 11 will let you experiment with the placement of modifiers.

<hr>

EXERCISE 11

Add the modifier to each corresponding sentence in two different locations. Then say the sentences aloud and listen to where the pitch of your voice rises. Explain the effect each placement would have on the intonation and the meaning of the sentence.

1. The book was banned in twelve countries.

   Modifier: controversial but insightful

2. The crew navigated the river.

   Modifier: high above flood stage

3. The Mad Hatter's ears twitched in the moonlight.

   Modifier: longer than a rabbit's

4. Joltin' Joe belted that home run.

   Modifier: sailing down the avenue

5. The bulldog of Canton roamed any street he wanted to.

   Modifier: an intimidating canine

6. The president wanted an ambassador for that difficult post.

   Modifier: strong-willed yet flexible

7. The price of petroleum kept many people home that summer.

   Modifier: rising each week

8. U Thant was the secretary-general of the United Nations during the Cuban missile crisis.

   Modifier: a man for all seasons

9. The candy company is developing a flavor.

   Modifier: bold and surprising

10. Laurie walked out of that movie.

Modifier: filled with clichés

COMPREHENSION QUESTIONS

1. What are adverbials?

2. Name four different types of adverbials.

3. What are dangling clauses? How can they be diagnosed?

4. What grammatical problems arise in the use of comparison clauses?

5. What are absolute phrases? How can you recognize their form?

6. What are adjectivals?

7. What is the punctuation rule for two or more adjectives inside a noun phrase?

8. When should hyphens be used inside a noun phrase?

9. How do relative clauses differ from subordinate clauses in structure?

10. What is the difference between restrictive and nonrestrictive relative clauses?

11. What are reduced relative clauses and participial phrases?

12. What considerations can help a writer determine when to place adjectivals before or after the noun phrase?

11

Structuring Information in Writing

PREVIEW *Knowing the structure of English, as it has been presented in the previous chapters, allows us to talk about and understand the variation between writing and speaking, particularly with regard to how we package information in both. This chapter will introduce some basic ideas about intonation, which writing lacks, and explain why, as a result, word order must be more tightly controlled in writing than in speech.*

Intonation

One of the most marvelous aspects of speech is intonation. When we speak, our voices go up and down. Our pitch rises and falls. Sometimes we tell jokes about the professor who speaks with a flat voice, but in reality no person truly speaks in a strict monotone. Everyone's voice changes in pitch, and it is a good thing that is so. It would be incredibly difficult to understand one another without intonation, because the changes in pitch give us clues about how to chunk together words when we are listening to someone.

Intonation is like a melody, and the human voice has a kind of music to it. We can see this by considering what the melody might sound like for an actual sentence. A line drawn above the following sentence signifies a typical intonational pattern:

All the intelligence and talent in the world can't make a singer.
(Willa Cather)

The peaks of the line show where the speaker's pitch rises. The valleys show where the pitch goes lower. There are a couple of things you might notice about this intonational pattern. First, the pitch tends to go up on the words that have more content. Thus, we see peaks on words like *intelligence* and *talent* but not on *in* and *the*. Second, the highest peak occurs at the end of the sentence, in this case on the word *singer*.

Intonation communicates a lot of information to listeners, including how we intend to structure the information of our sentences. In particular, intonation often corresponds to the way we package new and old information. Our sentences normally contain both types. The old information serves the very important task of linking everything we say to what we already know or what has already been said. Without old information in a sentence, we would have a very hard time figuring out the meaning and relevance of the sentence. The new information carries the discourse forward. Without new information, there would be no point to what we are talking about. Typically, the highest intonation peak of the sentence tends to fall on the new information. The old information or topic will usually be associated with a low pitch. This common intonational pattern is called **end focus.** The intonational peak draws a hearer's attention to the new information and makes it easier for him to identify and interpret its novel contribution to the sentence.

To get a feel for end focus, speak aloud the following sentences in a normal manner and listen to your own pitch:

(1)   My hardest class was organic chemistry.

(2)   That textbook cost $130.

(3)   Heart attacks may be caused by viruses.

(4)   Yak's milk is pink.

One of the great things about speech is that we are not limited to end focus; rather, we can elevate our pitch at any point in the sentence. Consequently, we can use many different word orders as well. For example, if the word *Judy* is the new information in a sentence, it might appear at the end, with end focus:

(5)   That delicious cake was baked by Judy.

However, I could also speak the sentence with the new information word *Judy* at the front if I place an intonation peak at that point:

(6)   JUDY baked that delicious cake.

A sentence like (6), though, may lead to a problem when it is used in writing. When we write, we don't draw squiggly lines above our sentences to show our readers what intonational pattern they should read with. Yet readers read with intonation: their internal voice rises and falls in pitch as they take in the words from the printed page. A reader will typically read a sentence with a typical intonational contour, which in many cases is end focus. However, writers sometimes write the way they speak. The new information is often paramount in their mind, which means that they put it first in the sentence. This leads to the kind of anomalies illustrated in the following sequences. Which one of the following paragraphs sounds more natural?

> (7)   I came home and found a delicious cake on the counter. I tried a slice, and it was fantastic. However, I wasn't sure who made it, so I called my roommate at work and confirmed my suspicions. This delicious cake was baked by Judy.

> (8)   I came home and found a delicious cake on the counter. I tried a slice, and it was fantastic. However, I wasn't sure who made it, so I called my roommate at work and confirmed my suspicions. Judy baked this delicious cake.

The two paragraphs are identical except for the last sentence. Paragraph (8) sounds slightly odd, although there is nothing unusual about its content. This oddness comes from intonation. A reader will tend to read each sentence with end focus. The end focus in the last sentence of paragraph (7) occurs on the word *Judy*, which conveys the information that is sought in the previous sentences. Hence, the paragraph reads naturally.

In the last sentence of (8), the end focus falls on the phrase *that delicious cake*. This, however, causes a problem. The highest intonation peak of the sentence should coincide with the words that convey the most important information in that sentence. However, the phrase *that delicious cake* is old information in the paragraph. The most important information in the last sentence is the identification of who baked the cake, but unfortunately that information appears at the beginning of the sentence, in a place where readers don't tend to expect it. Therefore, paragraph (8) has an awkward feel to it.

Now notice that if the above paragraphs were being spoken rather than written, then either one would work. Paragraph (8) would probably be spoken as follows:

> (8a)   I came home and found a delicious cake on the counter. I tried a slice, and it was fantastic. However, I wasn't sure who made it, so I call my roommate at work and confirmed my suspicions. JUDY baked this delicious cake.

The great advantage of speaking is the flexibility we have because of intonation. The reader can put stress on any word in any location in the sentence. Putting a greater stress on the word *Judy* allows the hearer to process the sentence easily, and so the exact location of the word *Judy* in the sentence is less important in speaking. Again, though, because we don't write intonational contours into our written sentences, we must make up for their absence by paying more attention to the arrangement of our words so that our readers will assign intonational peaks to the information we as writers consider most important.

Here is one more example of an intonational breakdown in a written paragraph:

(9)   Gus-Gus was a greedy mouse. Rather than attend to danger, he piled on kernel after kernel of corn in his arms, determined to bring every last one to his mouse hole. Gus-Gus was unable to see over the top of his pile of corn and so did not notice that his progress was suddenly halted by a barrier. Mean old Lucifer was standing in his way.

The new information is the phrase *mean old Lucifer,* yet if the reader puts end focus on the phrase *his way,* the sentence will sound awkward, and it will be less easy to understand.

New and Old Information

In our previous discussion, we saw how end focus relates to the presentation of old and new information. As we have seen, sentences in a piece of writing usually contain a combination of both. The reason for including old information is two-fold: it helps us to link each sentence to what has been said before so that the entire discourse has a sense of cohesion, and it also helps us to make sense of the new information, which is what spurs the reader.

The importance of combining old and new information can be seen if we look at extreme examples. What would a discourse look like if it had old information? It would be profoundly uninteresting. The reader would not continue reading because there would be no point to what was being said. It might look something like the paragraph in (10).

(10)   Grammar is important to all who use language. In addition, knowing how sentences are put together helps those who need to compose. Also, people would benefit from understanding the structure of English. Furthermore, a knowledge of grammar will aid them when they try to figure out the meaning of sentences they encounter.

Yes, quite bo-o-or-ing. Each sentence really only contains old information, so the paragraph doesn't develop.

What would a discourse look like if it contained all new information? It might look like

(11)   Grammar is important to all who use language. For example, determiners precede nouns in English. Also, spoken English includes intonational contours. Finally, verbs can be identified by looking for words with verbal suffixes.

The main problem with this paragraph is that each sentence lacks old information, the words that would help link it to something earlier in the text.

Discourse works much better when it has the kind of balanced structure shown in (12):

(12)

Old info . . . new info. Old info . . . new info.

Old info . . . new info. Old info . . . new info.

Old info . . . new info. Old info . . . new info.

Old info . . . new info. Old info . . . new info.

The old information is the hook that fits a sentence to previous context. The new information stimulates the reader to keep reading. It is difficult for a reader to maintain attention without a little bit of novelty in each sentence to move the discourse along.

The intonational pattern of end focus corresponds to this common ordering of old and new information. The highest intonational peak occurs at the end of the sentence, where the new information often appears. We can listen to where the intonational peaks occur in a sentence, and we can also evaluate the information of the sentence and observe where the old and new information are placed. Sometimes when we write, we fail to place information correctly in a sentence. It is not uncommon to hear a student say, "I write like I speak." This can lead to the following scenario: In composing a sentence, a writer grapples with the wording. For her, new information is uppermost in her mind, and so the sentence she composes begins with that information. However, starting the sentence with new information violates the reader's expectations. It doesn't correspond to the typical end-focus pattern we read with, so a breakdown in the cohesion of the text occurs. This is a prime reason why we cannot write the way we speak.

The following exercise asks you to evaluate some sentences for cohesion.

EXERCISE 1

Evaluate the following passages with respect to cohesion and breakdowns in the packaging of old and new information. Rewrite those that need correction. Some passages may be coherent as written.

1. Theaters have all kinds of superstitions. To say "Macbeth" is bad luck in one.

2. Many sports events use champagne to celebrate a victory. Milk is traditionally drunk by the winner in the Indianapolis 500.

3. If you hit the golf ball in the hole in the required number of shots, you score a par. One under par is a birdie. Two under par is an eagle.

4. Many people question the wisdom of the NBA for allowing high school players to be drafted before they enter the college, but we can't blame the NBA for starting the whole thing. The National Football League originated the college draft.

5. Our northern neighbor is Canada. Our southern neighbor is Mexico. Many people don't realize that Russia is our next closest neighbor.

6. Bad economies tend to threaten charitable giving. This has not generally affected the United Way. In 1991 when its president was indicted for embezzlement and fraud, donations were down that year. Otherwise since 1971 they have increased every year.

7. Astronomers were hoping to find a planet in that star system. A wobble in the first star was noticed by them.

8. There is a tension in every conversation. The speaker wants to produce speech efficiently. The hearer wants maximal distinctions and clarity in the words.

9. Randy thought Baby Red's injury was fully healed. Though the trail was muddy, all the way home he galloped that horse.

10. If you drink that, you will get sick. Flies are in the buttermilk.

Vague Errors

There is a real payoff to knowing the differences between spoken and written language. I remember getting term papers back from teachers with the comment "awk" written in red ink. I knew, then, that something was awkward in my sentences, but I didn't always know exactly what was wrong. "Awk" is an example of vague error correction. It is sometimes used when the teacher knows there is a weakness in a sentence but cannot pin down the exact fault. Vagueness in error identification is usually a hindrance to solving problems. If you can clearly identify a problem, you are that much closer to solving it. For developing writers and students who have difficulty diagnosing their own errors, vague error-correction hinders their attempts to revise, because they may not be able to correct a sentence with "awk" or some other vague error label without more help.

For those of you who are going to be teachers some day, suppose you come across a problem that you cannot diagnose with the wording in a student's paper. You write down something vague on the paper; the student knows there is something wrong but despite his best intentions is unable to pinpoint the problem. If he comes up to you and asks for some specific help, in particular, if he asks what the exact breakdown is in his writing, will you be able to help him? Or will you be forced to say, "There is something wrong. Just rewrite the sentence"? This can also hold true for you who are going to write and edit some day. Can you diagnose your own difficulties? A subgoal of this book is to help you be specific when you identify weaknesses in your own or someone else's writing.

The kinds of problems we looked at above are often areas that can lead to vague error labels. These are places where one senses some problem in cohesion yet finds no problem in the actual words or conveyed content. If you learn to listen for intonation, you can teach your students (or yourself) to listen for the reader's voice, how he might read a particular sentence in a way that clashes with the writer's intention, and then you can show the writer how she can reorder her words to take advantage of the reader's voice.

Reordering the Sentence

Because we do not mark intonation in writing, we must rely more heavily on word order. As a matter of fact, in addition to word choice, the ability to change the order of words in a sentence is one of the marks of a skilled writer. Besides the basic order of subject–verb–direct object, the English language provides a number of other patterns that change the intonational contour of the sentence and so allow for a different reading than end focus supplies. Now that you are familiar with the basic categories and phrases of the sentence, these alternative sentence patterns will be easier to understand. One of the things you can notice as you read is that when you come across an unusual sentence pattern, it normally has the effect of throwing more attention onto some part of the sentence that wouldn't get as much attention in its typical position. The following sections will discuss some of the patterns that change the intonation of the sentence and, along with that, its packaging of information.

Frank and Ernest

©1997 Thaves. Reprinted with permission. Newspaper dist. by NEA, Inc.

INVERSION Sentences with verbs like *be* and *come* can change the order of their subjects and subject complements or phrases that follow the *be*-verb. The following sentences are examples:

(13)   The climb was quite breathtaking.

(13a)   Quite breathtaking was the climb.   [inversion]

(14)   The storm comes over the mountains.

(14a)   Over the mountains comes the storm.   [inversion]

(15)   Garfield is composing a sonnet.

(15a)   Composing a sonnet is Garfield.   [inversion]

Inverted sentences may sound odd out of context, but they can be effective in a text where issues of cohesion and emphasis arise. One reason a writer might invert a sentence is to place the subject at the end of the clause so that it receives an intonation peak. The following paragraph demonstrates this tactic:

(16)   [1] Around the year 449, Germanic tribes began to invade Britain. [2] For over a century, they traveled to the British Isles, sometimes as settlers but often as conquerors. [3] From the northern half of Denmark came the Jutes. [4] Schleswig-Holstein in the south was the home of Angles. [5] Further south was the staging point for the Saxons. [6] These incursions changed the history of Britain forever and eventually led to the Germanic language we know today as English.

Sentences 3, 4, and 5 all exhibit **inversion.** The subjects (the Jutes, the Angles, and the Saxons) appear after their respective verbs in the location for end focus. These sentences as written draw attention to the names of the tribes rather than the geography from which they came.

PASSIVES We have already discussed passive sentences in Chapter 8. Now we can think about how passive constructions affect our writing. In the past, it would not be uncommon to hear a teacher discourage the use of passive sentences because they are wordier than active sentences. They also can be used ineffectively by developing writers. However, use of the passive voice is one technique in our arsenal for altering the intonational pattern of a sentence. If the information conveyed by a subject is new information or information that the writer wants to highlight in some way, a passive sentence might be appropriate. Consider the following active sentence:

(17)   A crocodile attacked Ludwig.

If *a crocodile* was the new information added to a text, this could be an instance where the passive version would work well. In the passive counterpart, the noun phrase *a crocodile* is moved toward the end of the sentence, into end focus position:

(17a)   Ludwig was attacked by a crocodile.

Notice how the following paragraph sounds with either (17) or (17a) in it:

(18)   version with sentence (17)

> Loyal friend and world-famous traveler, Ludwig Lloyd has had quite a year. After winning three bake-offs for his culinary creativity, Ludwig gained 25 pounds in one week to star in a movie about the infamous pool hustler Minnesota Fats. His Fourth of July party attracted over 3,000 people from ten different countries. He received awards from the presidents of three countries and wrote two books in Fijian and Swahili. Although you would never know it to look at him, <u>a crocodile attacked Ludwig</u>. And yes, the crocodile regretted the incident.

(18a)   version with sentence (17a)

> Loyal friend and world-famous traveler, Ludwig Lloyd has had quite a year. After winning three bake-offs for his culinary creativity, Ludwig gained 25 pounds in one week to star in a movie about the infamous pool hustler Minnesota Fats. His Fourth of July party attracted over 3,000 people from ten different countries. He received awards from the presidents of three countries and wrote two books in Fijian and Swahili. Although you would never know it to look at him, <u>Ludwig was attacked by a crocodile</u>. And yes, the crocodile regretted the incident.

Paragraph (18a) sounds more cohesive because the reader's voice would naturally peak on the noun phrase *a crocodile,* and the reader would unconsciously note that it is new information.

IT-CLEFTS Another way of focusing the reader's attention is by using **cleft sentences.** The *it*-cleft pattern consists of the pronoun *it* and some form of a *be*-verb at the beginning of the sentence. After this beginning comes one of the noun phrases from a standard sentence. The rest of the original sentence then becomes a relative clause. Sentence (19) thus becomes either (20) or (21):

> (19)   The new manager trimmed the yew tree.
>
> (20)   It was <u>the new manager</u> <u>who trimmed the yew tree</u>.
>   NP   Rel Cl
>
> (21)   It was <u>the yew tree</u> <u>that the new manager trimmed</u>.
>   NP   Rel Cl

This pattern throws emphasis on the phrase following *it* plus the *be*-verb:

> (19a)   The new manager trimmed the YEW tree.
>
> (20a)   It was the new MANager who trimmed the yew tree.
>
> (21a)   It was the YEW tree that the new manager trimmed.

The subjects of English sentences often do not receive an intonation peak, but notice how you can stress the subject phrase in (19) by placing it in an *it*-cleft, as in (20). Similarly, though the direct object phrase in (19) would normally receive end-focus stress, you can give it a contrastive stress by placing it in an *it*-cleft, as in (21), which would be appropriate for a context like that given in (21b):

> (21b)   I know you thought you saw pine branches on the ground, but <u>it was the yew tree that the new manager trimmed</u>.

This context sounds less natural with sentence (19):

> (19b)   I know you thought you saw pine branches on the ground, but <u>the new manager trimmed the yew tree</u>.

It-clefts are the kind of sentences that can be a problem for writers. Grammar checkers flag them, and writing teachers caution against their wordiness. However, they can be quite effective at the right location in a text because of their power to focus the reader's attention.

WH-CLEFTS Cleft sentences can also begin with a question word (*who, what, where, why, how, when*), as in

> (22)   What the new manager trimmed was the yew tree.

We can form a *wh*-cleft by separating one phrase from a standard sentence:

(23)   The new manager trimmed the yew tree.

↻

(22a)   <u>The new manager trimmed</u>   <u>the yew tree</u>
        S(gap)   NP

Then the appropriate question word is added to the sentence to make it a *wh*-clause.

(22b)   <u>What the new manager trimmed</u>   <u>the yew tree</u>
        Wh-Clause   NP

Finally, the appropriate *be*-verb is added between the *wh*-clause and the displaced phrase at the end of the sentence:

(22)   <u>What the new manager trimmed</u>   <u>was</u>   <u>the yew tree</u>.
        Wh-Clause   be-verb   NP

This also can be done with subjects and other phrases in the sentence, as in (23a–c):

(23)   The new manager trimmed the yew tree.

↻

(23a)   <u>trimmed the yew tree</u>   <u>the new manager</u>
        S(gap)   NP

↻

(23b)   <u>Who trimmed the yew tree</u>   <u>the new manager</u>
        Wh-Clause   NP

↻

(23c)   <u>Who trimmed the yew tree</u>   <u>was</u>   <u>the new manager</u>.
        Wh-Clause   be-verb   NP

The phrase that appears in end focus in a *wh*-cleft receives an intonational peak. Thus, this pattern allows a writer to emphasize what would otherwise be a subject, as in (23c). It also increases the emphasis for what would otherwise be a direct object. The noun phrase *the yew tree* in (23), which receives end focus there, would receive even greater stress in (22). The *wh*-cleft (22) is longer than the basic sentence (23), and the slightly longer time it takes to read the *wh*-cleft as compared to the basic sentence heightens the anticipation as the reader waits to find out what the new manager trimmed.

It-clefts and *wh*-clefts are not common in speech. A moment's reflection should tell us why. Cleft sentences have a more complicated structure than basic sentences, and this means that they are harder to compose during spontaneous speech. Furthermore, the speaker has all the resources of her intonation and can throw prominence on any word she wishes no matter where it appears in the sentence. Cleft sentences are more common in writing, where they are a good example of what writers must do to compensate for the loss of intonation. Writers cannot mark where their pitch goes up and down, but they can manipulate the order of words and phrases in their sentences, and good writers are masters at this.

The following exercise asks you to experiment with *wh*-cleft sentences.

EXERCISE 2

Write five ordinary sentences. Then change them into *wh*-clefts by displacing the verb phrase from each sentence. Finally, describe in your own words what systematic changes must be made to the sentence to make it a *wh*-cleft with a displaced verb phrase.

THERE-SENTENCES Sentences with *be*-verbs can be altered by adding the word *there* as the subject and moving the former subject after the *be*-verb:

(24)   A raging storm is bearing down on the coast.

(24a)   There is a raging storm bearing down on the coast.

This pattern, like inversion, has the effect of moving the subject to a later position in the sentence and thereby focusing more attention on it. This is why *there*-sentences commonly introduce stories and pieces of writing. They work well when a writer wants to introduce a character or situation into her prose. She can then treat her subject as new information, as is done with that well-known story beginning

(25)   Once upon a time, there was _____
                                        New Emphasis

Exercise 3 will give you practice in manipulating word order.

EXERCISE 3

Rewrite the following sentences according to one of the patterns listed above. Then state what effect it would have on the intonation and the meaning of the sentence.

1. Kaplan didn't like being a Capricorn or having a birthday on New Year's Day.

2. Prisoners captured by Venice were marched down the Bridge of Sighs.

3. The number-one killer in industrialized countries is heart disease.

4. The "ghost" who galloped the fastest was Red Grange.

5. A cow's sweat glands are in its nose.

6. He may have been an inventor, but Orville Wright flew for forty-three years without a pilot's license.

7. Americans eat more bananas than oranges.

8. You have to be at least thirty-five to become president of the United States.

9. Dr. Benjamin Spock led the National Committee Against the Vietnam War.

10. The cow jumped over the moon, and the dish ran away with the spoon.

OTHER VARIATIONS IN WORD ORDER Besides the general patterns listed above, still other ways exist to vary the order of words and phrases in a sentence. Elements inside the verb phrase can sometimes occur in more than one position.

(26)   The Quincys threw <u>a really, really big party</u> <u>two days ago</u>.

(27)   The Quincys threw <u>two days ago</u> <u>a really, really big party</u>.

Though the words and phrases are the same in both (26) and (27), what is conveyed by the two sentences changes with the alternate word order. In (27), the noun phrase *a really, really big party* receives more emphasis than it does in (26), and the time adverbial *two days ago* is de-emphasized. Every variation in word order alters the intonation our audience reads with and consequently their understanding of a text.

Similarly, phrases in the verb phrase can appear at the beginning of the sentence. Compare the basic sentence (28) with its alternate (28a):

(28)   Chance forgot to buy the mouthwash.

(28a)   The mouthwash Chance forgot to buy.

In (28), the old information is in the noun phrase *Chance*. In (28a), the old information is most likely to be in the noun phrase *the mouthwash*. There is also the possibility of an intonation peak on the noun phrase *Chance* in (28a), one that would not likely occur on the same noun phrase in (28):

The mouthwash CHANCE forgot to buy.

Hence, the word order in (28a) is one that allows the writer to make another phrase besides the subject the old information of the sentence and to place some emphasis on the subject that it would not otherwise receive in the basic sentence.

Placement of Modifiers

As seen in previous chapters, many adverbials and adjectivals in English can be placed in different positions in the sentence. For example, we saw in Chapter 9 how subordinate clauses can occur at the beginning, in the middle, and at the end of sentences. Variations in word order here have consequences for intonation and focus, just as they have for the patterns discussed above. Consider the three sentences in (29)–(31) with regard to the placement of the subordinate clause.

(29)   Before the ink was dry on the contract, Justine cashed the down payment for the ranch.

(30)   Justine cashed the down payment for the ranch before the ink was dry on the contract.

(31)   Justine, before the ink was dry on the contract, cashed the down payment for the ranch.

Each of these sentences has a different focus because of the word order. In (29), the focus is on what Justine did, her cashing the down-payment check for the ranch. In (30), the focus is on how quickly Justine cashed the check—"before the ink was dry."

Modifiers also become interesting when they are placed internal to the sentence. A sentence-internal subordinate clause is set off by commas before and after it. A comma usually affects the intonation of a sentence in two ways. First, it slows the reader down slightly; second, the word before the comma ends with a slight rise in pitch. If you read sentences (30) and (31) aloud, you should hear a difference in intonation on the word *Justine* in each sentence. These changes in how the sentence is read have the effect of throwing more attention on the word or phrase immediately before the comma. In the case of (31), more attention is drawn to the word *Justine*.

Word Choice and Intonation

One final way that writers influence the intonation of their readers is through word choice. In particular, certain words tend to attract intonation peaks because of their color and forcefulness. Compare the following two sentences:

(32)   Greta took me to a nice MOvie.

(33)   Greta took me to a stuPENdous movie.

The adjective *nice* is so mild and overused in English today that it often attracts little rise in pitch. The adjective *stupendous,* however, is much stronger; it is the most colorful word in (33). These are the kinds of words that draw intonational prominence to themselves.

Because words like *stupendous* attract our attention, they can also be used to withdraw it from some other aspect of the sentence. The word choice in sentences (34) and (35) demonstrates this shift in emphasis

(34)   We saw the conditions at the camp last night.

(35)   We saw the <u>absolutely appalling</u> conditions at the camp last night.

In (34), the reader's attention is likely to focus on either the prepositional phrase *at the camp* or the time phrase *last night.* In (35), however, the adjective phrase *absolutely appalling* is so strong that it draws the reader's attention to the noun phrase *absolutely appalling conditions* and away from the later phrases in the sentence.

Writers need to be aware of how their word choice affects intonation and focus. In academic writing, for example, they must avoid the tendency to overuse colorful words and phrases that distract their readers' attention from the real points they are trying to make and that cause their writing to sound too heated or emotional. They must learn to place vivid phrasing effectively so it underscores the points they wish to emphasize.

The next two exercises ask you to apply the concepts of this chapter to sentences in context.

EXERCISE 4

The following paragraph is in need of revision. Keeping the content the same, rewrite this text using the techniques discussed in this chapter for affecting word order and intonation. Make a list of the exact changes you make and explain how your word-order choices altered your reading of the text.

> Every technology takes a physical form. The technology will be used in some ways and not others because the physical form gives it a bias. The printing press had a bias to be used as a medium of language. Television has a bias. Its bias is toward images and spectacle and entertainment. The average shot on television is 3.5 seconds. Your eye never rests and always has something new to see. Concentration on ideas and the expression of uncertainty and nuance are not possible because of the swiftly moving action. Even the news becomes entertainment in this medium. Writing promotes depth of thought. Television promotes amusement and immediate gratification.

> (adapted from Neil Postman, *Amusing Ourselves to Death*)

EXERCISE 5

Bring in a printed page of a text you have written and exchange it with a class-mate. Then evaluate your classmate's prose with regard to cohesion and the au-thor's ability to control old and new information and focus the reader's atten-tion through word order and word choice. Make suggestions as to where the writing might be strengthened by altering word order or word choice.

This chapter has promoted the same message over and over again: word or-der matters in writing. It matters greatly because it is one of the primary tools writers have to convey their meaning and so compensate for the loss of intona-tion and other factors that we depend on when we speak and understand oth-ers' speech. Good writers also have good ears!

COMPREHENSION QUESTIONS

1. What is intonation? How does intonation help us to understand spoken language?

2. Why is it a disadvantage to write like we speak?

3. How are old and new information arranged in English sentences?

4. What is the drawback of vague error labels when evaluating our own or some-one else's writing?

5. What purpose does word order play in written English? What does it compen-sate for in spoken English?

6. Describe some of the possibilities that exist in English for changing the reader's intonation by altering word order and word choice.

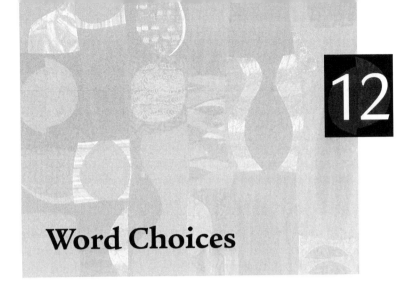

Word Choices

PREVIEW *Up to this point, we have looked at grammar as it applies to arranging words together. However, a lot of problems in writing really occur on the level of individual words. This chapter will spend some time examining this aspect of our English language so that you can have a more complete picture of all that takes place when we write.*

The Dictionary vs. the Lexicon

It will be helpful to start our discussion by talking about what you know when you know a word. This topic invites us to speculate about what is inside our heads. When we know a language, that knowledge includes details about a large number of words. If we could peek inside our brains at a level where we could see accurately how our knowledge is organized, what would we see?

Our discussion will be aided if we compare the knowledge of words in our head with what we find in a dictionary. We must have something like a dictionary in our heads, and linguists usually call that "mental dictionary" a **lexicon.** It turns out that a dictionary and our lexicon have some traits in common and some crucial differences as well.

Before you read this section, open up a good dictionary and make a list of what you find in there. What kind of information do you discover in each word entry, and what other sections does the dictionary contain?

As I look at a dictionary in front of me, I can see that the entries for words contain the following: the spelling of the word, its pronunciation, its parts of speech, its meaning in terms of definitions, and an etymology, or information on where the word came from. Sometimes there is a picture or diagram that shows more concretely what the word means. There might also be a list of syn-

JUMP START reprinted by permission of the United Feature Syndicate, Inc.

onyms, a statement of the word's usage, or some sentences displaying how the word is used.

How does this kind of dictionary compare with the lexicon in our heads? First, we might notice that not all of our lexical entries contain information on spelling. There might be some words that we have only heard or that we have not seen on the written page often enough to have remembered their spelling. Conversely, we might have pronunciation information for most words we know, but not necessarily every word. There may be some words that we have encountered in reading but that we have never heard pronounced.

We would have part-of-speech information for the words in our lexicon. We may not be able to consciously verbalize what those categories are, but the evidence we have that information is that we use the word correctly and that we understand when other speakers use it.

We certainly have meanings associated with the words in our lexicon. However, the definitions in our heads must be encoded very differently from the definitions in a dictionary. While definitions in a dictionary are given in terms of other words, almost certainly there are very few words in our heads defined that way. Suppose we discovered that some random word in our lexicon was defined in our heads in terms of other words. That would force us to ask what the meanings of the words were that were in the definition. If those words were defined in terms of other words, then we would need to see the definitions of these new words. Eventually, we would run out of words that could serve as the basic definitions for the rest of the lexicon. Clearly, there must be words, at least beginning words, in our heads that are defined by something besides other words. If we reflect on what it must have been like when we acquired our very first words, maybe *Dada* or *Mama,* we realize that we did not learn those words by using other words because we didn't have other words in our lexicon.

When we are asked to give definitions of words in our own native language, it is a very difficult task. We usually struggle giving definitions. If we are asked to define many of our most common words, the function words such as *the* and *a/an,* we run into all kinds of difficulty. This is another piece of evidence that the definitions in our heads are not encoded by means of words. Perhaps the only words whose explicit definitions are stored there are the very few technical terms that we have learned in school and not in the course of ordinary life.

Another difference with the definitions in our head is that even the best dictionary is limited as to how much it can tell us about the meanings of individual words. The entry for a word with multiple definitions won't capture all of the ways we actually use it.

For example, the *American Heritage Dictionary* offers fourteen basic definitions for the adjective *high:*

1a. Having a relatively great elevation; extending far upward: *a high mountain.*

b. Extending a specified distance upward.

2. Far or farther from a reference point: *too high in the offensive zone to take a shot.*

3a. Being at or near the peak or culminating stage: *high summer.*

b. Advanced in development or complexity.

c. Far removed in time; remote: *high antiquity.*

4a. Slightly spoiled or tainted; gamy. Used of meat.

b. Having a bad smell; malodorous.

5a. Having a pitch corresponding to a relatively large number of sound wave cycles per second: *the high tones of a flute.*

b. Raised in pitch; not soft or hushed: *a high voice.*

6. Situated relatively far from the equator.

7a. Of great importance.

b. Eminent in rank or status.

c. Serious; grave.

d. Constituting a climax; crucial.

e. Characterized by lofty or stirring events or themes: *high drama.*

8. Lofty or exalted in quality or character: *high morals.*

9a. Greater than usual or expected, as in quantity, magnitude, cost, or degree.

b. Favorable: *a high opinion of himself.*

10. Of great force or violence: *high winds.*

11a. Filled with excitement or euphoria.

b. *Slang* Intoxicated by alcohol or a drug, such as marijuana.

12. Luxurious; extravagant.

13. *Linguistics* Of or relating to vowels produced with part of the tongue close to the palate, as in the vowel of *tree*.

14. Of, relating to, or being the gear configuration, as in an automotive transmission, that produces the greatest vehicular speed with respect to engine speed.

The entire entry is detailed and even includes a number of idioms. Nonetheless, it is not exhaustive. It does not tell us in any of its definitions that while we can say "a high building," we cannot refer to a human being's stature with the word *high*. The sentence

(1)   The high basketball player missed the open shot.

does not mean the player is tall. When referring to height, somehow you just know that the word *high* is used for inanimate objects and not for humans and animals.

This is not an argument against dictionaries. Because of their space limitations, it would be impossible for even the largest dictionaries to capture all the definitions stored in our heads.

Are there pictures or diagrams associated with the words in our heads? There might be for some entries. However, for most words we probably don't have etymological information associated with them. When we learn a word in our youth, we don't learn the history of the word. Only those who specifically study such matters know about the origins of words. Yet all English-speakers know and use English without this sort of formal training.

We have established that there is information in a printed dictionary that is not in our lexicon. There is also information in our lexicon that is not in the dictionary. Another way the two storage systems differ is in the ordering of their entries. In a printed dictionary, entries are ordered alphabetically based on spelling. They are not ordered that way in our heads. If they were, then whenever we mentally searched for a word in our heads, we would move through lists of words based on spelling, but that is not what we do. If I give you a word and ask you to think of other words, you are not likely to give me a list of all the words you know whose spelling would put them near that word in a dictionary. Additionally, the words in a dictionary are arranged in a formal linear order, which also does not appear to correspond to the order of words in the lexicon.

How are words organized in our lexicon? This is a very difficult question that linguists are only beginning to understand. One way that words might be arranged in our lexicon is via sublexicons, smaller organized parts of the whole lexicon. That is, there may be words that are linked together because they are used to talk about the same slice of life. For example, if you like to cook, words that apply to cooking might be linked together in your mind, such as *roast, poach, boil, braise,* and *brown.* One way to demonstrate this theory would be to see whether you are likely to offer these cooking terms if I mention one to you and ask you to think of words that came to your mind.

The entries in our lexicon are very sophisticated and involve subtle shades of meaning and nuance. For example, a speaker normally conveys the same attitude whether she uses the singular or plural form of the same noun. There is no difference in attitude whether a speaker says (2) or (3):

(2)   How are your classes?

(3)   How is your class?

However, there is a difference in attitude between sentence (4) with the plural noun and sentence (5) with the singular noun:

(4)   Where are the kids?

(5)   Where is the kid?

Sentence (4) is relatively neutral, but sentence (5), by using *the kid* to refer to a child rather than the child's name, conveys a certain gruffness or perhaps a demeaning attitude toward the child. The difference between (4) and (5) is not something that anybody ever teaches us, but somehow we acquire this kind of nuance as we learn the language and grow up in an English-speaking culture. You also would not find this kind of information in a printed dictionary, but the lexical entries in our heads include this kind of subtle distinction.

Another important type of information in our lexicon has to do with the way individual words combine in grammatical patterns. Earlier in this book, we looked at the basic patterns for combining words into English sentences. We saw, for example, how nouns and adjectives and determiners combine to make noun phrases and how verbs combine with various phrases to make verb phrases. We looked at the patterns that were most common and most general, and it might even seem as if we could account for all of English grammar with our analysis. However, the facts are not actually that simple. There are many exceptions to the general patterns we looked at earlier, and these exceptions can generally be associated with individual words of the language.

For example, we described adjectives as words that precede nouns in noun phrases. While this generalization holds for the great majority of adjectives, it does not hold for every adjective. We cannot say, "*the asleep man," though *asleep* is an adjective. This means that the entry for *asleep* in our lexicon includes information that says it is an adjective but that it is not the kind of adjective that can appear before nouns.

Commonly Confused Words

Knowing about the lexicon gives us a way to think about the many words that are easily confused in writing. This includes pairs (and triplets) like the following:

> its vs. it's

> there vs. their vs. they're

We can also throw in here mistakes in writing such as

> suppose to instead of supposed to

A more novel kind of mistake arises when a writer pens

> doggy dog world

in a sentence like

> (6)   With all of the economic competition today, we can see that this is a doggy dog world.

when she intended to write

> (6a)   With all of the economic competition today, we can see that this is a dog-eat-dog world.

The lexicon gives us a way to understand such errors in more depth. These errors seem to be linked to the central question of how words (and phrases) are stored in our minds. Unlike in printed dictionaries, where words are listed by spelling, probably most words in our lexicon are stored primarily by their pronunciation. This is because we learn to speak before we can read and continue to acquire our language more through sound than through sight (reading). One of the differences between written and spoken English is that many words that are pronounced the same are spelled differently. Likewise, a number of words that are spelled the same are pronounced differently.

With regard to the former situation, we encounter something quite intriguing. Though the words are separate in our mind with regard to their meaning, they are stored very similarly in terms of their sounds. That makes it problematic when we write, because we may pull the wrong word out of the lexicon when we commit it to paper.

Some writers, though, are fairly proficient in putting down the correct word when they write. What separates them from those who struggle with writing the correct form? Visual storage. When we go to school and learn to read and write, we are enhancing our lexicons and adding to them a visual storage of words in addition to the auditory storage. Once we have attended enough school, we have in our heads words that are stored or encoded both by sight and by sound. Those who have the strongest visual storage of words will be those writers that most consistently make accurate choices when it comes to choosing *their* versus *there* versus *they're.*

There's a moral to this tale. If you struggle with these kinds of mistakes, then it shows how much you are relying on auditory storage rather than visual storage. You could sit down and try by brute force to memorize words, but this will not be as nearly effective as vigorously immersing yourself in the printed page. Read, read, and read whatever you like, because thereby you will enhance your visual storage so that the words in your head are organized by both sight and sound.

If you plan to be a teacher some day, then this explanation may give you some guidance. You should now realize the limitations of simply red-inking spelling errors that are based on a lack of visual storage. Such action will not by itself improve their writing because it does not address students' basic problem. The real solution is to encourage these students to read and read and read and thereby strengthen the visual storage of words in their heads. Your curriculum should devote time and space to the purpose of reading for reading's sake.

English Spelling

The previous section alludes to one bane of the English language—the dreaded system of spelling. English has been a written language for many centuries. At various times in the history of the language, very intelligent men have proposed reforming the spelling system. These ambitious spelling reforms generally have gone nowhere, but that hasn't stopped people even today from proposing (or at least wishing) that English spelling were not so ornery.

However, if English spelling is as atrocious as people claim, then it seems reasonable to ask why it has lasted so long. If the spelling system were broken, if it didn't work, then we would have expected it to change a long time ago. It may be that there is something about the spelling of English that is actually beneficial. If we examine English spelling more closely in light of the themes discussed in this book, we will find that there is a reason why English spelling works despite its difficulties.

For those who favor spelling reform, the usual idea is that spelling should match the way words are pronounced. English has many homophones, separate words that are pronounced the same way. If we wrote words as they are pronounced, we might end up with sentences like the following:

(7)   *Tu cats came tu the river tu.

Once we learned such a system, writing would be much easier for us, but what would happen to reading? Reading would be undoubtedly harder. A reader would be able to figure out what word each *tu* represented above, but not as easily as he would with our present system.

In other words, the spelling system favors readers over writers, because it often maximizes the differences between homonyms—distinct words that are pronounced the same. This is a kind of redundancy (see Chapter 1). A person reading the sentence above would by his knowledge of grammar be able to figure out what word each *tu* designated, but having a more complicated spelling tells the reader right away what word is present. In the equation between sender and receiver, the receiver wants clear distinctions between words in the message, and the sender wants ease of delivery. The spelling system in English favors the receiver (reader) over the sender (writer).

This makes good sense. In real-world writing, there are multiple readers for every writer. If you are fortunate enough to write texts for publication, you will have an audience of hundreds, thousands, maybe even millions. If the task of writing is eased, that helps one person but complicates things for many people. It is much better to complicate the writer's task and make the reading process more efficient.

Subject-Verb Agreement

We have been talking about the detailed information that is stored in the lexical entries in our heads. Most of this information is unconscious—we don't realize what we know until someone points it out to us. Some of the details in our heads are connected to the phenomenon called subject-verb agreement. As we saw in Chapter 10, *agreement* refers to the form words take to show their connection to one another. Depending on the singularity or plurality of a noun, the form of the determiner changes. We use *this* and *that* with singular nouns:

this cat   that dog

We use *these* and *those* with plural nouns:

these cats   those dogs

Agreement is another example of the redundancy we find in language. It is as if we marked the singularity or plurality of the noun phrase in two locations, once on the noun and once on the determiner.

Strictly speaking, the English language doesn't really need both *this* and *these* or both *that* and *those*. We don't have two forms for the determiner *the*. The word *the* is used with both singular and plural nouns. Nonetheless, we do have some cases of determiner-noun agreement in English.

The most prominent area of agreement in English is between subjects and verbs. Just like determiner-noun agreement, subject-verb agreement is limited. It doesn't apply to all verbs but only to those in the present, present-perfect, and present-progressive tense. Likewise, the changes in form apply only to third-person-singular subjects. In this very specific case, the verb takes the *-s* suffix.

If you think about this case for a minute, it may strike you as a very odd thing. Why does the verb change form only with third-person subjects? Why doesn't the verb take a different ending when the subject is plural or another ending when the subject is first person or second person? (This does happen with *be*-verbs.) Why don't past-tense verbs vary their endings depending on the subject? Where did such a strange system come from?

We can't answer all these questions, but we can talk a little bit about where the system came from. In earlier stages of the language, English had a more exacting system of agreement. In Old English, verbs appeared in many different forms to signal agreement with subject. What happened over the centuries was that English lost most of its subject-verb agreement forms but not all of them. It shouldn't come as a surprise that if a language were to change, it might lose some of its redundancies. Basically, the same information can be conveyed without the presence of agreement. The interesting question is this—why didn't English lose all of its subject-verb agreement? Why did it keep just this one case? We don't know enough about language to give a good answer to either question. All we can do is live with the language that we have today.

DIFFICULTIES IN SUBJECT-VERB AGREEMENT It might seem as if subject-verb agreement is straightforward. Actually, it is not. In English it is quite complex, as the following list of guidelines demonstrates.

1. Collective nouns, nouns that refer to a collection of things, may take either singular or plural agreement, depending on how they are conceived by the writer.

   (8)   Judith's team <u>win</u> most of their matches.

   (9)   Judith's team <u>wins</u> most of its matches.

   Often an element in the sentence will clarify whether the collective noun is conceived of as a single entity or in terms of its members. In (10), the possessive pronoun *its* tells us that the team is being viewed as a single entity:

   (10)   The team <u>has</u> changed <u>its</u> strategy.

In (11), the possessive pronoun *their* tells us that the team is being viewed in terms of its members:

(11)   The team <u>have</u> changed out of <u>their</u> uniforms.

2. Singular nouns that have a plural form take plural agreement.

(12)   The cut is jagged because the scissors <u>are</u> dull.

3. Plural numbers when applied to distance, money, or time take singular agreement when the amount is conceived of as a single entity.

(13)   Six thousand dollars <u>is</u> too much to pay for that car.

Compare sentence (13) with sentence (14):

(14)   Six thousand dollar bills <u>are</u> floating in this pool.

These three generalizations tell us that subject-verb agreement is determined by both form (rule 2) and meaning (rules 1 and 3). In your reading be sure to pay attention to the subject-verb agreement of skilled writers to get a feel for what is appropriate.

4. When the subject contains the coordinate conjunction *or*, the verb agrees with the noun phrase it is closest to.
     We can conjoin a plural noun phrase with a singular noun phrase using the conjunction *or*. It turns out that the order of the conjuncts matters for subject-verb agreement. Compare the following sentences:

(15)   <u>Three professors</u> or <u>one dean</u> is all the college can afford to hire
                Plural NP   Sing. NP

         this year.

(16)   <u>The band leader</u> or <u>the drummers</u> are likely to be at that party after
              Sing. NP   Plural NP

         the concert.

In (15), the singular noun phrase *one dean* agrees with the singular verb *is*. In (16), the plural noun phrase *the drummers* agrees with the plural verb *are*.
     When these kinds of subjects appear in questions, then the verb will be closest to the first conjunct and agree with it:

(17)   **Does** <u>your boss</u> or <u>your colleagues</u> stay late at the office on a regu-
                  Sing. NP   Plural NP

         lar basis?

(18)   **Do** <u>the workers</u> or <u>their union representative</u> wish to file a
                Plural NP   Sing. NP

         grievance?

In (17), the singular noun phrase *your boss* agrees with the singular verb *does*. In (18), the plural noun phrase *the workers* agrees with the plural verb *do*.

5. Verbs agree with the head of the NP.

We saw in Chapter 2 how every noun phrase contains a noun that heads that phrase. However, we also know that noun phrases may have more than one noun inside them, particularly if the noun phrase contains a prepositional phrase:

(19a)   a <u>fly</u> in the <u>ointment</u>

(19b)   the <u>peas</u> in his <u>soup</u>

(19c)   the <u>woman</u> of my <u>dreams</u>

When such noun phrases are the subject, we must make sure that the verb agrees with the head of the noun phrase:

(20)   The <u>peas</u> in his soup <u>are</u> juicy.

(21)   The <u>woman</u> of my dreams <u>is</u> in the next room.

In (20) and (21), the noun closer to the verb is part of the prepositional phrase that modifies the head noun, so it would be easy to mistakenly make the verb agree with the closer noun.

Sometimes the head of a noun phrase is a number or a quantifier. In this case, the verb still agrees with that head:

(22)   <u>One</u> of the paintings <u>is</u> missing.

(23)   <u>Every one</u> of the keys <u>has</u> been duplicated.

6. When the subject is distant from its verb, it still must determine agreement with the verb. It is possible to put adverbials between a subject and verb, and sometimes this makes it difficult to determine what form the verb should take:

(24)   The east <u>stairwell</u>, an addition made to the building in 1660 by French carpenters, <u>is</u> a fine example of the classical influence of the period.

Again, we must be careful not to make the verb agree with the noun closest to it.

Rules 5 and 6 illustrate the value of understanding the structure of English sentences. We know how to find subjects and verbs and how to distinguish adverbials from the necessary stuff of the sentence. We know how to identify the head of a phrase. Thus we know exactly what we are looking for when we need to diagnose or correct a subject-verb agreement error.

The following exercise will give you some practice with subject-verb agreement.

EXERCISE 1

Identify the specific subject-verb agreement error in each sentence and then correct it. Some sentences may be correct as written.

1. Do the president or his advisors plan to attend the conference?

2. Surprisingly, that student, even though his teachers gave him excellent grades, have decided to skip college.

3. Foster's pants is imported from Indonesia.

4. Three of the players on that team scores most of the points.

5. Fourteen miles are a long way to hike to see another waterfall.

6. The grievance committee has handed in their resignations in protest.

7. The cabinet have expressed its disapproval of the grievance committee's actions.

8. Janice's bifocals needs cleaning before she can continue her beadwork.

9. Our coach or her players is due to win an award after this fine season.

10. The ewok, Endor's most gregarious furry bipeds, are ferocious when one approaches in battle armor.

Gender in Language

Reference to gender is a source of unending lexical controversy. It would seem as though English has a serious defect in its pronoun system. The language has three third-person singular pronouns—*he, she,* and *it. He* refers to a male, *she* refers to a female, and *it* refers to something that is neither male or female nor human. This same distinction marks the object pronouns—*him* refers to a male, *her* refers to a female, and *it* refers to a nonhuman object—and the possessive pronouns *his, her,* and *its.* What English lacks is a singular pronoun referring to a human that is neutral with respect to gender.

I find in discussions with students that there are often two views on the topic. One view says that women cannot be referred to with masculine pronouns. Another says that masculine pronouns can refer to either gender. How do we decide between the two?

If it were possible, a useful thing to do would be to examine the lexicons of the people holding these views. What would the entries for pronouns contain for each group? This problem illustrates another aspect of our mental lexicons—they do not all contain the same information. Looking at a printed dictionary can give one the impression of a great uniformity about the meaning of words. However, the lexicon in your head will be different from the lexicon in your neighbor's head. We all don't know the same words. Neither do we understand all words in the same way. Some words may be quite familiar to us and not to others. Even words that we all know well may be encoded differently in our heads. When can the adjective *old* be applied to a person? When he's 70? 60? My small daughter has applied it to 30-year-olds.

If we peered at the entries for personal pronouns in the lexicons of a diverse group of people, we would probably find that some people use *he* and *she* very strictly to refer to males and females, respectively. We can infer this by their language behavior. We listen to how they speak and note that they consistently use *he* to refer to a man and *she* to refer to a woman. On the other hand, we also would probably find that some people use *he* as a generic pronoun to refer to an indefinite individual who may be male or female. Again, we can infer this by language behavior.

Observing language behavior can be useful to you as a writer. You may be writing someday to an audience whose lexical entries for personal pronouns differ along the lines described above. Knowing this will help you to make informed rhetorical choices. If you know that your audience contains readers who use *he* and *she* strictly for men and for women, and you wish to respect that audience and appeal to them, then you will certainly not choose to use *he* to refer to an individual who may be male or female. Alternatives to *he* will be discussed in the next section.

Gender-Neutral Language

The missing neutral singular-pronoun in English causes a lot of problems today for writers who wish to write about topics that pertain equally to men and women, which includes most writing topics. Unfortunately, there has not yet emerged a good alternative. Writers have pursued a number of strategies to avoid gender reference, all with their own drawbacks.

One strategy is to use expressions like *he or she* or *s/he*, which tends to be cumbersome. Another is to alternate between *he* and *she* within the same passage. The observant reader will have noticed that this has been the approach taken in this textbook, where I have used feminine pronouns for a speaker and a writer and masculine pronouns for a hearer and a reader. This strategy gives equal time to both men and women and avoids favoring either gender over the other, but it still might seem confusing to some readers who wonder why some sentences got the *he*'s and some the *she*'s.

Another strategy is to avoid singular pronouns by using plural nouns and the pronouns *they, them,* and *their.* This avoids gender reference, but sometimes a writer wants to or needs to refer to a singular noun.

A more controversial strategy is to use *they, them,* and *their* in tandem with singular nouns. That is, a writer can use singular gender-neutral nouns for her sentences. Then when she wants to refer back to those nouns, she uses *they, them,* or *their.* The rationale behind this choice is that the pronoun agreement is based on the meaning of the sentence rather than the form of the noun. We all recognize in the following sentence

(25)   When choosing <u>a family physician</u>, make sure that <u>they</u> care more about <u>their</u> patients than about <u>their</u> income.

that the clause *when choosing a family physician* refers to a general situation of choosing doctors; the noun phrase *a family physician* does not refer to a single specific physician. A plural pronoun in a follow-up clause or sentence refers to the whole group of physicians that is described by the previous clause. That is, the plural pronoun points to the *meaning in context* of the noun phrase, not to the *singular form* of the noun phrase.

There are two things that could be said in favor of this strategy. First, third-person-plural pronouns have been used with singular antecedents at earlier stages of the English language, so this solution is not alien to the system. Second, this strategy exhibits sensitivity to meaning, as opposed to form. (Recall our earlier discussion, in the section Subject-Verb Agreement, about the two kinds of linguistic processes that characterize English, one sensitive to form and another sensitive to meaning.)

It is important to know that many writers and readers object vigorously to this use of third-person-plural pronouns and will not accept this strategy for avoiding gender reference. Your grammar teacher may easily be one of them! However, this usage is becoming more common today, and it holds promise as an efficient means of avoiding gender reference while using resources provided by the system of English itself.

The following exercises will give you the opportunity to compare a printed dictionary with your own knowledge of words and with another printed dictionary.

EXERCISE 2

Without looking at a dictionary, think of ten words that you know and write down five pieces of information you can think of for each word. Then consult a good dictionary and compare the information stored in your lexicon with the information in the dictionary entry. What information did you have in your head that was not listed in the dictionary entry? What information did the dictionary entry have that was not stored in your lexicon?

EXERCISE 3

Find two dictionaries published by different companies. Then make a list of ten random words and look them up in each dictionary. What differences do you find in the lexical entries of each word? Can you discern any differences between the goals of each dictionary or between the audiences each dictionary is intended for? Why do you think these differences exist?

COMPREHENSION QUESTIONS

1. What are the differences between a dictionary and our lexicon?
2. What do commonly confused words tell us about the way words are stored in our heads?
3. What benefit does English spelling have in the process of reading?
4. What does subject-verb agreement show about our lexicon?
5. What factors determine subject-verb agreement?
6. What options are there for the writer who wishes to avoid gender reference?

The Written Standard and Oral Varieties of English

PREVIEW *This chapter will look at Black English and Appalachian English in order to explore the relationship between the written standard of English and spoken varieties of English.*

Linguistic Diversity

One intriguing aspect of language is its variety. It is estimated that there are over 5,000 languages in the world today, all with their own unique system of syntax and sounds and word meanings. We tend to admire people who can speak many languages. When people discover I am a linguist, the first question they ask me is, "How many languages do you speak?" Unfortunately, I have to confess that I don't speak many at all. When we do meet a real polyglot, however, we are amazed at their prowess. Their ability might be a consequence of years of study, or perhaps they have lived in interesting places around the world, or maybe they simply have that gift of picking up languages without much effort. In any case, I am always jealous and wish I could speak as many languages as some of the people I have met.

This diversity also appears within a single language as well. There are many varieties of English in the world, just as there are of French and Chinese and Swahili and of any other language that covers a large enough area and has a diverse group of speakers. If you have traveled within the United States widely enough, you may have noticed that people in the south speak a "southern" variety of English and that people in the northeast speak a "New England" variety of English. As a matter of fact, there is no southern English and no New England English. There are many varieties of English throughout the south and the northeast and everywhere else in the country. Some may be more noticeable, and some may go underneath our radar, but varieties are everywhere.

Some people are shocked to learn that everyone speaks a variety or, to use a more common but loaded term, a **dialect** of English. Though the general population treats *dialect* as a pejorative word, linguists sometimes use the term to refer to varieties of the same language that are mutually intelligible. Now, you may be saying to yourself, "No, I don't speak a dialect; I speak standard English," but strictly speaking this is not true, because (surprise again!) there is no such thing out in the real world of everyday speech as standard English—an unmarked variety of speech that is neutral with respect to all other varieties of English. Standard English is an ideal, like a Santa Claus figure. He is real enough to serve a useful purpose, and we can all recognize him when we see him, but there is no Santa Claus in the real world. We often think of standard English as the kind of English we hear on the nightly news or from some telephone operators or recorded messages. However, what we are really hearing is a variety of English. It may seem very similar or even identical to our conception of "standard English," but subtle characteristics always reveal a unique dialect.

One reason people want to maintain that they speak standard English is their low view of dialects. Curiously, we don't always have the same admiration for these varieties of English as we do for different languages. Here is where a little knowledge can make a big difference. Each variety or dialect of a language is as much a language as are national languages such as French, Chinese, Swahili, and so forth. To take a specific example, Black English is as much a language, a linguistic system, as French. It has rules that govern its structure, its word formation, and its sound system. One of the things we will do in this chapter is look at some of the formal characteristics of two varieties of English, Black English and Appalachian English, so that you will know the linguistic system underlying them. It is one thing simply to say that these varieties are legitimate forms of speech. It is another thing to show the rules that govern them so that you know the true nature of these (and every) variety of speech.

The System of Black English

Black English (BE), also called African American Vernacular English in the literature, is one of the most distinctive varieties of English. It is a variety that has been at the center of a fair amount of controversy; in 1996 the Oakland, California, School Board proposed using Black English, or Ebonics, in the classroom to help their students' academic achievement. Strong voices were raised both for and against the proposal. This text will not argue the merits of the case one way or another. Rather, it will address the troubling reality that many debaters made arguments that were factually untrue. Some argued that Ebonics should not be taught because Black English was not a real language but rather some deficient form of street talk. This shows a lack of understanding about language. BE, as noted earlier, is rule governed and systematic, as are all varieties of English. It has rules that are different from written standard English, but it is not devoid of them. Rather, it exemplifies a different system, a different form of complexity than that of standard English. As we look at some of the rules in the next few pages, keep in mind that variation exists among BE speakers, as among speakers of other dialects. Not all BE speakers will manifest the entire range of characteristics described below. Nor are they all African Americans.

VERB FORMS One of the first characteristics people notice about BE is the lack of tense and the lack of person marked on verbs. For the most part, BE uses the same forms for past and present (1) and the same forms for singular and plural subjects (2):

(1)   I <u>look</u> for him last night.

(2)   She <u>have</u> us say it.

This lack of verb endings bothers a lot of people who think that BE is somehow uncultivated or unintellectual. However, if BE were deficient as a language system, then we would find verbs arbitrarily showing up sometimes with tense and person endings and sometimes without, but that is not what we find. The lack of verb endings in BE is as consistent as the use of verb endings in other varieties of English.

This may raise a question in your mind about the usefulness of verb endings. Is standard English superior because it marks past tense and singular third person on the verb? Here are some considerations that might help us answer this question.

First, one might suppose that standard English is more informative because the verb form by itself gives us temporal information. When we read the following sentence,

(3)   The Jones family ate étouffée.

the verb form tells us we are reading about an event in the past. The corresponding BE form below,

(4)   The Jones family eat étouffée.

does not narrow down the time by itself. However, this does not really turn out to be a serious problem, because language is not used in a vacuum. The context almost always makes clear the time period to which a sentence is referring. If my conversation partner is talking about what happened at the Jones's house last night, the temporal aspect of sentence (4) is immediately clear.

Second, even in standard English, there are verbs that don't mark past tense, such as *cut*. The temporal aspect of the sentence

> (5)   The players cut the cake.

is not specified. However, this does not derail the usefulness of standard English nor the usability of the verb *cut*.

A reader might raise the perceptive question, "Why does BE lack tense and person marking on the verb?" In fact, BE has simply carried out the same process that standard English began, but carried it out further. If we go back to the earliest stages of the English language, to Old English, which dates from approximately 500 to 1100 C.E., we find a language that had many more verb forms than Modern English.

For example, in Old English the verb *help* was *helpan*. In Modern English, this verb takes regular forms: *helped, helps, helping*. However, in Old English, it was an irregular verb and took the forms *healp* (first-person singular and third-person singular preterite), *hulpon* (plural preterite), and *holpen* (past participle). If this verb had come down to us today based on its Old English forms, it would be irregular in Modern English, for example, and we might say

> (6)   Ursula and Buster hulp the Red Cross by donating time and money. (instead of *helped*)

> (7)   It could not be holpen that the river flooded the town. (instead of *helped*)

What happened in the evolution of English was the same process that has taken place in BE. Speakers of English unconsciously began on a case-by-case basis to treat certain irregular verbs as regular, *help* being one of those verbs. This process made for a simpler and more efficient system of language, and it is not uncommon to see this kind of tendency toward regularity in the languages of the world. This process in English, though, has never been carried through to its ultimate conclusion, so that that verbal system that we have today is mixed: English has both regular and irregular verbs.

Thus, standard English has been losing verb endings and regularizing verbs throughout its history. BE has simply moved beyond standard English to what really is a more consistent system. Unfortunately, BE is stigmatized for this, but now that you know the linguistic nature of BE verbs, you can avoid making linguistic misjudgments about verbs in this variety of English.

BEEN AND *DONE* AND *BE* You might be wondering, if BE does not mark tense on the verb, whether it uses other means besides context to convey time information. In fact, BE has developed a system that involves the use of *been* and *done*. The *been*-form is used to convey an event that began in the past but that continues up to the present, as in the following sentences:

(8)   He been there before.

(9)   He been gone a day.

This construction is usually equivalent to present-perfect constructions in standard English. Thus (8) and (9) translate in standard English to

(10)   He has been there before.

(11)   He has been gone a day.

The *done*-form in BE produces a sentence like

(12)   I done finish my work today.

It usually conveys that an event has ended and is similar to the present perfect in standard English (which has a wide range of uses):

(13)   I have finished my work today.

Finally, another notable BE verb form involves the use of the verb *be* to convey habitual action. The BE sentence in (14) corresponds to a standard-English sentence like (15):

(14)   Bill be running.

(15)   Bill is usually running.

These verb forms are clearly different from the kind I enumerated in Chapter 8. Are the BE forms loose ways of speaking? Despite its apparent randomness, it turns out that the use of *been, done,* and *be* in BE is part of a system.

If *been* and *done* correspond to the present perfect in standard English, then we would predict that they would be subject to the same kind of restrictions. For example, the present perfect cannot appear with a past-time adverbial like *yesterday.* I can say in standard English,

(16)   I have finished my work today.

but not

(17)   *I have finished my work yesterday.

BE works the same way. The forms *been* and *done* cannot appear with a past-tense adverbial:

(18)   *She been tardy twice last semester. (*She has been tardy twice last semester.)

(19)   *I done finish my work yesterday. (*I have finished my work yesterday.)

The use of *be* in BE supplies a useful form that standard English lacks. Languages such as Swahili and Czech actually have verb forms that convey habitual action. Standard English is forced to rely on adverbials for this purpose.

What we see here is that BE has a different system than standard English, but not a deficient system.

DOUBLE NEGATIVES Another distinctive characteristic of BE is the common occurrence of double (and even triple and quadruple!) negatives. Standard English has a clear preference for single negatives. Thus, the standard English utterances in (20) and (22) have an extra negative in BE, as in (21) and (23):

(20)   I can trust <u>no</u> one.   Standard English

(21)   It <u>ain't</u> <u>nobody</u> I can trust.   Black English

(22)   <u>None</u> of these dudes can beat me.   Standard English

(23)   <u>Ain't</u> <u>none</u> of these dudes can beat me.   Black English

What we see in sentences (21) and (23) is that besides the negation within the sentence, the sentence as a whole takes a negation.

Again, we must wonder what is going on here. Unfortunately, a lot of ignorant things have been written about double negatives. A typical response is to claim that two negatives make a positive or that negatives cancel each other out. Then such a knowing person comes along and says that sentence (21) means "I can trust everyone." This would make good sense if sentences were math problems and meaning were the same as pure logic. However, language is more complex than mathematics, and meaning is richer than pure logic. It is no good telling a speaker of Black English that sentence (21) means "I can trust everyone," when every speaker of Black English knows that it means the same as sentence (20). Instead, we must ask what system of language underlies BE, and the answer is that in BE, as in many other languages of the world, double negatives simply mean a negative sentence. In other words, the negatives don't cancel each other out in BE. Rather, the same negative meaning is marked in more than one place in the sentence.

This is similar to the way standard English uses the word *any*. Take the sentence

(24)   I saw some movie stars on vacation.

and turn it into its negative counterpart. We wouldn't say,

(25)   *I <u>didn't</u> see <u>some</u> movie stars on vacation

but we could say,

> (26)   I <u>didn't</u> see <u>any</u> movie stars on vacation.

In addition to adding *not* to the sentence, we also change the determiner *some* to *any*. In this kind of standard-English sentence, the negation affects the sentence in two places.

Double negation is found in numerous languages around the world, including Bantu languages and Romance languages like French, Spanish, Portuguese, and Italian. It also occurs in earlier stages of English and Dutch. Shakespeare revels in double negatives:

> I can<u>not</u> goe <u>no</u> further   (*As You Like It*)
>
> I haue one heart, one bosome, and one truth,
>
> And that no woman has, <u>nor neuer none</u>
>
> Shall mistris be of it, saue I alone.   (*Twelfth Night*)

Hence, there is nothing defective about the BE use of double negatives. It is simply a different system from that of standard English.

The following exercise will give you practice in understanding double negatives.

EXERCISE 1

Translate the following sentences with double negation into their equivalents in Standard English.

1. Won't nobody do nothing about that.

2. There ain't never a man in this town who won't tell you about the fire.

3. Can't nobody touch that shot.

4. She didn't have no occasion to buy a car.

5. Henry never said nothing last night.

6. We tried to fix the dike, but it wasn't no use.

The System of Appalachian English

The speech of Appalachia is a variety of English associated with a geographic area, a region that includes parts of Kentucky, Virginia, North Carolina, Tennessee, and West Virginia. Historically, this mountainous area was isolated by its terrain from the surrounding parts of the United States, and so a variety of English emerged here, many of whose distinctive features have survived into the twenty-first century. It is also a variety that has sometimes been looked down upon, but as is true with Black English, its forms and pronunciations are part of a different system of language. Like Black English, Appalachian English (AE) is systematic and rule governed, not random and haphazard.

This discussion of AE is based on research done in West Virginia by Walt Wolfram and Donna Christian and presented in their monograph *Appalachian Speech*. Let's take a look at some of the more distinctive patterns of this variety of English, many of which can be found in speech outside Appalachia, but many of which are also disappearing.

AE adheres to most of the basic patterns of standard English. For example, AE speakers put subjects before verbs and direct objects after them:

> "Oh, we played hop scotch, baseball, ring around the roses, little kid games."
> (Wolfram and Christian 169)

> "I love that." (Wolfram and Christian 169)

They put adjectives before nouns:

> "We always planted . . . tender beans, tough beans a little later on. . . ."
> (Wolfram and Christian 170).

In fact, most structures of AE are the same as those in other varieties of English. If you looked at a stretch of AE, you would understand most or all of it. This is evidence that your variety of English shares many of the same structures with AE. However, systematic differences between AE and other varieties of English do exist.

THE *A*-PREFIX   One of the forms that many people quickly associate with Appalachia and other rural areas is the *a*-prefix that occurs primarily on *-ing* verb forms, as in the following sentence:

(27)   Let's go a-fishing this afternoon.

Wolfram and Christian point out that the *a*-prefix seems to be dying out, because it appears most frequently in the speech of older speakers of AE. Nevertheless, what does the *a*-prefix show? Is it a mark of ignorance? Does it show some deficiency in the language? It turns out that the *a*-prefix is rule governed, not arbitrary. It occurs systematically in some places and fails to occur systematically in others. For example, it does not occur on all uses of *-ing* forms. It does not appear on the *-ing* forms when they are used as nouns (28) or adjectives (29):

(28)   *A-fishing is fun.

(29)   *Those a-flashing lights in the mirror bothered me.

That is, AE speakers make the same kinds of grammatical distinctions in their minds that other speakers of English make between *ing*-forms used as verbs and *ing*-forms used as nouns and adjectives.

Other rules govern *a*-prefixing. For example, the *a*-prefix is not attached to words that begin with an unstressed syllable. The word *discover* has its stress on the second syllable—disCOVer, not *DIScover. We don't find sentences like the following in AE:

(30)   *Jody was a-discovering a whole new way of life.

Similarly, the *a*-prefix doesn't show up on words that begin with a vowel:

(31)   *The folks were a-eating barbecue.

Both of these conditions are related to the kinds of rules we find in all varieties of English. In the first case, we rarely find words that begin with two unstressed syllables. Usually, a word of English has a stress on either the first syllable (TAble) or on the second syllable (comPUter).

In the second case, words in English rarely have two vowel sounds in a row. What these conditions show is the systematic, rule-governed nature of AE. They also show that AE has the same kinds of rules as other varieties of English.

IRREGULAR VERBS   Standard English has both regular and irregular verbs. Regular verbs are very well behaved when it comes to their past-tense and past-participle forms: they end in *-ed:*

(32)   The stranger jumped over the fence.

(33)   The stranger has jumped over the fence.

Irregular verbs form their past tense and past participle in a number of different ways:

(34)   The guests came late.

(35)   The guests have come late.

Many dialects tend to regularize irregular verbs and make them conform to the regular verb pattern; otherwise they use different irregular patterns. This tendency is characteristic of AE. Sentence (36) gives an example of an AE speaker using the *-ed* suffix on the irregular verb *throw:*

(36)   We throwed them a birthday party. (instead of *threw*)

We see an irregular pattern for the verb *come* in the sentence below, where the past participle form of *come* has been applied to the simple past:

(37)   Finally the state come by and they pushed it all out. (instead of *came*)

By marking tense in these sorts of ways, AE is continuing a trend that has been going on for centuries in the English language. In Old English, the language had a larger number of what we would now call irregular verbs, verbs that conformed to the less-common patterns. Over time, speakers of English moved certain irregular verbs into the regular patterns.

Like many varieties of English, AE has simply moved irregular verbs into the regular category. This is an example of the human mind seeking regularity, a good thing. One might even say that if the English language was maximally efficient, then all verbs would form their past tense by adding -*ed*.

The following exercise asks you to explore the characteristics of an AE text.

EXERCISE 2

Analyze the following examples of spoken Appalachian English. How is AE different from Standard English?

1. "Oh, they was twelve of us kids, not at that time, after I got old enough to work, two of the girls was married, the rest of us was home we farmed and grew about everything we eat, other than coffee and sugar, you know, the things that you can't grow around here. We raised our hogs and had cows, we had our milk and butter and cornmeal and now we didn't raise no wheat, we bought our flour but outside of that we grew the rest of it, our cornbread, butter and buttermilk, sweet milk and molasses, we made them and I used to love them things . . . The old cane molasses." (Wolfram and Christian 175)

2. "Well, if they're sick or their parents or the boys are sick and disabled to work why, I'm in favor of 'em having it. But they's a lot of 'em on there that is stout, able-bodied men and boys and they could make it on their own. Now, I'll tell you, people say, 'Oh, I can't find a job, I can't find a job.' They's a job for you if you want it. If you'll hunt for it. It may not come to you, but it's there." (Wolfram and Christian 175)

Standard English and Dialects

All languages are rule governed and systematic, and all varieties or dialects of language are rule governed and systematic as well. Nonetheless, many people have strong feelings about the legitimacy of dialects. Some people who criticize dialects are concerned about academic standards and educational excellence. On the other hand, speakers of dialects may feel threatened or marginalized by the apparent attacks on their speech.

No matter what your position is on these issues, it is important for teachers, writers, and users of language in general to understand the relationship between standard English and the various dialects of English. We might picture this relationship using the following diagram:

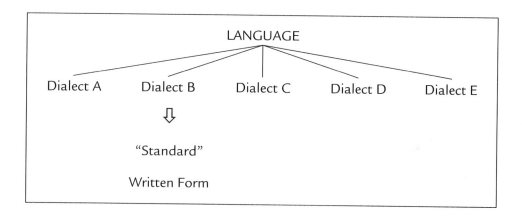

Any language that is spoken over a large enough area will have a number of dialects or varieties associated with it. The standard variety of a language itself typically develops from one of those dialects that is spoken by those people who have political or economic power in the country. Eventually, this dialect is associated with power and success and influence and is viewed in a favorable light by society in general. During the emergence of the standard variety, the written form of the language develops as well, and this dialect becomes the basis for written communication.

Once a dialect becomes a standard variety of a language, it takes on a life of its own. In particular, its expressive resources expand as the written language grows and develops. New words and terminology are introduced into the

JUMP START reprinted by permission of the United Feature Syndicate, Inc.

language, and certain grammatical patterns useful in writing become prominent, because the written form of the language will begin to influence the spoken form.

Hence, one of the major differences between a standard variety of English and other varieties such as Black English and Appalachian English is that it has all of the resources of written English to draw upon. Dialects rarely have extensive written traditions; they are much more likely to have survived in their spoken form.

Descriptive vs. Prescriptive

People are always making judgments about other people's language. However, deciding what is correct in language depends on having a standard to judge by.

Linguists distinguish between making descriptive judgments and prescriptive judgments. Descriptive judgments are the judgments of the scientist, who wishes to accurately describe what people do as they use language without making value judgments about what they do. Most linguists, who study language for a living, focus on making descriptive judgments. When linguists describe the *a*-prefix of Appalachian English, they are describing rather than judging an aspect of the English language.

Prescriptive judgments are the judgments of those who want language users to conform to a standard. For example, we all grow up learning in school that the word *ain't* is not "proper" English. What is the basis for this judgment? The word *ain't* is used in certain dialects of English, where it exists primarily as a spoken, not written, form. However, it is not part of the dialect that formed the basis for standard English and is considered substandard.

What exactly is standard English? In a country like the United States, this is not a simple task to determine, because the rules are not written down in some definitive form as the laws of the land are. If you consult a number of grammar handbooks or textbooks, you will find a great consensus about many matters of language use but not complete agreement by any means. Some aspects of "correct" English are fiercely debated by those who are concerned about the English language.

This uncertain state of affairs leaves many teachers and writers feeling uneasy. One way for you to avoid this discomfiture is to become knowledgeable about the areas of agreement and disagreement among grammarians. Teachers are sure to want to stay close to agreed-upon conventions in the classroom, and writers will need to know where an audience might react to choices they make in their writing that are seen as straying from acceptable usage.

COMPREHENSION QUESTIONS

1. How does linguistic variety manifest itself in languages? How does linguistic variety manifest itself in dialects?

2. Is Black English a defective form of speech? Why or why not?

3. What are some of the characteristics of Black English? What do they demonstrate about the language?

4. Is Appalachian English a defective form of speech? Why or why not?

5. What are some of the characteristics of Appalachian English? What do they demonstrate about the language?

Appendix: The Grammatical Analysis of Literature

PREVIEW *This appendix gives examples of how an understanding of structure and language can be applied to literature.*

One area in which grammatical analysis can be applied is the close reading of texts. This is of value to anyone whose livelihood depends on reading something carefully: from lawyers to businesspeople to students studying literature. The concepts discussed in this book give readers a framework and a vocabulary for determining the meaning of texts and also for justifying those interpretations on the basis of linguistic structure. This chapter will show how grammar is useful for the close reading of literature, the kinds of texts studied in English classes, but its principles are relevant to many other areas as well.

Metrical Analysis

There are a number of ways that linguistics can be brought to bear on literature. The area in which the most work has been done is in the metrical analysis of poetry. Meter refers to the placement of stressed and unstressed syllables within a line of poetry, with an eye toward uncovering the patterns that govern its rhythm. While not all poetry in English observes such conventions, many poems do follow a metrical pattern.

The most celebrated metrical pattern in English is iambic pentameter. *Pentameter* describes a line of poetry that has five feet. A *foot* consists of a sequence of two or more syllables that are connected rhythmically. An *iamb* refers to a pattern of two syllables where the first is unstressed and the second is stressed. Thus, iambic pentameter describes a line of ten syllables that consists of alternating unstressed and stressed syllables:

U S	U S	U S	U S	U S
Foot	Foot	Foot	Foot	Foot

Here is an example of a line of poetry from Robert Browning that could be read in iambic pentameter:

Ah,	but	a	man's	reach	should	exceed	his	grasp,
U	S	U	S	U	S	US	U	S

There are numerous issues that arise in the study of meter. One issue is that a reader may read a line of poetry in multiple ways, and the change in stress patterns and intonation brings to light interpretive possibilities for the poem. For example, a possible reading of the above line could be the following:

Ah,	but	a	man's	reach	should	exceed	his	grasp,
S	U	U	U	S	U	US	U	S

However, if we read the line in strict iambic pentameter, we find stress occurring on the words *but, man's,* and *should,* but no stress on the word *reach*. This leads to a different reading. A stress on the conjunction *but* highlights a contrast with preceding lines in the poem. A stress on *man's* draws attention to humanity's potential. A stress on *should* strengthens the poet's request to the reader to live on a higher plane. We have already seen how crucial intonation is to meaning and to written language. Paying attention to the metrical dimensions of a poem helps the reader to consider the many nuances and shades of meaning that can emerge from a piece of literature.

There are several other interesting questions that arise in metrical analysis. Sometimes, a line of iambic pentameter may have more or fewer than ten syllables. In other words, some of the feet may not be iambic. This raises the issue of how to form the feet of such a line. It also leads to a means for evaluating an interpretation of a poem. Do the non-iambic feet signal a significant meaning or change of meaning in the poem? If you are interested in this approach, I would encourage you to pick up one of the many books that discuss metrical analysis.

Grammatical Analysis of Poetry

Though it is not as widely discussed as metrical analysis, the grammatical structure of sentences in poetry can also be analyzed in a way that enhances the adventure of interpretation. Good writers make grammatical choices that bring a lot of power and expression to their writing, and readers can probe and consider those grammatical choices based on a knowledge of how English structure works.

One of the poets who is best know for exploiting grammar is e. e. cummings, and a sample poem that illustrates well cummings' technique is "Anyone Lived in a Pretty How Town."

anyone lived in a pretty how town
(with up so floating many bells down)
spring summer autumn winter
he sang his didn't he danced his did.

Women and men(both little and small)   5
cared for anyone not at all
they sowed their isn't they reaped their same
sun moon stars rain

children guessed(but only a few
and down they forgot as up they grew   10
autumn winter spring summer)
that noone loved him more by more

when by now and tree by leaf
she laughed his joy she cried his grief
bird by snow and stir by still   15
anyone's any was all to her

someones married their everyones
laughed their cryings and did their dance
(sleep wake hope and then)they
said their nevers they slept their dream   20

stars rain sun moon
(and only the snow can begin to explain
how children are apt to forget to remember
with up so floating many bells down)

one day anyone died i guess   25
(and noone stooped to kiss his face)
busy folk buried them side by side
little by little and was by was

all by all and deep by deep
and more by more they dream their sleep   30
noone and anyone earth by april
wish by spirit and if by yes.

Women and men(both dong and ding)
summer autumn winter spring
reaped their sowing and went their came   35
sun moon stars rain

A phrasal analysis of the first line turns up a few oddities:

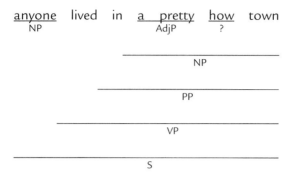

First, the word *how* is in a strange position. *How* can be used as a question word or as a qualifier (*how pretty*) but in line 1 it looks like it is being used as an adjective. Instead of cummings' writing "how pretty a town," he chose the wording in line 1. One of a poet's creative tools is using a word as if it belonged to a new word category. It slows the reader down to think about the significance of a line. The creative use of words may enhance the aesthetic pleasure we receive from poetry or may make the poet's point even stronger.

If you were discussing cummings' poem in a class, this grammatical oddity could provide you with a nice opportunity to speculate as to why he chose to write "a pretty how town" rather than "how pretty a town." You might suggest that he is describing the location ironically as the kind of small town that one would expect to be picture-postcard picturesque but that is not really so perfect in his estimation. Or you might propose, on the contrary, that cummings is actually emphasizing how beautiful the town is. By using a qualifier (*how*) as an adjective, he might be expressing the extent to which the town is pretty, similar to saying "pretty and how." These and other interpretations could be exchanged in a class and then checked against the rest of the poem to see what was viable in context.

The other oddity of line 1 is the subject *anyone*. *Anyone* is an interesting word in English because it cannot be used in just any kind of sentence. For example, we can say (1) but not (2), and (3) but not (4):

(1)   Anyone can live here.

(2)   *Anyone lives here.

(3)   I haven't met anyone new today.

(4)   *I have met anyone new today.

We do not have space here to get into all the intricacies of the quantifier *any*, but a "quick and dirty" observation of sentences (1) to (4) suggest that *anyone* can be used when the sentence is describing a situation that is not actual or real. Sentence (1) describes what is possible but not what is actual. Sentence (3) describes what has not happened. Both sentences (2) and (4) describe actual situations, and *anyone* makes the sentence ungrammatical.

However, cummings uses *anyone* in a sentence where it is not grammatical, and this suggests he is using *anyone* differently, just as he used *how* differently. If we look for words similar to *anyone* that cummings might have in mind, we might think of *everyone* and *someone*. cummings' meaning could be either "Everyone lived in a pretty how town" or "Someone lived in a pretty how town."

The first possibility sounds somewhat implausible, but what we must really do is find further evidence in the poem to clear up the mystery, and we find that evidence in line 4:

> he sang his didn't he danced his did

The only thing so far in the poem that the pronoun *he* might refer back to is *anyone* in line 1. This is good evidence that cummings is using the word *anyone* to mean *someone* or, more specifically, that he is using *anyone* as if it were a proper name, the man named "Anyone." If we examine all the rest of the uses of *anyone* in the poem, they confirm that cummings is using the word to refer to a specific man.

What is the effect of calling a specific person "Anyone"? A number of possibilities come to mind. It may be that this man in the poem is so nondescript and ordinary that he is an "anyone," someone who, at least on the surface, is no different from every other person in the town, someone whom you would never notice in a crowd.

Later on in the poem, we encounter the noun phrase *noone* in line 12. cummings has misspelled "no one," and this should alert us that he might be using this phrase the same way he used *anyone*. In line 14, we find the pronoun *she*, which appears to refer back to *noone*, and this is the clue that tells us that *noone* is being used as the name of a woman whom Anyone loves. If Anyone is nondescript, Noone's name suggests that she is equally unimportant in the town she lives in.

This analysis shows how grammar can be brought to bear on questions of interpretation. Sometimes the structure of a sentence may be so simple and straightforward that we don't need to consciously identify phrases and sentence patterns. However, poets can also choose to use grammar or, in cummings' case, to exploit grammar to convey meaning. When they do, we should be able to identify explicitly what the structure of a sentence is—and, based on that structure, what the meaning is.

The following exercise will ask you to apply your part-of-speech knowledge to this poem.

EXERCISE 1

Make a list of all the words in cummings' poem that are used in non-standard word classes. Then offer a possible interpretation that arises from these novel uses of words.

PARALLELISM Parallelism, which we looked at in Chapter 9, is also a tool writers use to add beauty and durability to their writing. Lines 2–4 of Robert Frost's "Mending Wall" illustrate a poetic use of parallelism:

> Something there is that doesn't love a wall,
>
> That <u>sends the frozen-ground-swell under it</u>
>
> And <u>spills the upper boulders in the sun;</u>
>
> And <u>makes gaps even two can pass abreast</u>.

These lines combine three verb phrases, whose parallelism propels the reader along the current like a moving river. As you wade out into the poem, the river drags you downstream and before you know it you are caught up in the narrator's sentiment, his attitude toward walls. Parallelism builds a kind of force; it piles up the evidence for the point the poet wants to make—in this case, that the tendency of walls to decay is due to the general dislike of walls the narrator senses in the world.

The next exercise gives you the opportunity to look for parallelism in two poems.

EXERCISE 2

Find the parallelism in the following poems. Identify what kind of phrases are parallel. Then interpret the effect that the parallelism has on the meaning or sense of the poem.

from The Love Song of J. Alfred Prufrock
T. S. Eliot

> But though I have wept and fasted, wept and prayed,
> Though I have seen my head (grown slightly bald) brought in upon a platter,
> I am no prophet—and here's no great matter;
> I have seen the moment of my greatness flicker,
> And I have seen the eternal Footman hold my coat, and snicker,   5
> And in short, I was afraid.

And would it have been worth it, after all,
After the cups, the marmalade, the tea,
Among the porcelain, among some talk of you and me,
Would it have been worth while,   10
To have bitten off the matter with a smile,
To have squeezed the universe into a ball
To roll it towards some overwhelming question,
To say: "I am Lazarus, come from the dead,
Come back to tell you all, I shall tell you all"—   15
If one, settling a pillow by her head,
    Should say: "That is not what I meant at all.
    That is not it, at all."

Poetry
Marianne Moore

I, too dislike it: there are things that are important beyond all this fiddle.
    Reading it, however, with a perfect contempt for it, one discovers in
    it after all, a place for the genuine.
        Hands that can grasp, eyes
        that can dilate, hair that can rise   5
            if it must, these things are important not because a

high-sounding interpretation can be put upon them but because they are
    useful. When they become so derivative as to become unintelligible,
    the same thing may be said for all of us, that we
        do not admire what   10
        we cannot understand: the bat
            holding on upside down or in quest of something to

eat, elephants pushing, a wild horse taking a roll, a tireless wolf under
    a tree, the immovable critic twitching his skin like a horse that feels a
    flea, the base-
        ball fan, the statistician—   15
        nor is it valid
            to discriminate against 'business documents and

school-books'; all these phenomena are important. One must make a
    distinction
        however: when dragged into prominence by half poets, the result is
            not poetry,
        nor till the poets among us can be   20
        'literalists of
        the imagination'—above
            insolence and triviality and can present

for inspection, 'imaginary gardens with real toads in them,' shall we have
   it. In the meantime, if you demand on the one hand,   25
     the raw material of poetry in
       all its rawness and
       that which is on the other hand
         genuine, you are interested in poetry.

Nonstandard Structures

We have seen numerous examples in this book of the typical word order of English: subject—verb—direct object, for example. Our language, however, also allows less-common word orders, which are often exploited by poets. Sometimes the unusual word order creates a rhythmic or aesthetic effect, but we also know that word order is used to convey meaning, because different word orders lead to different intonational patterns.

The following lines from Ezra Pound's "The River-Merchant's Wife: A Letter" show an example of nonstandard word order:

> While my hair was still cut straight across my forehead
> <u>Played</u> I about the front gate, pulling flowers.
> You came by on bamboo stilts, playing horse,
> You walked about my seat, playing with blue plums.

In line 2, Pound has inverted the word order so that the verb appears before the subject. Compare the first two lines as Pound wrote them to the hypothetical version below with standard word order:

> While my hair was still cut straight across my forehead
>
> I played about the front gate, pulling flowers.

What is the difference between the two? One effect is that Pound's version highlights the verb *played*. Generally, the main verb of a sentence, especially when it occurs in its standard position, receives no important intonational peak. When it is put elsewhere in the sentence, more attention is drawn to it. The verb *play* is emphasized again in the next two lines through repetition. His lines focus on the playful relationship between the couple.

Another way that poets achieve their intended effects is by leaving out words and phrases that are necessary for grammatical sentences. A fine example of this is found in Ezra Pound's short poem "In a Station of the Metro":

In a Station of the Metro

The apparition of these faces in the crowd;
Petals on a wet, black bough.

This poem consists of two noun phrases and no verbs. It is an example of imagist poetry, an art form in which the poet tries to avoid abstractions in favor of concrete images. The second noun phrase in Pound's poem, *petals on a wet, black bough,* evokes an image that is placed next to the image suggested by the first noun phrase, *the apparition of these faces in the crowd.* The lack of verbs here gives an effect that is similar to looking at two photographs side by side. It is almost as if the poem were a painting rather than a display of poetic language. However, what is interesting for our purposes is how Pound achieves this effect *through* language, by using noun phrases rather than sentences, not *in spite of* language.

Exercise 3 gives you more practice in using grammatical structure to analyze poems.

EXERCISE 3

Answer the questions for each of the poems below.

Anne Rutledge
Edgar Lee Masters

Out of me unworthy and unknown
The vibrations of deathless music;
"With malice toward none, with charity for all."
Out of me the forgiveness of millions toward millions,
And the beneficent face of a nation   5
Shining with justice and truth.
I am Anne Rutledge who sleep beneath these weeds,
Beloved in life of Abraham Lincoln,
Wedded to him, not through union,
But through separation.   10
Bloom forever, O Republic,
From the dust of my bosom!

1. Identify all incomplete sentences in this poem. Then identify all complete sentences in the poem.

2. What effect(s) do the incomplete sentences have on the meaning? Why do you think Masters begins the poem with the grammatical structures he chooses?

Charles Carville's Eyes
E. A. Robinson

A melancholy face Charles Carville had,
But not so melancholy as it seemed,
When once you knew him, for his mouth redeemed
His insufficient eyes, forever sad:
In them there was no life-glimpse, good or bad,   5
Nor joy nor passion in them ever gleamed;
His mouth was all of him that ever beamed,
His eyes were sorry, but his mouth was glad.

He never was a fellow that said much,
And half of what he did say was not heard   10
By many of us: we were out of touch
With all his whims and all his theories
Till he was dead, so those blank eyes of his
Might speak them. Then we heard them, every word.

1. Identify the subject and the direct object of the sentence in line 1. What does the word order of this sentence contribute to the meaning of the poem?

2. Where is the subject of the sentence in line 5? What does the word order of this sentence contribute to the meaning of the poem?

3. What is the subject of the sentence in line 10? Is this sentence active, passive, or neither? What is the effect of voice here?

God's World
Edna St. Vincent Millay

O world, I cannot hold thee close enough!
    Thy winds, thy wide grey skies!
    Thy mists, that roll and rise!
Thy woods, this autumn day, that ache and sag
And all but cry with color! That gaunt crag   5
To crush! To lift the lean of that black bluff!
World, World, I cannot get thee close enough!

Long have I known a glory in it all,
    But never knew I this;
    Here such a passion is   10
As stretcheth me apart,—Lord, I do fear
Thou'st made the world too beautiful this year;
My soul is all but out of me,—let fall
No burning leaf; prithee, let no bird call.

1. Identify the two examples of parallelism in the first stanza. What effect do they have on the poem?

2. The first three sentences in the second stanza have nonstandard word order. Identify the phrases and structure of these sentences. (Hint: first convert the sentences into their standard word order to help you locate where everything is.) What effect does the nonstandard word order have on the poem?

The Snow Man
Wallace Stevens

One must have a mind of winter
To regard the frost and the boughs
Of the pine-trees crusted with snow;

And have been cold a long time
To behold the junipers shagged with ice,   5
The spruces rough in the distant glitter

Of the January sun; and not to think
Of any misery in the sound of the wind,
In the sound of a few leaves,

Which is the sound of the land   10
Full of the same wind
That is blowing in the same bare place

For the listener, who listens in the snow,
And, nothing himself, beholds
Nothing that is not there and the nothing that is.   15

1. How many sentences are there in this poem? How can you tell?

2. What is the grammatical relationship between the four verb phrases in lines 1, 2, 4, and 7?

3. What phrase makes up the fourth stanza?

4. What phrase makes up the last stanza?

5. How do the structural relationships identified above contribute to the meaning of the poem?

LINE BREAKS One technique poets use to evoke multiple meanings is line breaks. The poet can choose to end one line of poetry in a way that leads the reader to a particular interpretation. However, when the reader encounters the next line, the continuation changes the grammatical structure of the previous line, and a further interpretation arises. Consider the first line from Amiri Baraka's "The Bridge":

> I have forgotten the head

This line seems simple enough. It can stand alone as a self-contained sentence, and though the reader may speculate about what "the head" refers to, he won't feel as if something is missing from the line's grammatical structure.

The first line and a half of the poem, though, reads as follows:

> I have forgotten the head
> of where I am.

When the reader comes to the second line, he realizes that his reading of the first line was incomplete. In his mind he must go back and alter the structure he had assigned to line 1. Now he knows that the direct object of the verb *forgotten* was not just the noun phrase *the head* but rather the noun phrase *the head of where I am*. Or maybe the poet intends for the reader to consider two possibilities—that he forgot both "the head" and "the head of where I am."

Take a look now at the entire first stanza of Baraka's poem:

> I have forgotten the head
> of where I am. Here at the bridge.   2
> bars, down the street, seeming
> to warp themselves around my fingers, the day,
> screams in me; pitiful like a little girl   5
> you sense will be dead before the winter
> is over.

The move from line 4 to line 5 confronts us with another question of how to interpret the grammatical structure of the poem. Should we read the last phrase of line 4 as the subject of "screams" in line 5? This would give us the reading

> the day <u>screams in me</u>
>   VP

Or should we read lines 4 and 5 as giving us a list of things that "warp themselves around my fingers"? That would give us the reading

> seeming to warp themselves around <u>my fingers</u>, <u>the day</u>, <u>screams in me</u>;
>   NP   NP   NP

The word *scream* is one of those forms that can be either a verb or a noun, and this leads to the possibility of more than one reading for lines 4 and 5. Note that the punctuation choice of a comma at the end of line 4 favors the second reading, but the line break Baraka chooses certainly invites the reader to consider the first reading as well.

The next exercise asks you to work with line breaks.

EXERCISE 4

Examine the line breaks in the following excerpts by Emily Dickinson. Analyze the grammatical possibilities based on her choice of line breaks. Then describe the possible meanings that arise based on the different ways of analyzing the poem's grammatical structure.

1) I died for Beauty—but was scarce
   Adjusted in the Tomb
   When One who died for Truth, was lain
   In an adjoining Room—

2) This was a Poet—It is That   5
   Distills amazing sense
   From ordinary Meanings—
   And Attar so immense

(Attar ➲ "fragrant oils extracted from flowers")

Frank and Ernest

© 2003 Thaves. Reprinted with permission. Newspaper dist. by NEA, Inc.

Grammatical Analysis of Prose

We have primarily concentrated on poetry so far in this chapter, but grammatical analysis can be brought to bear on prose as well.

"The Short Happy Life of Francis Macomber" by Ernest Hemingway tells the story of a married couple, Francis and Margot Macomber, on their first safari. During this trip, Francis must confront his personal fears. He initially fails badly. While hunting a lion, he runs in fear from the charging beast and is humiliated in front of his wife and the safari guide, Robert Wilson. Later on, though, Francis finds new courage while hunting buffalo. Below are two paragraphs that describe what Wilson thinks of Francis—first after Francis has run in fear and second, after Francis has found his courage.

It was a good morning, Wilson thought. There was a heavy dew and as the wheels went through the grass and low bushes he could smell the odor of the crushed fronds. It was an odor like verbena and he liked this early morning smell of the dew, the crushed bracken and the look of the tree trunks showing black through the early morning mist, as the car made its way through the untracked, parklike country. He had put the two in the back seat out of his mind now and was thinking about buffalo. The buffalo that he was after stayed in the daytime in a thick swamp where it was impossible to get a shot, but in the night they fed out into an open stretch of country and if he could come between them and their swamp with the car, Macomber would have a good chance at them in the open. He did not want to hunt buff with Macomber in thick cover. He did not want to hunt buff or anything else with Macomber at all, but he was a professional hunter and he had hunted with some rare ones in his time. If they got buff today there would only be rhino to come and the poor man would have gone through his dangerous game and things might pick up. He'd have nothing more to do with the woman and Macomber would get over that too. He must have gone through plenty of that by the look of things. Poor beggar. He must have a way of getting over it. Well, it was the poor sod's own bloody fault.

It had taken a strange chance of hunting, a sudden precipitation into action without opportunity for worrying beforehand, to bring this about with Macomber, but regardless of how it happened it had most certainly happened. Look at the beggar now, Wilson thought. It's that some of them stay little boys so long, Wilson thought. Sometimes all their lives. Their figures stay boyish when they're fifty. The great American boy-men. Damned strange people. But he liked this Macomber now. Damned strange fellow. Probably meant the end of cuckoldry too. Well, that would be a damned good thing. Damned good thing. Beggar had probably been afraid all his life. Don't know what started it. But over now. Hadn't time to be afraid with the buff. That and being angry too. Motor car too. Motor cars made it familiar. Be a damn fire eater now. He'd seen it in the war work the same way. More of a change than loss of virginity. Fear gone like an operation. Something else grew in its place. Main thing a man had. Made him into a man. Women knew it too. No bloody fear.

Before you read any further, analyze these paragraphs and write down the grammatical differences you notice between them

Two big differences jump out at us in the paragraphs above. The first paragraph is rather ordinary as far as grammar is concerned. The sentences are not unusual as Wilson describes his contempt of Francis. In the second paragraph we find something different. Once we get past the first sentence, where probably the narrator is speaking, the later sentences, which express Wilson's thoughts, are almost all short. Compare these two sentences from the first paragraph to some sentences from the second paragraph.

First Paragraph

> If they got buff today there would only be rhino to come and the poor man would
> have gone through his dangerous game and things might pick up.
> He'd have nothing more to do with the woman and Macomber would get over that too.

Second Paragraph

> Look at the beggar now, Wilson thought.
> It's that some of them stay little boys so long, Wilson thought.
> Sometimes all their lives.

There is no doubt that the sentences have shrunk in the second paragraph.

Another difference is that many of the short sentences in the second paragraph are incomplete sentences, or fragments.

Fragments

> Sometimes all their lives.
> The great American boy-men.
> Damned strange people.
> Damned strange fellow.
> Probably meant the end of cuckoldry too.
> Damned good thing.
> Don't know what started it.
> But over now.
> Hadn't time to be afraid with the buff.
> That and being angry too.
> Motor car too.
> Be a damn fire eater now.
> More of a change than loss of virginity.
> Fear gone like an operation.
> Main thing a man had.
> Made him into a man.
> No bloody fear.

The difference in grammatical structure is largely what makes these paragraphs so effective. The first paragraph is constructed along conventional lines, thereby conveying typical structure, and it conveys Wilson's run-of-the-mill criticism of Francis Macomber, the kind of criticism he has made many times of past clients. The second paragraph is filled with short sentences and fragments, and it conveys Wilson's excitement as he witnesses Macomber confront his fear and transform into a real man, very unlike his former milquetoast self. If you watch for these kinds of grammatical influences in prose, you can be alert to what a writer may be conveying through structure.

The following two exercises will give you practice in analyzing prose.

EXERCISE 5

Identify the phrase or phrases in the sentence fragments listed on the previous page.

EXERCISE 6

Rewrite the second paragraph on page 250 so that it contains longer, complete sentences. Then compare your paragraph to Hemingway's version and discuss how the difference in grammatical structure changes the meaning and mood of the paragraph.

COMPREHENSION QUESTIONS

1. What is metrical analysis? How can a knowledge of intonation inform the study of poetry, especially with regard to meter?

2. How can grammatical analysis be applied to the study of poetry?

3. What can parallelism and nonstandard structure contribute to the meaning of a poem?

4. How do line breaks in poetry invite multiple readings of a poem?

5. How can grammatical analysis be applied to the study of prose?

Selected Answers to Exercises

Chapter 2

EXERCISE 1

Sentence 1

NOUNS: president, clothes, number, sandwiches, counselor

ADJECTIVES: thoughtful, pretty, largest, greasy

EXERCISE 2

1. N ➲ ants; pizza pie; V ➲ devoured; Adj ➲ delicious; Adv ➲ slowly, surely

3. N ➲ clubhouse, child, babysitter; Pron ➲ your, you; V ➲ run, yelled;
Adj ➲ naughty, flustered; Adv ➲ quickly

5. N ➲ god, name; Pron ➲ I, my; V ➲ am, is; Adj ➲ famous; Adv ➲ definitely

7. N ➲ adjective, word; Pron ➲ he; Proper Noun ➲ Spud, *deleterious;*
V ➲ wanted, write, think, was

9. N ➲ administration building, eagles, sky; V ➲ was carried; Adj ➲ giant

11. Proper Noun ➲ Andy, Barney, (Mayberry, North Carolina); V ➲ patrolled

13. N ➲ earth, tons; V ➲ weighs

15. N ➲ rodeo clown, life, star cowboy, rival, love; Pron ➲ his; V ➲ saved;
Adv ➲ bravely

EXERCISE 5

1. *Skis* is a noun. It is preceded by the determiner *the.*

3. *Jessie* and *Bobbie* are proper nouns. They name people. *Them* is a pronoun. It
cannot be preceded by a determiner as nouns can.

5. No errors.

7. *Ex-nun* is a noun. It is preceded by the determiner *an.*

9. *Blue* is an adjective. It can be preceded by qualifiers like *really. Bag* is a noun. It
is preceded by the determiner *that.*

Chapter 3

EXERCISE 1

1. Det ➲ the; Prep ➲ with, of

3. Det ➲ the; Quant ➲ every, some; Coor Conj ➲ yet

5. Det ➲ the; Prep ➲ for (2x); Num ➲ two

7. Det ➲ the; Prep ➲ before; Pron ➲ you, us; Sub Conj ➲ when; Inf Mkr ➲ to

9. Det ➲ this, the; Prep ➲ to, for, of; Pron ➲ I, you

11. Det ➲ the; Prep ➲ as

13. Det ➲ the; Pron ➲ I; Qual ➲ very; Sub Conj ➲ if-then; Neg ➲ not

15. Det ➲ the; Prep ➲ from; Pron ➲ she, her; Coor Conj ➲ or; Inf Mkr ➲ to

Chapter 4

EXERCISE 1

Sentence 1

PHRASES: he; the brake; pulled the brake; he pulled the brake

EXERCISE 4

1. 1 clause: <u>we have been doing grammar all day long</u>

3. 0 clauses

5. 3 clauses: <u>since Gigi confessed</u>; <u>not a lot has changed in this town</u>; <u>since Gigi confessed, not a lot has changed in this town</u>

7. 1 clause: <u>Because I love you</u>.

9. 3 clauses: <u>the Texans play the Cowboys on Sunday</u>; <u>and the Steelers play the Eagles on Monday</u>; <u>the Texans play the Cowboys on Sunday, and the Steelers play the Eagles on Monday</u>

11. 2 clauses: <u>that he might not finish his education</u>, <u>the thought that he might not finish his education renewed Edgar's determination</u>

Chapter 5

EXERCISE 1

1.

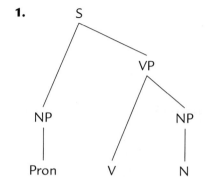

3.

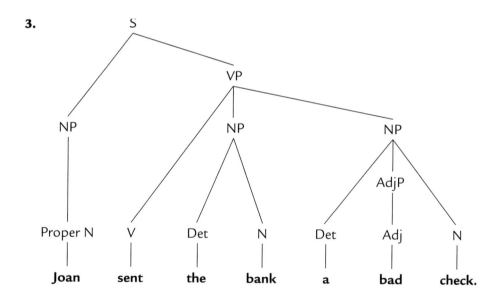

5.

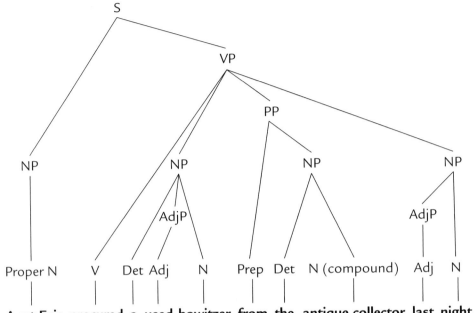

7.

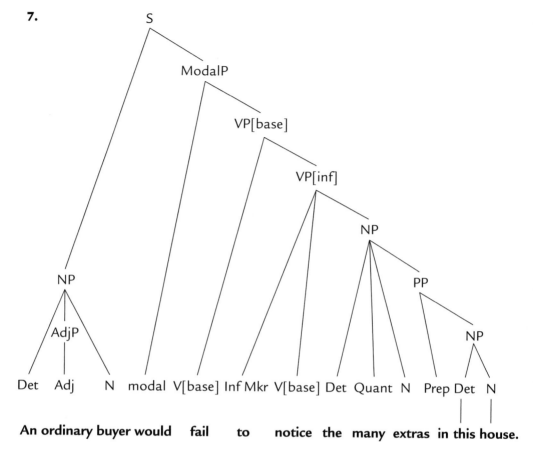

9.

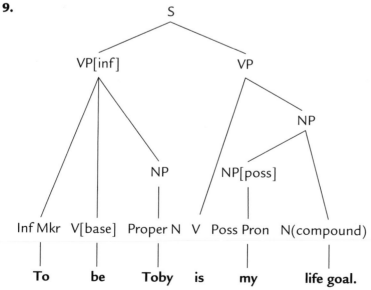

11.

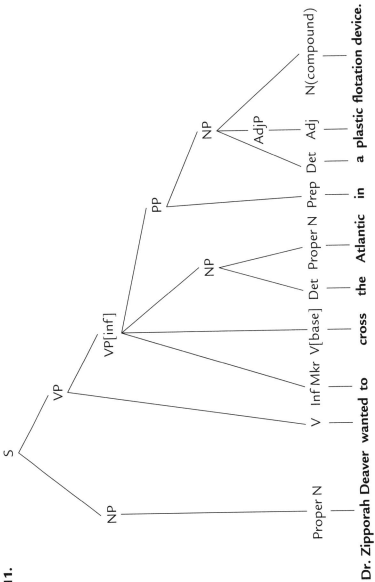

13.

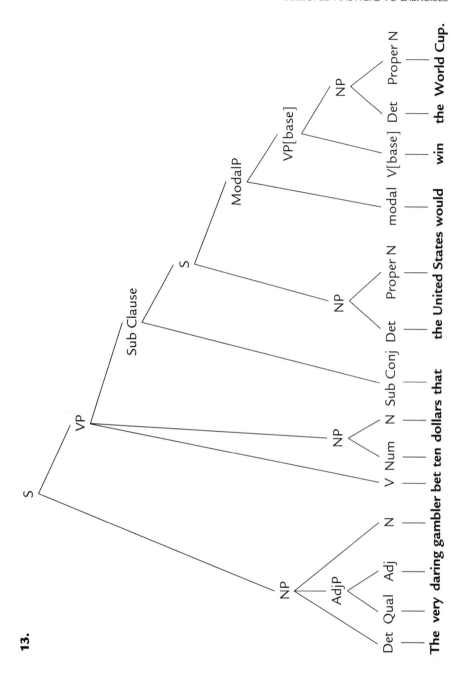

15.

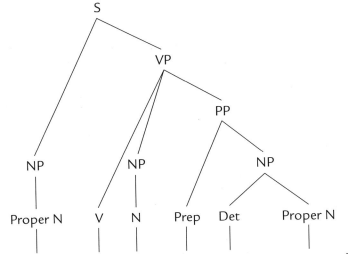

New York City gets water through the Delaware Aqueduct.

17.

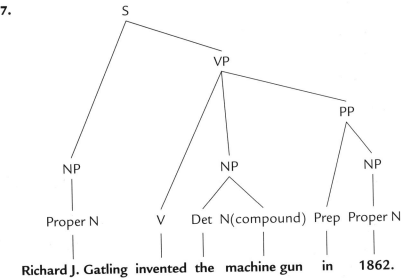

Richard J. Gatling invented the machine gun in 1862.

EXERCISE 4

Sentence 1

PROBLEM: noun phrases

Chapter 6

EXERCISE 1

1. Subj ➲ Mervin; Dir Obj ➲ trivial pursuits

3. Subj ➲ Brandy; Subj Comp ➲ sick

5. Subj ➲ the local philanthropist; Ind Obj ➲ the town; Dir Obj ➲ $50,000

7. Subj ➲ this babysitter; Ind Obj ➲ Susie; Dir Obj ➲ a book about reptiles

9. Subj ➲ Betsy; Dir Obj ➲ the room; Obj Comp ➲ a deep shade of purple

11. Subj ➲ the tongue; Subj Comp ➲ the strongest muscle in the body

13. Subj ➲ the quartet; Dir Obj ➲ a Bach cantata

15. Subj ➲ the new carpenter in town; Ind Obj ➲ the Ridleys; Dir Obj ➲ a fantastic back porch

Chapter 7

EXERCISE 1

1. location: off my bike

3. temporal: late; cause: because his car had broken down

5. manner: hard; purpose: in order to go to medical school

7. manner: barefoot; location: on the cover of *Abbey Road*

9. cause: on account of the rain; temporal: till next Saturday

11. none

EXERCISE 2

1. PP: on Memorial Day

3. VP[inf]: to keep the blues away

5. Sub Cl: after he played football at Florida State

7. NP: forty-eight times

9. NP: last night; Sub Cl: though the orange crop probably survived

11. Sub Cl: while they were warming up; PP: from the pool area

13. PP: inside the tunnel, with great fervor

EXERCISE 3

1. at this plant ➲ location, PP; during the fall ➲ temporal, PP

3. after you leave work ➲ temporal, Sub Cl; to the store ➲ location, PP

5. around the corner ➲ location, PP; at Kelly's house ➲ location, PP; three weeks ➲ temporal, NP

7. undoubtedly ➲ manner, AdvP; in that song ➲ location, PP

9. once Camille unscrewed the lid ➲ temporal, Sub Cl; into the hall ➲ location, PP

EXERCISE 4

1. Subj ➲ Napoleon's army; Dir Obj ➲ canned foods; Adverbial ➲ first

3. Subj ➲ crass rudeness; Ind Obj ➲ you; Dir Obj ➲ nowhere; Adverbial ➲ with that division head

5. Subj ➲ that cheese; Subj Comp ➲ rancid; Adverbials ➲ in two weeks, unless you put it in an airtight container

7. Subj ➲ Anne; Ind Obj ➲ the children; Dir Obj ➲ a story about knights in shining armor; Adverbial ➲ at the orphanage (It is also possible that the indirect object is **the children at the orphanage.**)

9. Subj ➲ Ralph; Dir Obj ➲ a bowling ball; Adverbials ➲ carelessly, on his big toe, outside the alley

Chapter 8

EXERCISE 1

1. modal

3. simple past

5. present perfect

7. simple present

9. modal

11. present progressive

13. simple past

15. simple present

EXERCISE 3

1. neither

3. active

5. neither

7. passive

9. passive

11. active

13. active

15. passive

EXERCISE 4

1. past progressive, neither

3. present progressive, neither

5. simple present, active

7. present progressive, active

9. past perfect, active

11. simple present, active

13. past progressive, passive

15. modal, neither

EXERCISE 5

1. simple present. Half a pineapple is crushed for this recipe.

3. present progressive. A mistake about Mr. Davenport is being made by Shea.

5. modal. I may be entertained by them for free.

7. simple past. The highest mountain in Florida—"The Matterhorn" at Disney World—was climbed by the Potter family.

9. past progressive. A fly was being swallowed by Cleo, Pinocchio's pet goldfish.

11. past perfect. That fish had been landed by Sinead before her brother inadvertently knocked it back into the water.

13. simple present. Fat, not water, is stored by camels in their humps.

15. modal. The tournament might be canceled by our school if there are not enough entries.

EXERCISE 6

1. simple present. The U.S. treasury depicts the White House on the back of a U.S. twenty-dollar bill.

3. present perfect. The doctors have healed Shirley of her cancer.

5. present progressive. The Hillman Players are staging a comic rendition of *Macbeth*.

7. simple present. The amount of time you spend with Sheila amazes us.

9. past progressive. People with low seniority were driving the Mattoon-Decatur route in the seventies.

11. simple present. Your symptoms puzzle me.

13. simple past. Richard Nixon made the first U.S. presidential trip to China in 1972.

15. simple past. People named the monkey wrench after the English blacksmith Charles Moncke.

EXERCISE 7

1. simple present, active. Rocks are skipped by Freddie across Lake Bartholomew.

3. simple present, neither.

5. present progressive, active. York's art teacher is being met by Zoe tomorrow.

7. present perfect, active. Bric-a-brac has been sold by yours truly for forty years at this flea market.

9. present perfect, active. National Squid Day has been observed by Moira for almost thirty years.

11. modal, active. Next week ZSU will be beaten by our fencing team.

13. present perfect, passive. The staff has scoured the kitchen, and they have unclogged the drains.

15. past perfect, active. That book on pottery had been requested by Karnov the Magnificent through interlibrary loan.

Chapter 9

EXERCISE 3

1. correct

3. correct

5. correct

7. "Kline was the culprit, because I saw him leave the building at 2:30."

9. The computer, once Smythe replaced the motherboard, worked like a dream

11. correct

13. The roof, whenever it rains, leaks like a sieve.

EXERCISE 5

1. <u>A bricklayer</u>, <u>a carpenter</u>, and <u>an electrician</u>
  NP   NP   NP

3. <u>in</u>, <u>on</u>, and <u>under</u>
 Prep Prep   Prep

5. <u>to pick up the phone</u>, <u>to dial the number</u>, and <u>to call your boss immediately</u>
  VP[inf]   VP[inf]   VP[inf]

7. <u>met all her staff</u>, <u>evaluated their performance</u>, and
  VP[past part]   VP[past part]

  <u>made her salary recommendations</u>
        VP[past part]

9. <u>The food is cooked</u>, <u>the apartment is decorated</u>, and <u>the guests are here</u>.
        S   S   S

11. <u>tallied her receipts</u>, <u>swept the floors</u>, and <u>closed her shop early</u>
        VP   VP   VP

EXERCISE 6
(possible corrections)

1. AdjP, AdjP, Adj P. correct

3. VP[-ing], VP[-ing], NP. Working for the IRS, being a volunteer dad, and playing cricket may not be the typical description of a suburban Denverite.

5. VP[base], VP[base], VP[base]. correct

7. AdjP, AdjP, AdjP. correct

9. VP, VP, NP. The members of the band strum guitars, bang drums, and play keyboards.

11. NP, NP, VP. Lady Macbeth gave me the creeps, the willies, and a thorough fright during the University Players' performance of *Macbeth*.

EXERCISE 9

1. correct

3. Comma combines two noun phrases. My money and your brains are the key to success.

5. correct

7. Comma needed between two sentences joined with *and*. Daddy was a plumber, and Mommy was a carpenter.

9. Semicolon appears between an independent clause and a subordinate clause. My neighbor filed a complaint with the city after his yard was flooded during last night's rains.

11. correct

13. correct

Chapter 10

EXERCISE 1
(possible corrections)

1. correct

3. Putting aside my objections, the counselor suggested I take a long vacation.

5. Though her new drug was not yet tested, the scientist was confident it would cure male-pattern baldness.

7. Whether he is coming or going, a smile can always be found on Sammy's face.

9. correct

11. After we came to an agreement, the meeting was continued at the coffeehouse.

EXERCISE 3
(possible corrections)

1. correct

3. The capital of Maine is smaller than the capital of Louisiana.

5. Steak with potatoes is more typical than steak with peas.

7. The Polecats of Dogpatch sold more Kickapoo Joy Juice than the Polecats of Sioux City.

9. Dumbo the Elephant has more knees than I have.

11. The boss gave Yolanda more perks than she gave Wyatt.

EXERCISE 4

1. correct

3. a tall, dark stranger

5. that sad, leafless tree

7. his grimy, seedy house

9. a wise strategic decision *or* a wise, strategic decision

EXERCISE 5

1. correct

3. The Double Cross Gang found an old abandoned mine at the end of the logging trail.

5. We only sell juicy, spicy burgers at this greasy spoon.

7. The expensive deluxe upgrade was never a big seller.

9. correct

EXERCISE 6

1. correct

3. correct

5. Dell works at a crocheted-sweater shop part-time on the weekends.

7. Vanna turns vowel-letter boxes with less enthusiasm than she turns consonant-letter boxes.

9. A once-in-a-lifetime opportunity awaits you if you call within the next ten minutes.

EXERCISE 7

1. The president, who is staying at Camp David this weekend, must decide whether or not to veto the new bill passed by Congress.

3. correct

5. correct

7. Carol shifted the schedule that you agreed on forward one hour.

9. correct

EXERCISE 8

1. Clouds gathering on the horizon threatened the community cleanup.

3. The lawn, sprinkled with dew, sparkled like a diamond.

5. The Scillibus, sunk in 1504, is likely to be the wreckage you see off the coast.

7. In this picture are teeth suffering from years of neglect.

9. correct

EXERCISE 9

1. Her term papers piling up, Lizzie had too much to do before the end of the semester.

3. Her brother's condition worsening, Aunt Betty sent for a doctor.

5. All three candidates stayed awake during the night, the election too close to call.

7. The earth looking inviting, the alien piloted his star cruiser towards our solar system.

9. His pace superb, Sykes ran his first mile under four minutes last June.

EXERCISE 10

1.

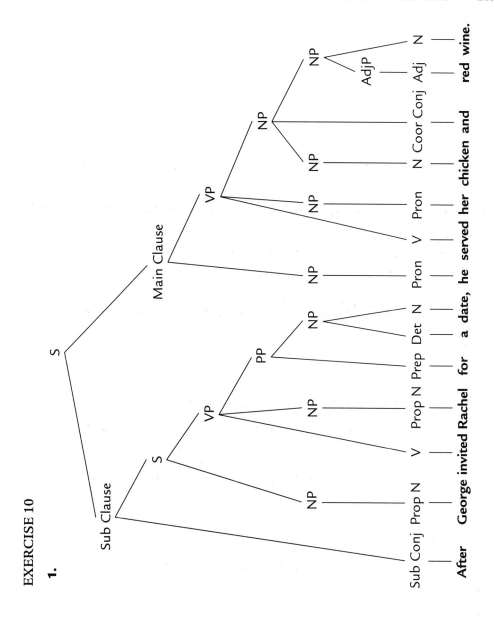

The sentence: After George invited Rachel for a date, he served her chicken and red wine.

3.

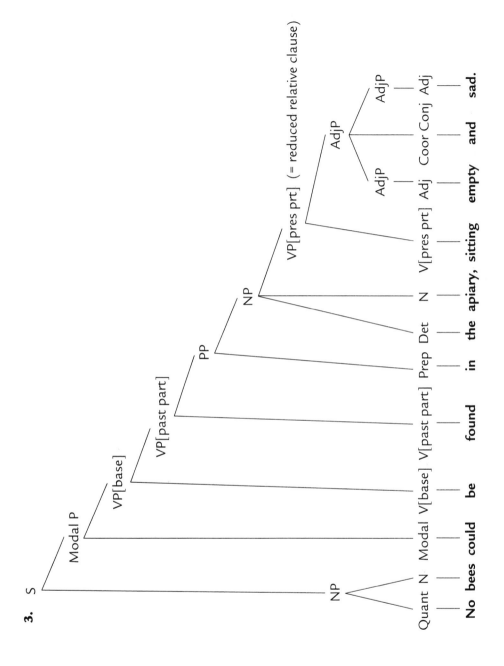

5.

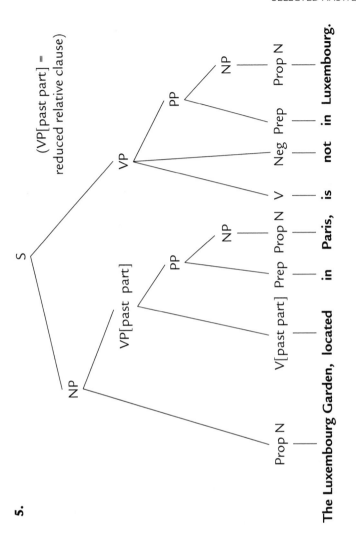

(VP[past part] =
reduced relative clause)

7.

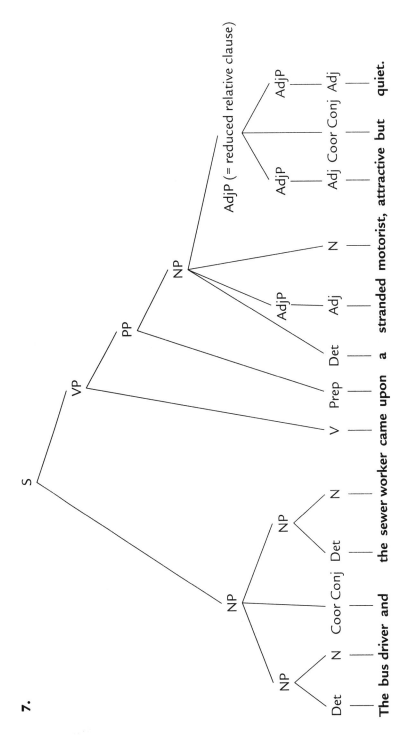

S

VP

NP   PP   NP   AdjP (= reduced relative clause)

NP   NP   AdjP   AdjP

Det N Coor Conj Det N   V   Prep Det AdjP   N   AdjP Coor Conj Adj

                                             Adj   Adj   Adj

The bus driver and the sewer worker came upon a stranded motorist, attractive but quiet.

9.

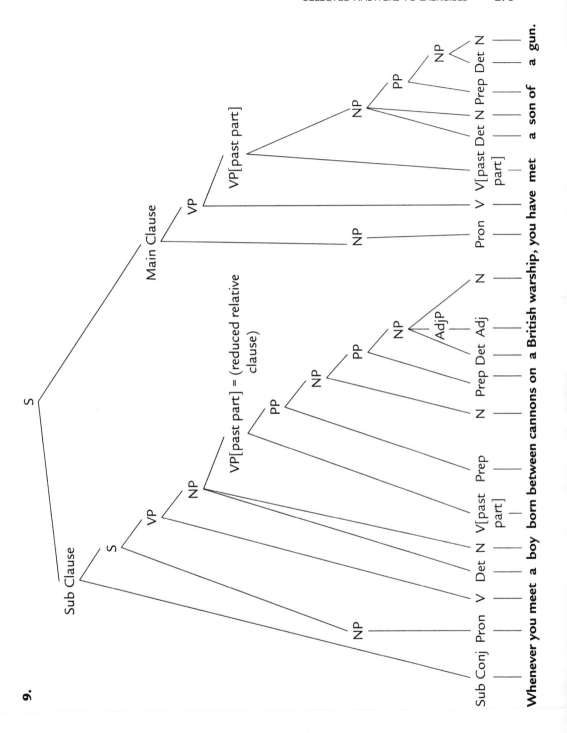

Whenever you meet a boy born between cannons on a British warship, you have met a son of a gun.

Chapter 11

EXERCISE 1
(possible corrections)

1. Theaters have all kinds of superstitions. For example, it is bad luck to say "Macbeth."

3. no change needed

5. Our northern neighbor is Canada. Our southern neighbor is Mexico. Many people don't realize that our next closest neighbor is Russia.

7. Astronomers were hoping to find a planet in that star system. They noticed a wobble in its first star.

9. Randy thought Baby Red's injury was fully healed. All the way home he galloped that horse, though the trail was muddy.

Chapter 12

EXERCISE 1

1. Rule 4: the verb *do* should be *does* to agree with the closer phrase *the president*.

   Does the president or his advisors plan to attend the conference?

3. Rule 2: the plural form of *pants* takes plural agreement.

   Foster's pants are imported from Indonesia.

5. Rule 3: plural numbers when applied to distance take singular agreement.

   Fourteen miles is a long way to hike to see another waterfall.

7. Rule 1: the pronoun *its* shows that the collective noun *cabinet* is being conceived as a singular entity.

   The cabinet has expressed its disapproval of the grievance committee's actions.

9. Rule 4: the verb *is* should be *are* to agree with closer phrase *her players*.

   Our coach or her players are due to win an award after this fine season.

Chapter 13

EXERCISE 1
(possible answers)

1. Nobody will do anything about that.

3. Nobody can touch that shot.

5. Henry didn't say anything last night.

Glossary

absolute phrase   A type of adverbial that is formed by deleting a *be*-verb from a complete sentence.

active voice   A characteristic of verbs and sentences that occur with a direct object.

adjectival   A phrase inside a noun phrase that is not needed to make the noun phrase complete.

adjective   A word class whose members typically modify nouns.

adjective phrase   A phrase that is headed by an adjective.

adverb   A word class whose members modify verbs or sentences.

adverb phrase   A phrase that is headed by an adverb.

adverbial   A phrase inside a sentence or verb phrase that is not needed to make the sentence complete.

article   A subclass of determiners that consists of *a, an,* and *the.*

aspect   See *tense-aspect.*

base form   The form of a verb that takes no suffix or other changes. It is identical to the dictionary entry of that verb.

clause   A phrase that consists of a subject and a verb phrase.

cleft sentence   A sentence whose structure is reordered by adding a new subject and a *be*-verb and moving one phrase to another position in the sentence. This changes the intonation and emphasis of the original sentence.

closed class   A word class that does not easily add new members. Pronouns, conjunctions, and prepositions are examples of closed classes.

comparative   The form of adjective that is used in *-er* comparisons.

compounds   Two or more words that combine to make a new word.

coordination   A means of combining equal grammatical units using coordinate conjunctions: *and, or, nor, for, but, yet,* and *so.*

conjunct   A general term for words or phrases that are combined by coordinate conjunctions.

dangling clause   A clause whose missing subject does not match the main subject of the sentence.

demonstrative   A closed-class part of speech. Demonstratives (*this, that, these, those*) describe the distance (physically or metaphorically) between a speaker and an object.

determiner   A closed-class part of speech. Determiners occur before and modify nouns. Articles, demonstratives, possessive pronouns, numbers, and quantifiers all are specific kinds of determiners.

dialect   A variety within a single language, such as Black English or Appalachian English.

direct object   A grammatical role that applies to noun phrases that convey the individual(s) acted upon by (the action of) the verb. Only certain verbs can occur with direct objects.

ellipsis   A term that describes when necessary elements are left out of a clause or phrase.

-en verb form   Another name for a past participle.

end focus   A pattern of intonation in which the highest pitch occurs toward the end of the sentence.

function tests   Tests that identify which part of speech closed-class items belong to, based on how they function in a sentence.

grammatical roles   Labels we give to phrases, in particular, noun phrases, that describe what relationship they have to their verbs.

head   The particular word in a phrase that determines the phrase type. Nouns are the heads of noun phrases, verbs are the head of verb phrases, and so forth.

homonym   One of two or more words that sound the same but have different meanings. *Bank,* a financial institution, and *bank,* the sloped edge of land on a body of water, are homonyms.

indirect object   A grammatical role that applies to noun phrases that convey the recipient of the action. Only certain verbs can occur with indirect objects.

infinitive marker   A closed-class part of speech. This class contains a single word, *to,* when it is used to make an infinitive-verb phrase.

infinitive-verb phrase   A verb phrase based on an infinitive marker plus a verb in its base form.

interactional language   Language that is primarily used to promote or affect human relationships. Most speech is interactional in nature.

intonation   The rise and fall of our voices as we utter sentences. Intonation directs a hearer's attention to the content of a sentence that a speaker wants to emphasize and conveys the overall mood and purpose of the sentence.

intransitive verb   A verb that can make a complete verb phrase by itself.

inversion   A term that describes sentences in which the subject and the subject complement switch places. This changes the intonation and the emphasis of the sentence.

lexicon   The dictionary in our heads.

locative   A kind of phrase that designates a location.

meaning tests   Tests that identify which part of speech a word belongs to, based on the meaning of the word.

modal   A closed-class part of speech. Modals modify verbs and introduce information related to moral/ethical judgments and to possibility or necessity.

modal phrase   A phrase that is headed by a modal.

modifier   Words and phrases that modify other elements in a sentence. Adjectivals and adverbials are the two main kinds of modifiers.

negation marker   A closed class part of speech for words that negate, such as *not*.

noun   A word class whose members designate people, places, things, and other abstractions.

noun phrase   A phrase that is headed by a noun.

number   A closed-class part of speech that consists of numbers, such as *one, two, three,* and so forth.

object complement   A grammatical role that applies to noun phrases and adjective phrases that complement or describe a direct object in a sentence. Only certain verbs can occur with object complements.

open class   A word class that easily adds new members. Nouns, verbs, adjectives, and adverbs are open classes.

paralinguistic cues   Characteristics of speech that are outside of language itself. These include voice quality, facial expression, posture, and gestures. They aid the hearer in interpreting a message. Crucially, writing lacks paralinguistic cues.

parallelism   When members of a series share similar characteristics. Grammatical parallelism means that the members belong to the same part of speech. Conceptual parallelism means that the members have similar content.

part of speech   The traditional name for a word class.

passive voice   A term that describes verbs and sentences in which the subject of the sentence conveys the object of the action expressed by the verb.

past participle   The traditional name for the verb form that appears in the present-perfect and past-perfect tenses. It also appears in passive constructions. This textbook also refers to past participles as *-en* verb forms. They may be difficult to recognize because they take many different forms.

past perfect   A tense that consist of a past-tense form of the verb *have* plus a past participle.

past progressive   A tense that consists of a past-tense form of the verb *be* plus a present participle.

possessive   A form of pronouns, nouns, and noun phrases when they are in a possessive relationship to another noun.

preposition   A closed-class part of speech that combines with noun phrases. Examples include *on, by, at, from,* and *of.*

prepositional phrase   A phrase that is headed by a preposition.

present participle   The traditional name for the verb form that appears in the present-progressive and past-progressive tenses. It is easy to recognize because it is formed by adding the suffix *-ing* to the base form of the verb.

present perfect   A tense that consists of a present-tense form of the verb *have* plus a past participle.

present progressive   A tense that consists of a present-tense form of the verb *be* plus a present participle.

pro-form   Words that stand in for phrases. Pronouns, which can take the place of noun phrases, are the best-known example of pro-forms.

pronoun   A closed class part of speech. Pronouns stand in for noun phrases.

proper nouns   An open class part of speech that names persons, places, and things. Proper nouns often constitute an entire noun phrase by themselves.

qualifier   A closed-class part of speech. Qualifiers modify adjectives and adverbs.

quantifier   A closed-class part of speech. This subclass of determiners conveys the idea of how much or how many.

redundancy   In language, a term meaning that information is signaled by more than one means. For example, a reader knows that the sequence *the kite* consists of two words, *the* and *kite,* based on (1) knowledge of English spelling and (2) the space between the words. The space, then, is redundant.

relative clause   An adjectival that consists of a relative pronoun and a sentence with a missing element.

relative pronoun   A pronoun that is used to construct relative clauses. Examples include *who, which,* and *that.*

simple past   A tense that consists of a past-tense form of the main verb of the sentence and no other participles, except in the case of passive sentences.

simple present   A tense that consists of a present-tense form of the main verb of the sentence and no other participles, except in the case of passive sentences.

situational transparency   A characteristic of most face-to-face speech situations where the setting makes clear what a sentence is about. Writing lacks situational transparency because the writer is removed from the reader in time and place.

structure tests   Tests that identify which part of speech a word belongs to, based on the position a word occupies or the form of the word.

subject complement   A grammatical role that applies to noun phrases and adjective phrases that complement or describe subjects in the sentences. Only certain verbs can occur with subject complements.

subordination   A means of combining grammatical units in an unequal manner by using subordinate conjunctions such as *if, though, because,* and *when.*

superlative   The form of an adjective that expresses the highest or lowest degree of the attribute conveyed by that adjective.

tense-aspect   In English, the verb system displays tense-aspect information. *Tense* refers to time, and *aspect* refers to how the action or state of the verb is being viewed — as complete, incomplete, or habitual.

time phrase   An adverbial that conveys time.

transactional language   Language that is primarily used to convey information. Most formal writing is transactional in nature.

verb   A word class whose members convey the action or state expressed in a sentence.

verb phrase   A phrase that is headed by a verb.

voice   The aspect of a sentence that describes the relationship between a transitive verb and its noun phrases. In English, the two main voices are active and passive.

Credits

Excerpts from *A Short History of Nearly Everything*, by Bill Bryson, Broadway Books, 2003. Reprinted with permission of Random House, Inc.

Copyright © 2000 by Houghton Mifflin Company. Adapted and reproduced by permission from *The American Heritage Dictionary of the English Language*, Fourth Edition.

Copyright © 2000 by Houghton Mifflin Company. Adapted and reproduced by permission from *The American Heritage Dictionary of the English Language*, Fourth Edition.

"anyone lived in a pretty how town." Copyright 1940, © 1968, 1991 by the Trustees for the E.E. Cummings Trust, from *Complete Poems: 1904–1962* by e.e. cummings, edited by George J. Firmage. Used by permission of Liveright Publishing Corporation.

Excerpt from "Mending Wall" from *The Poetry of Robert Frost* edited by Edward Connery Lathem. Copyright © 1967 by Lesley Frost Ballantine, © 1958 by Robert Frost, © 1969 by Henry Holt and Company. Reprinted by permission of Henry Holt and Company, LLC.

"The Lovesong of J. Alfred Prufrock," from *The Complete Poems of Plays* by T.S. Eliot, 1958. Reprinted with permission of Faber and Faber Ltd.

Reprinted with the permission of Scribner, an imprint of Simon & Schuster Adult Publishing Group, from *The Collected Poems of Marianne Moore* by Marianne Moore. Copyright © 1935 by Marianne Moore; copyright renewed © 1963 by Marianne Moore and T.S. Eliot.

Reprinted with permission from *Pound: Poems & Translations* (New York: The Library of America), 2003. First published in Ezra Pound's volume *Cathay*.

Reprinted with permission from *Pound: Poems & Translations* (New York: The Library of America), 2003. First published in Ezra Pound's volume *Lustra*.

The poem "Anne Rutledge" from *Spoon River Anthology* by Edgar Lee Masters. Originally published by Macmillan Co.; permission by Hilary Masters.

Reprinted with the permission of Scribner, an imprint of Simon & Schuster Adult Publishing Group, from *The Collected Poems of Edwin Arlington Robinson* by Edwin Arlington Robinson. © 1935, 1937 by The Macmillan Company; copyright renewed © 1963, 1965.

Excerpt from "God's World" by Edna St. Vincent Millay. Copyright 1913, 1941 by Edna St. Vincent Millay.

From *The Collected Poems of Wallace Stevens* by Wallace Stevens. Copyright © 1954 by Wallace Stevens and renewed 1982 by Holly Stevens. Used by permission of Alfred A. Knopf, a division of Random House, Inc.

"The Bridge", from *Preface to a Twenty Volume Suicide Note*, 1961, Corinth Books. Reprinted by permission of SLL/Sterling Lord Literistic, Inc. Copyright by Amiri Baraka.

Index